HEARTS

OF

DARKNESS

HEARTS

OF

DARKNESS

SERIAL KILLERS,
THE BEHAVIORAL SCIENCE UNIT,
AND MY LIFE
AS A WOMAN IN THE FBI

JANA MONROE

FOREWORD BY JOE NAVARRO

ABRAMS PRESS, NEW YORK

ABRAMS The Art of Books
195 Broadway, New York, NY 10007
abramsbooks.com

For the too many victims of violent crime
and the loved ones who grieve their loss.

CONTENTS

FOREWORD
BY JOE NAVARRO

JANA MONROE IS THE SINGLE most influential woman to ever
serve in the FBI. Jana is too humble to write this herself, but it
needs to be said. Yes, she coached Jodie Foster for her role as Clarice Starling in *The Silence of the Lambs*. Jana was the only female
FBI agent in the Behavioral Science Unit when the adaptation of
Thomas Harris's novel was being filmed at the Bureau's Quantico,
Virginia, campus. To me at least, Jana's stamp is all over Jodie's
portrayal. And, yes, Jana went on to an illustrious career as a special agent in charge. All that will become apparent as you read this
highly personal account of some of the most significant cases in
the history of the FBI. From working mob cases to serial killers,
Jana did it all. Yet few know her personal side as I do.

Every May for more than thirty years, I've received a birthday card from Jana and her wonderful husband, Dale, which she
signs simply "from your bud." That's how we greet each other:
"Hey, bud." No names needed. Even though I was Jana's senior in
the Bureau by eight years, she and I developed a special bond. We
worked closely together on cases that are still classified. I also flew
surveillance missions with Dale, who was an accomplished Marine
pilot. We sat in boring all-night watches together, ate together,
commiserated together. And in that closeness, I got to see things
no one else had time to see about Jana.

As a former police officer, Jana came to the Bureau with a great reputation, and when she arrived in the Tampa Division her presence was immediately felt. She was sharp, witty, and clever, with great street smarts. In the Bureau, we rate each other based on investigative skill, credibility, the agility to think and improvise, how you worked the cases and the streets, and how well you got along with others. Jana had it all, and by that alone she had great influence.

Young agents routinely get hazed, especially young female agents, but you could not do that with Jana. She was too sharp, too accomplished, and too fearless. There was no job she wouldn't do, no matter how dangerous. I loved working with her because I could always count on her. Everyone else around her believed that as well.

I knew Jana was headed for greatness in the FBI when she left for the Behavioral Science Unit at the FBI Academy in Quantico, Virginia. What I did not expect is that she would nominate me to become the next criminal profiler in Tampa and later would support my nomination to the National Security Division's elite Behavioral Analysis Program. Both acts of kindness came to define my career in the FBI and later led me to become the FBI's body language expert and to a writing career after I retired.

Because I was so close to Jana, I also saw the effect she had on others. She was a stalwart, a giant among agents. When it came to duty, she set the standard for many of us. For female agents, she defined what could be achieved—that there was no glass ceiling that hard work, intellectual robustness, investigative acuity, an agile, compassionate mind, humor, and camaraderie could not overcome. She opened doors and commanded respect by virtue of who she was and set an example that few have equaled. In a Bureau that had plenty of "dinosaurs" left over from what had long been an all-male workforce, Jana silenced critics, humbled the mediocre, crushed the incompetent, swayed leaders, and provided a light for others to follow. She made the FBI a better place, she made us better investigators, and she did it by her example, with her hard work and a deep caring that went beyond the institution.

Jana won't say it, so I must: This book is about great, sometimes horrifying cases and the scary people who walk among us, but it's also the memoir of a great woman, a great human being, and a great friend who has helped to define what is possible in law enforcement but few will ever achieve . . . unless, that is, you are my bud, Jana Monroe.

—Joe Navarro, 2022

Joe Navarro was an FBI Special Agent for twenty-five years, specializing in counterintelligence, and a founding member of the Bureau's elite National Security Division Behavioral Analysis Program. He is the author of *Three Minutes to Doomsday* and the international bestseller *What Every BODY Is Saying*.

PROLOGUE:
JUST ANOTHER DAY AT THE OFFICE

YOU KNOW HOW OFFICES ARE. You fall into routines. One day becomes pretty much like another. You don't think a lot about your surroundings. You just get the job done.

That's the way it was at the FBI's Behavioral Science Unit, which I joined in 1990. The BSU—it has gone by many iterations since—sounds almost like an academic research center, and, indeed, we did a lot of research into arcane subjects. But the unit's charge is about as grim as it gets in law enforcement—or in any other line of work, for that matter: understanding and teasing out the secrets of tormented people who do unspeakably ghastly things, mostly by confronting head-on the ghastly things they have done.

The workload was onerous: During my five years with the unit, I was involved in roughly 850 cases, almost all of them homicides. Sometimes I would piece together the likely traits and characteristics of the killer, or I might do a case link analysis to determine if multiple murders had a likely single perpetrator. One afternoon I might be consulting a manual on the various ways in which flesh decays. The next day I would be comparing decapitations with my morning coffee.

I wasn't new to murder or grisly crime scenes. In Tampa, Florida, where I had been assigned before joining the BSU, I had dealt with a triple homicide—a mother and two teenage daughters—that haunts me still. Nor was I naïve about the work ahead of me when I shifted jobs: The BSU was where many of the FBI's most gruesome cases eventually migrated for help if they couldn't be puzzled out at the field office level. But in Tampa the crime diet was leavened (if that can possibly be the right word) by bank robberies, property theft, the whole broad banquet of crime. Here, it was essentially all murder all the time. The ghoul factory never closed down.

Victimology was also a big part of my work. What did the bodies themselves tell us? Or the crime scenes? If a case was headed to trial, I might advise on jury assessment and selection. As I will discuss later, I almost never saw a case through to closure. At BSU, we walked in and out of the gore. Since a lot of those 850 cases involved serial killers, I dealt with far more dead bodies than that—not one of them pretty to contemplate in its final battered, too-often gutted state.

The BSU was soon to be famous, thanks to Thomas Harris's runaway bestseller *The Silence of the Lambs* and the Oscar-sweeping 1991 film based on it. I can claim a role in that. As I'll get into later, I coached Jodie Foster (Best Actress) when she was cast as Clarice Starling for the movie. In a way, that was inevitable: Clarice was a fictional trainee at the BSU, and I was sole woman in the unit, the only one who could walk Jodie through our peculiar world from a woman's point of view. Along with all my colleagues, I also recognized many bits and pieces of the psyche of Hannibal Lecter, maybe the ultimate screen villain.

But to us the BSU was our workplace, not a film set, and to describe its visual appeal as "upscale low-rent" is to do it a major favor. Mind you, the FBI Academy and its five-hundred-plus acres carved out of the massive U.S. Marine base at Quantico, Virginia, is a spectacular facility. Opened in 1972 as the Bureau's training facility for new agents, it was later expanded to include a national academy for training selected police officers and sheriff's deputies. The BSU, though, did not get the best part of it.

For starters, our office space was two stories underground, in a repurposed site that had been designed to be longtime FBI director J. Edgar Hoover's underground bomb shelter—if and when the Cold War came to a head and if and when there was warning sufficient for Hoover to skedaddle the thirty-six miles from FBI headquarters in DC. We had no windows, of course. That wasn't the idea, but that part of Virginia can be both sweltering hot and dripping humid in summer, and to combat that and the mildew, mold, and everything else that comes with high heat and punishing humidity, we kept the air-conditioning on high from late May into September, and I worked (literally) in a parka in what seemed like fifty-degree temperatures, periodically rising to ground level as if entering a sauna.

The floor above us—still underground—mostly served as office space for the instructors who trained new FBI agents and the police officers attending the National Academy. Two floors above was the gun vault and the gun-cleaning room, the latter directly above my office down in the dungeon below. I spent my workdays with the distinct aroma of Hoppe's No. 9 gun bore cleaner wafting down through the ceiling vents. The aroma of Hoppe's still brings back vivid memories.

Not to mention the sewage. Once every eight to ten weeks, as if on government schedule, the bathrooms on our sub-subfloor would overflow, and we'd have, well, you-know-what flowing down the hall. The custodial crew would clean it up right away, but the underlying problem—plumbing from the Ice Age—got addressed only when someone anonymously contacted OSHA. I swear it wasn't me, but heartfelt thanks to whoever was responsible.

At any rate, within this underground paradise was my office space—four walls, a desk, filing cabinets, a door—and I used it the way anyone else would. (Connectivity back then was out of the question, at least for me, both because of our subterranean location and because this was the FBI, where "computer" would continue to be a dirty word for another decade.) My desk stayed mostly clear for current projects. Old ones, or ones on hold, got filed away, and the walls I used for evidence, visual reminders of what I was working on, prompts to both my conscious and subconscious awareness. Sometimes answers to deep conundrums just popped off those walls.

That's the state I left my office in one afternoon before departing for a three-day meeting on the West Coast. When I returned, the BSU was in an uproar, and I seemed to be at the heart of the problem.

"What happened?" I asked.

It turned out that while I was gone, one of the unit's biggest congressional supporters had made a quick visit, just to gauge the state of things and familiarize a few of his staffers in tow with our work. Most of the briefing was handled by John Douglas, my boss and the BSU unit chief, but at the end our friend on the Hill asked if he could show his team one of our offices, and John, knowing I was away, volunteered mine. That's where the trouble began.

The small entourage had no sooner walked into my office than one of the staffers—a guy, I was told, in his thirties—had a look around my walls, fainted dead away, cracked his head on my desk as he fell, and left a major puddle of blood on the floor before they could get some pressure on the wound.

"You injured him!" John told me, half in jest.

Injured him? I wasn't even there! But when I opened my office door, I looked around to see what might have been the matter. The walls were decorated with a series of photos that were the only traces we had of a serial killer who had been preying on homeless women in Philadelphia. All of the victims had been eviscerated from below the navel all the way up to the neck. The forensic photographer, I should add, had done a thoroughly professional job—not only in preserving the evidence without tainting the crime scene but also in capturing the full horror of the crime itself.

Who knew, I thought, that congressional staffers were such delicate flowers? But a few days later a new ruling was promulgated for the BSU: If you're going to be out of the office for even a day, clear the damn walls.

For that matter, who could have predicted that a girl who practically from the cradle wanted to right the wrongs of the world would end up in such a peculiar corner of law enforcement?

As noted earlier, I stayed with the BSU only half a decade. The psychological toll of the place was immense. I wanted to inhabit a larger, more varied world, and I did. Ruby Ridge and the Branch Davidian standoff at Waco, Texas; the school massacre at Columbine; the assault on the El Al ticket counter at Los Angeles International; the Texas Seven—they all became part of my résumé to a greater or lesser degree. I barely slept for what seems like months after 9/11. Eventually, I launched the FBI's new Cyber Division and ended my Bureau career as special agent in charge at the Phoenix field office.

All that is part of this memoir, but my half decade with the Behavioral Science Unit and the hearts of darkness I lived with there colored everything that followed. The BSU is not an experience you can just close the door on.

1.
DAYS AND NIGHTS WITH DIRTY HARRY

IF YOU'VE NEVER HEARD OF St. Edward, Nebraska, don't despair: Almost nobody has. St. Edward is a tiny town in northeastern Nebraska with a population of slightly under seven hundred people, about the same as it was when my dad was born there in 1905. In 1939, just as the Depression was easing and before a new war settled in, Dad and his teenage bride, also from St. Edward, joined the stampede to Southern California, and that's where I was born fifteen years later in Long Beach, their only child.

My mother was a fastidious housekeeper. Even our towels and washcloths were carefully ironed. I loved her dearly, but early on I knew that her life wasn't for me. Cooking was a chore for Mom, not any kind of pleasure, and her meals showed it. She had no girl-friends that I can remember, nothing like a network of acquaintances. Neither she nor my father were active in the community. They didn't attend a church. Their only social activity was bowling twice a week. The other constant in Mom's life was repainting the kitchen every Fourth of July weekend. Rather than escape the boredom of St. Edward, they seemed to have dragged it with them to the West Coast.

Dad had no more ambition than Mom did and made no more effort to broaden their social circle, but as far I was concerned, he couldn't have had a better job. Dad was the projectionist at the

Mom and Dad. He was fifteen years her senior,
and I was their only child.

West Coast Theater in Long Beach—a 3,000-seat throwback to the golden age of movies, bigger than just about anything up the road in Los Angeles—and that's basically where I was raised, on double-feature movies, and not just one showing. I would watch them again and again as the day wore on, and Dad played reel after reel. And believe me, I paid attention.

By the time I hit my teens, I could quote at length from all the Clint Eastwood movies, especially the *Dirty Harry* series, supposedly based on a real San Francisco police officer. It's probably a stretch to say that Dirty Harry was my babysitter, but Eastwood's character, Harry Callahan—ruthless, fearless, confident, willing to dig in and get his hands dirty to get the job done—was definitely a formative influence.

Even when the bad guys were supposed to be lovable, I wasn't biting. Paul Newman and Robert Redford were definitely eye candy in *Butch Cassidy and the Sundance Kid*, and they got all the good banter. But the line I remember most of all was the one they uttered in amazement when the posse was doggedly pursuing them: "Who *are* those guys?" Whoever they are, I thought, I want to be one of them.

Remember, this was the 1960s. John F. Kennedy was assassinated when I was nine; Martin Luther King Jr. and Bobby Kennedy were shot when I was just entering my teens. All three of those murders devastated me. Other kids my age were tuning in and turning on to the counterculture, ready to drop out and do acid. All I could think about was righting the wrongs of the world, beginning with the wrongs right in my own backyard at Washington Junior High School.

Our part of Long Beach was a mixed area to begin with, and busing made the school more mixed still: Asian Americans, Mexican Americans, African Americans—the whole SoCal rainbow experience. We even had our own little street gang. Almost every day at lunchtime, which we ate outside, the gang would go from group to group, shaking down kids for their pocket change or demanding their sandwiches or oranges or whatever was in the lunch bags.

Being a stickler even then for the rule of law, I naturally reported this behavior to one of my teachers; being someone not to look for trouble, she naturally did nothing about it. So, a few days later, when one of the gang members knocked my sandwich out of my hand—not to eat it but just to show he could—my inner Dirty Harry took over and I got really aggressive with him, meeting him face-to-face with only inches between us. My invasion of his space and my unwavering stare seemed to be the impetus that sent the entire gang running, but not before a lunch monitor hauled me off to the principal's office for starting the whole thing. That resulted, per school rules, in my parents being summoned, and *that* brought my interest in law enforcement out into the open where they could no longer ignore it.

Everyone—my mom and dad, the principal, the whole chain of adult authority above me—assumed this was just a phase I was going through. "Oh, next week she'll want to be ballerina, and the week after that a nurse," the reasoning went. "Jana will outgrow this."

I didn't. In fact, that same year I went on my first official law enforcement mission, although "official" and "mission" might overstate things. Our neighbor's son was with the Long Beach Police Department, so I asked if I could ride along with him for a couple nights, and he said, "Sure."

I can't say it was very exciting—I keep thinking of the old TV series *The Mod Squad* in trying to describe those few nights—but on the second evening we finally saw some action. A bartender had called in a disturbance, so we raced over there with siren blaring and arrived the same time as another policeman, who had been summoned as backup in case alcohol was involved, which it was—in quantity.

A very attractive (and also very inebriated) woman in a stylish trench coat had turned rowdy and obnoxious, and increasingly athletic and voluble. Just as we arrived, she climbed up on a table and let loose with a foulmouthed torrent that couldn't be ignored.

"I'm sorry, ma'am," my neighbor's son said, in his best guy-takes-charge voice, "we're going to have to arrest you."

And with that, she stripped off her long trench coat, revealing she was completely naked underneath. I remember laughing in surprise at that moment, along with most of the patrons in the bar, but my two male police officer companions were far from amused. Where do we touch her? Are we even allowed to look at her? And the handcuffs—how in the hell do we get those on?

I was a ride-along, mind you, barely a teenager, zero help other than to observe. Still, I couldn't help but notice that, in the midst of this small-neighborhood-bar debacle, the two male police officers were standing around with their thumbs up their noses, with no idea what to do next. Law enforcement, I thought, was definitely in need of additional training, especially in situations requiring interactions with the opposite gender. Maybe there really was space for a woman's sensibility.

By junior high, I was already trying to right the wrongs of the world.

2.
GIRLS ARE GIRLS, COPS ARE COPS

AS EYE-OPENING IN MULTIPLE WAYS as that first law enforcement foray was, it did little to prepare me for what I would eventually encounter as a "real" police officer and, later, FBI agent, but it did steel my resolve. I knew I could do this—that policing was within my skill set—and I was not going to be told no, even though I was told just that time and again.

At Long Beach State University, I majored in criminology, but when I graduated in 1976, Proposition 13 was still strangling state and municipal budgets in California, and no police departments—at least, that I could find—were hiring. I continued working at the local department store where I had started when I was fifteen years old, stayed all through college, and eventually became a junior assistant buyer—not exactly what my college training had prepared me for, but at least it fed my lifelong interest in fashion.

Meanwhile, I kept looking for female role models to guide me on the way. In fact, I probably would have done better to search for Amelia Earhart's remains. Almost invariably, the only women in the policing-related movies I watched were uniformed secretaries or file clerks for square-jawed, no-nonsense cops or leggy secretaries for wisecracking private detectives.

On NBC's procedural series *Police Woman*, Angie Dickinson's portrayal of Sergeant Suzanne "Pepper" Anderson gave me some hope that a female could succeed in a male-dominated world, but I didn't see myself going undercover as a prostitute, flight attendant, or dancer to help bag the bad guys. Even if I had, though, nothing in *Police Woman* would have prepared me for my very first job in law enforcement: a short stint just out of college at the Youth Training School (YTS) in Chino, California. YTS sounds like a nice, polite place for kids, and in a better world it might have been just that. But despite its benevolent name, YTS was nothing more than a prison for juveniles, and its youthful inmates were the worst of the worst. Convicted of crimes like homicide, grand theft, rape, assault, and battery, most of the "residents" at YTS deserved to be in adult prisons but were too young to be sent there. However, here was the truly shocking thing: All the men I worked with were worse than the prisoners. They leered at me, made constant sexual comments, and used the F-word like it was "Hello." Of the kids, I

As this photo suggests, my tenure as a probation officer was heavy on paperwork.

quickly had few if any expectations. Of the adults, I kept hoping forlornly for better.

TV's Pepper Anderson didn't do me much good either when the Proposition 13 drought broke and I was finally able to land real law enforcement–related jobs, first with the probation department in Ontario, then with the Chino and Upland police departments, all in Southern California.

Women by then were no longer absolute rarities in law enforcement. The feminist movement had noticed that this large sector of American employment had long been closed to half the American population, especially at the operational level, and a class action lawsuit was already working its way through the courts to force the FBI to open its doors as well. But even when women managed to secure police work, our male colleagues generally had no idea what to make of us.

Partially this was old-fashioned chivalry, partially chauvinism. A fair amount of male pigheadedness and confusion entered into the mix as well. Policing could be rough business; women were the fairer sex. What to do?

The answer, at least in the places I worked early on, was to designate the new females on the force as "quick-draw" officers, which meant basically that we would do everything the men didn't want to do. Babysitting, for example.

People seldom think of police forces as being in the kiddie care business, but Child Protective Services (CPS) exists for that very purpose. If we were heading out to make an arrest and knew there were likely to be small children in the house, we would give CPS a heads-up so they could arrive simultaneously and take the children into temporary custody. CPS, though, didn't seem to operate on exactly the same clock as we did. Often there would be a gap between our departure and their arrival, and that's when a female officer proved particularly handy.

"Quick, draw something with these kids," one of the guys would shout over his shoulder at someone like me, and then someone like me would sit for sometimes hours at a time, trying to humor scared little boys and girls who had just seen their mommy and/or daddy being handcuffed and led out the door by a bunch of heavily armed officers.

Fun, this wasn't, but obviously the job needed doing, and as far as my male colleagues were concerned, this was women's work, plain and simple.

One time, the wait for CPS stretched so long into the evening that I finally took two adorable little kids home with me—probably illegally and certainly stupidly, since if anything had happened to them while they were in my care, I would have been on the hook and out of a job—but the three of us survived the night, and the kids were rested and well-fed when I turned them over to CPS the next morning.

The older kids I dealt with during my brief time with the San Bernardino Probation Department were often the exact opposite of whatever "adorable" is. These were juveniles who frequently came into their teens already trailing criminal records and were probably eventually headed to the Youth Training School in Chino I had worked at earlier, or a similar facility, on their way to an adult life in and out of confinement.

I remember one thirteen-year-boy in particular—a small, skinny, extremely violent kid with one of the foulest mouths I've ever encountered, adult or child. His parents had basically given up on him, and he had clearly given up on complying with the terms and conditions of the probation he was already on for crimes I have long since forgotten. After the fourth or fifth such violation, we had no choice but to arrest him and haul him down to San Bernardino's Central Juvenile Hall.

At first, the job looked easy. The parents knew we were coming—in fact, they wanted us to come—and they assured us their son was asleep in his bed, which he was. So my male partner and I woke him, told him who we were and what we were doing there, and were about to haul this scrawny little guy wearing nothing but boxer shorts away to an uncertain fate when some inner mothering instinct took hold of me and I asked him if he didn't want to get dressed first.

"Sure," he said, and started for his closet, then cut right, jumped through his second-floor window, hit the ground, and took off running.

Speed afoot was not my partner's long suit, but I eventually ran the kid down, cuffed him, and was waiting by the road when my partner pulled up in his cruiser, explained that he'd had another call, and asked if I could drive the kid the forty minutes back to San Bernardino. (We'd come in separate cars.) With that, he ran us back to my car and took off, and I sat the boy in the back seat, tightened the legs restraints we always used in these circumstances, and set off for Juvenile Hall.

About ten minutes into the trip, this normally voluble cursing machine was so quiet that I adjusted the rearview mirror and took a peek at him, and he was sitting there with both hands free, picking his nose. This was before steel screens between the front and back seat, before back doors that couldn't be unlocked from the inside, before all sorts of protections. If the kid had had the sense to reach down and undo his leg restraints, he could have jumped me in the front seat or taken a chance and thrown himself out the back door. Instead, I slammed the brakes on, wrestled him onto the ground, used flex-cuffs this time—I'd failed to notice that his wrists were so thin, he could slip right out of the standard cuffs— and proceeded on to San Bernardino with a new and profound gratitude for the training I had to date and hungry for more.

• • •

TRAINING, THOUGH, CAN PREPARE YOU for only so much, as the cow on Central Avenue in Chino so effectively proved.

Chino today is a bustling city of more than 90,000 people, but back then, in the very early 1980s, it was still a farm town at the heart of one of the largest dairy centers in the state, a fact you could smell long before you got to Chino proper. The city was surrounded by milk cows, some of which occasionally slipped through open gates or downed fences and meandered around until they found someplace highly inconvenient to the general population, then refused to move a step farther.

This particular cow had decided to station herself on a bustling thoroughfare dead at the heart of Chino, which naturally caused a massive traffic jam. Naturally, also, the Chino PD turned this problem over to its "quick-draw" officer—me—which is how I found myself in the middle of a sea of honking cars and irritated drivers, trying to reason with a half ton of cow flesh. I had a vague memory that cows, unlike horses, can kick sideways, not just backward, which kept me head-on with the cow, in a perfect position to be stampeded if this major traffic obstruction took off running. Maybe because I was a woman, I also couldn't help but notice that her udders looked close to bursting, which couldn't be improving her temperament.

Other than that, though, I had no idea what to do. Nothing in my training—no scene in any of the movies I had watched at my dad's movie theater—had prepared me for this moment. To the best of my knowledge, Dirty Harry had *never once* faced a circumstance like this. But I knew with dead certainty what the guys back in the squad room would have to say once this was over: "What? You can't even get a cow out of the middle of Central Avenue? Women!"— which is pretty much exactly what they did say once one of the dairy farmers stuck in the traffic took charge of the situation and got Bessie off the street, and Chino could go back about its business.

Was the cow control gig a setup? Sure, in a way. I can just see the police dispatcher's face breaking into a big smile when someone called in a heifer problem on Central Avenue.

"Who should we give this one to?" he might have called to the guys around the station house. And they would have answered in unison: "The quick-draw officer!"

In fact, though, I brought some of this razzing down on myself. I'm not physically imposing, but I was trying to make my way in what had always before been a man's world, and I was determined not to be disregarded or dismissed. I did all the "lady cop" work that was asked of me to the best of my ability—and, in the cow's case, to the limits of my experience. Looking after kids while we waited for Child Protective Services was a form of stereotyping, but it was still important work. There was never a child in my custody during that time who was happy about the situation they had been placed in. How could they be? They had just seen their parents cuffed and hauled off to jail. But as a woman, I was less threatening to them than a man would have been in those circumstances, especially since the arresting officers were almost without exception males.

Similarly, interviewing female victims of battery or rape or whatever the crime—another of the regular quick-draw assignments—was an essential use of the new female component on police forces. Women can talk more easily with each other about all kinds of subjects, including the awful things that sometimes happen to them precisely because they are women. But was I happy doing "lady cop" work? No, of course not. I felt like a second-class citizen, a child being handed busywork to placate them. And I was determined the role wouldn't last.

If there was "man's work" to be done, I volunteered for it. If the opportunity to volunteer didn't arise, I would pester the guys on the force to take me along. And when they did take me along, I sometimes went out of my way—maybe too far out of my way—to show that I could be tough as nails, too. There's an old saying that goes: "If you can't find a seat at the table, bring a folding chair." That's what I did. I set up that chair as close to the table as I could get it, and, in what I think of as my own quiet way, I demanded to be noticed and included. I would be shocked, and maybe even a bit disappointed, if my male colleagues didn't sometimes refer to me as "that pushy broad," in the language of the times. But you can't learn on the job if you are not given the opportunity, and if I forced the opportunity, it was always with the goal of learning more and more and more.

Sometimes the results were grudging at best. I had never worked drugs, but I'd gone to coffee with a bunch of the guys who did, and while we were talking I said, "Next arrest, please include me if you need additional help." A few days later they did.

I was never told what the arrest plan was, and I didn't ask. It was going to be a controlled vehicle stop—that much I did know—and vehicle stops are never optimal. They have too many moving parts, figuratively and literally. But there were seven of us in on the arrest and only two targets in the car. That put the odds in our favor, and the bad guys seemed to realize that. They stopped the car without incident, exited on command, and were standing there, showing no sign of resistance, when the case agent turned and threw me the handcuffs.

"Here," he said, "you put 'em on."

In different circumstances, that might have been an honor. He might have even meant it that way, but I was so unprepared for the moment that I barely caught the handcuffs and was still fumbling with them when the bad guys conveniently held out their arms for me to cuff them. Clearly, they had had a lot more experience with this than I did. In any event, on went the cuffs, and off they both went to booking.

• • •

OTHER TIMES, MY OFF-AND-ON INITIATION into what I considered "real policing" bordered on the farcical, such as the first time I was allowed to handle the "knock-and-announce." As I'll get to later, this is an especially big deal in the FBI, but it wasn't small potatoes in this instance, either. The guys had taken me along on a response to a domestic disturbance in progress, and Dispatch had advised us the suspects might have a gun in the house. When we got there, my colleagues said, completely out of the blue, "Okay, Jana, you make the arrest. You go through the door."

Maybe it was the fact that the man and woman on the other side of the door were screaming so loudly at each other that none of the other officers wanted to risk getting between them. Maybe it was an expression of grudging respect for my iron determination to be a "full cop," not just a quick-draw one. Maybe it was just another test: Would she do this, knowing there might be a gun on the other side of the door? And if so, how badly would she screw it up?

Whatever had motivated the offer, I took the bit in my teeth, marched up to that door, gave it a good, loud bang, and shouted out, "Police! Open up!" With that, the door, which hadn't been latched, flew right open, and the two people on the couch inside—who up to that moment had been vehemently angry with each other—suddenly verbally attacked me with such vigor and enough suggestions of physical violence to follow that I drew my weapon to calm things down. And that's when the real trouble began.

The problem was twofold. First, I was wearing hoop earrings because, even when I was in uniform, I liked to look my best. Second, I also was carrying a shoulder bag and had no time to run it back to the squad car before the knock-and-announce. Normally, this combination would not have been cause for alarm, but somehow, in drawing my gun, I hitched up my shoulder and when I did, the strap for my bag got tangled up in my hoop earring. I quickly reholstered my gun when it became apparent the warring couple had no weapons at hand, but by then my shoulder bag was basically hanging from my right earlobe, which hurt like the devil and soon began to bleed.

All in all, this amounted to a pathetic enough situation that my colleagues took charge of the couple while I untangled my makeshift ear ornament with one hand while stemming the blood flow with a large wad of tissue. On the plus side, my sideshow seemed to quickly defuse the domestic disturbance, or maybe it just united the combatants in mutual derision of their would-be arresting officer. Either way, it wasn't long before peace was restored, and we were on our way back to the station, chuckling at the unique way this situation had been resolved.

THROUGH ALL THESE "COULDAS" AND "shouldas," I kept learning, kept gaining experience, kept hardening myself and building self-sufficiency, so that when I finally did make it to big-city policing in 1982—a temporary assignment from the Upland PD to Los Angeles—I felt confident I could work cases and ride the streets in the 77th Division, including Watts, which had been torn apart by riots in 1965 and would erupt again in 1992 following the acquittal of four LAPD officers involved in the beating of Rodney King.

By then, I'd even had my own brush with gunfire—something that I will stress throughout this book isn't at all common in law enforcement work. I was out on a gangland-related drug surveillance with two Upland detectives when the bad guys spotted us as they were driving by, started shooting, and hit our driver in the knee. Or at least that's what we originally thought. By the time we got through the after-incident report, though, it became apparent that in the heat of the moment the detective in the back seat had

had a Barney Fife moment—not only shooting out our own wind-shield but also firing the bullet that hit the other detective's knee. I still consider it a minor miracle that the gunfire didn't also hit me in the passenger seat. Friendly fire can be as deadly as incoming.

Undeterred by that incident or maybe hoping for an improved experience, I asked my new colleagues in the 77th Division to let me ride along as an observer on an arrest, but these guys saw things differently.

"This would be a really stupid place for you," one of them told me. "This isn't juvie work"—his way of telling me this wasn't a quick-draw assignment. "We're going to a really dangerous place, and a white blonde like you would stick out like a sore thumb."

My first reaction was my usual internal response in such situations: "I am woman. Hear me roar!" But it didn't take me long to see that this officer was right. If I were along, these guys would inevitably be in protection mode, at least to some extent. And in a firefight, if it came to that, you need a hundred percent of your attention on the bad guys. I wanted the experience of course—I always did; I was starving for it—but not at the expense of endangering fellow officers.

3.
GETTING SERIOUS

POLICING WAS A MAN'S WORLD when I started out, far more so than it is today. Time and again I had to push my way forward, into and across the gender gap. But other critical issues were at play, too—issues that continue to plague law enforcement and society as a whole—and I was thrown right in the middle of them as well.

One of the jobs I drew early on—almost certainly because they couldn't think of where else to put me—was as a community school police officer, the cop who worries about kids who would rather smoke down an alleyway than show up for math class. A few acts of truancy were generally forgiven, but after a set number I was summoned, and the school would set up a hearing with a student's parent or parents or guardians or whoever was in theory responsible for them, and half the time a "responsible adult" wouldn't even show up. When they did, it was often almost worse: Some parents or guardians were drunk; others were under the influence of something almost certainly illegal. Even the ones who did appear and clearly cared were often barely making a living or even holding their lives and families together.

Was it depressing? Sure, and sad, of course, and in its own tortured way even educational. After a while I began to think that the kids who were off hustling during the school day instead of nodding off half comprehendingly in class were the resourceful ones—the ones better training themselves for their world as it is, not the world as we want it to be for them.

My time as a probation officer and doing presentencing investigations for the Superior Court was equally frustrating. It wasn't like the work was unimportant. Part of my job was to make recommendations for a juvenile-court process known as a "fitness" or "transfer" hearing, in which a judge determines whether or not a minor should be transferred to face criminal changes in adult court. In effect, I was helping to determine what tier of punishment would be imposed: jail or prison time or perhaps probation for those found guilty in adult court; a relatively comfy juvenile hall or a much tougher youth correction facility such as the one I worked at in Chino, or again probation for those too young for a "fit and proper" adult hearing.

I took the work seriously because I felt I had to. My recommendations could affect the course of an entire lifetime. But the caseload was ridiculously high, and way too often when I recommended after much consideration that someone's probation be revoked, the judge would glance at his docket, think about how crowded the incarceration options already were, and say no. With that, whoever it was would go back on the street, and the whole cycle would start over again.

That scrawny kid I mentioned earlier—the one I ran down after he leaped out his bedroom window? He was in constant violation of the terms and conditions of his probation. He'd fled arrest; he was walking, talking evidence that, without meaningful intervention and counseling, recidivism is all but guaranteed, and after I hauled him in, the judge socked him with a weekend detention in juvenile hall. Big whoopee.

So many of the teenagers I dealt with lived at the intersection of youthful abuse, poverty, racism, terrible decision-making skills, and boiling rage. I remember one eighteen-year-old who had been sexually molested by an adult male as a child and was still confused about his own sexual identity. He repeatedly told the psychiatrists who examined him that he was evil, bad to the core. By then there was evidence to that effect.

The eighteen-year-old had recruited two accomplices—one age fifteen, the other twenty-one—to help him rob a thirty-something gay couple at their home in Upland. That part was easy, and the haul was a bonanza: nearly $10,000 in cash and valuables stored in the house. Only afterward did it dawn on the eighteen-year-old that the two men could readily identify him, so he and his ad hoc crime team appropriated a car rented by one of the victims, stuffed the two men in the trunk, dropped off the twenty-one-year-old, and drove into the mountains before stopping, beating both men unconscious, and throwing their bodies down a steep thousand-foot slope. One survived and by morning had scrambled back to the stop of the slope, where he was helped by joggers and connected with the Upland police. By noon that day, the eighteen-year-old and his fifteen-year-old partner were hunted down. They were still driving the dead man's car.

One could argue with the light sentencing in the case: The twenty-one-year-old was handed a life sentence even though he wasn't present at the murder site, but he was given the possibility of parole; the fifteen-year-old was remanded to Juvenile Hall, where he would remain until he reached age twenty-one. For the eighteen-year-old, though, life was over. He was tried as an adult and sentenced to life in prison without possibility of parole. Essentially, the court agreed with his own self-assessment: Whatever had made him that way, he was really and truly bad to the core.

Don't despair: There are positive tales from those days—upbeat counterbalances to all those young men who had been abused in one way or another as children and grown into rageful and sometimes homicidal teenagers. There had to be: The job would have been unbearable without them. But even the positive stories from those days were always in danger of tumbling into negative territory. At one level, Orlando Montoya was a typical problem kid: in a lot of trouble at an early age, deep into one of the few gangs in Upland, and with minimal prospects ahead of him. But he somehow managed to get himself into the Marine Corps— or more likely was given the option (available back then) of "enlist-ing" in the Corps or going to jail—and the Marines turned him totally around.

By the time I transferred from the Chino to Upland police forces, Orlando was a year or two out of the Marines and had become the best hope for a lot of area kids growing up much as he had. Orlando mentored them through after-school programs, especially boxing, which was popular in the Latino neighbor-hoods. He was always available for kids in crisis or for our police force in understanding the deeper issues often behind those crises.

In my own mind, I can still project a future for Orlando that might have included local or state political office, maybe even Congress and beyond, but none of that was to be. One evening, as Orlando Montoya was minding his own business, he was killed in a drive-by shooting, whether intentionally or not we could never prove. Orlando had lived by the gang growing up; he might have died by the gang as well.

Which gets me to the gang members themselves, who also made my early policing work so difficult and educational. Los Angeles was then and remains to this day the gang capital of America. The suburbs and exurbs where I learned policing were no match for that big city, but the gangs were steadily metastasiz-ing out of downtown LA and degrading everything in their path.

The crimes were getting worse by the month, it seemed, and the gang members we arrested ever younger. I can remember hauling in and talking with eleven- and twelve-year-olds who already had the equivalent of Murder One on their juvenile rap sheets. More and more, I wanted to understand the deeper *why* of all that—not just what had precipitated the violent acts that had brought these kids to our attention, but what had attracted them so powerfully to gangs in the first place. To that end, I began to read up on the meaning of the various tattoos that gang members were covered with. It was like a mystical, nonverbal language that actually told you a great deal: not only the specific gangs they belonged to but the types of crimes they were most likely to commit as acts of loyalty. I also read whatever I could find on the psychology of gangs and gang behavior and on the developmental and socioeconomic issues that underlay all that.

The gang kids I worked with were often far from unintelligent. They might have been too immature to imagine the consequences of whacking a rival gang member, but they clearly knew right from wrong. Many of them had older brothers and cousins already in prison for similar acts. They might even have seen them behind bars. And yet they had pulled that trigger. Why?

The best answer I could come up with was the simplest one. Yes, these kids had been dealt a bad hand. Role models like Orlando Montoya were few. Their schools were almost uniformly lacking. Violence was often endemic in their neighborhoods. All that played a role, but above it all was the power of belonging. Gang membership entails certain obligations: Only kids willing to be badasses need apply. But gangs also gave them the definition and meaning they hungered for, and prison by those terms was less a punishment than a badge of honor.

Whether all this speculating I was doing on the nature of evil presaged my eventual tenure with the FBI's Behavioral Science Unit, I have no idea, but it wasn't long before I became the go-to person among my colleagues for questions about gang members. Maybe that's what began to urge me toward operating in a larger venue like the FBI, but I think it had been in the back of my mind all along. There were, however, two serious impediments to that: my boss and my then husband.

LET'S START WITH THE EASIER of those two: my captain in Upland.

"These assignments I'm getting," I told him. "I feel like I'm going nowhere with them, so I've applied to the FBI. I want a broader range of experience."

His response wasn't exactly encouraging: "The FBI won't take you."

"I don't know why not," I said. "I think I can do it." And I honestly did. By then I had worked everything from truancy to homicide, at least glancingly, including a fatal encounter during "Bat Night" at Dodgers Stadium. Two inebriated fans of the opposing teams attacked each other with the miniature wooden bats given away in the promotional, one with enough fury to smash in the other's skull. Los Angeles police had jurisdiction, but the assailant was from nearby Ontario, where I was working, and enough bits and pieces of the case fell my way that I got a good taste of what a homicide investigation entails. (Bat Night giveaways throughout Major League Baseball turned almost immediately to lightweight plastic bats—better for America's forests and humanity generally.)

I had also seen enough dead bodies laid out on slabs with medical examiners probing them to know that both my stomach and my psyche could handle violent death and its aftermath. The first of those was an act of nature, not man—a twenty-year-old water-skier struck by lightning—but as the medical examiner went to great pains to point out, the damage to the young man's body was broad and immense.

I was also among the very few women in law enforcement, and I was applying to an FBI finally awakening to the need for women in its ranks.

None of that had much meaning to my boss, but he at least grunted an "Okay" and then quickly added, "I'll bet you fifteen bucks you're not going to get in, but if you do get through the written part of it, I'll write you a letter of recommendation."

For me, that was victory enough, and I think my captain, in his own gruff way, was pleased when I did pass the written exam and the numerous additional tests—psychological; physical health, ability, and agility; firearms strength-trigger pull; and several interview sessions—and was waiting to head off to the FBI Academy for the far more demanding sixteen weeks of training. Even then, though, he wasn't ready to come fully on board. He paid off our bet, but the two bills—a $5 and a $10—arrived laminated onto a plaque that read: "Good Luck in Butte." This was a reference to J. Edgar Hoover's preferred punishment for agents who had seriously embarrassed the Bureau but not sufficiently to fire them: banishment to the Butte, Montana, office, the equivalent in Hoover's mind of Russia's Eastern Front. (Nothing against Butte, by the way. It's a great city.)

Doug, my husband, was a more complicated matter. We had married young—twenty-one on my part, twenty-three on his, almost commonplace in those days—and we both hoped that time would iron out our differences. Doug wanted a traditional 1950s housewife you'd see on television—someone like Harriet Nelson or June Cleaver who would be waiting at home when he returned from the office or got back from a hard week on the road, with a warm meal in the oven, nicely scrubbed kids, and amusing tales of school triumphs, neighborhood pranks, and the like. I told him early on that life wasn't for me. I was going to

CONGRATULATIONS, JANA
- Good Luck In Butte -
CAPTAIN A.
JULY 1985

My boss bet me fifteen dollars the FBI would never accept me . . .
then paid me off with two bills glued to a plaque.

have a career in law enforcement no matter how many obstacles sprung up in my path.

Still, he tolerated my winding path through the San Bernardino Probation Department and the Chino and Upland police departments because he believed my feminist determination to succeed in law enforcement would yield over time to a woman's natural desire to bear children and mother them above all else.

For my part, I tolerated his downplaying of my ambitions because he was a decent man who surely would come around to understanding that the woman he wanted me to be wasn't the woman he married, nor one I had ever pretended to be. There had been warning signs all along that this wasn't going to happen. At every stage of my early career, he seemed shocked not only that I got the job but also that I succeeded in every police assignment

I landed. However, this wasn't the first marriage that pitted hope against experience, and it surely won't be the last.

In short, we were on a collision path, and my applying to and being accepted by the FBI didn't help matters—or maybe it just hastened the inevitable. I don't know if the Bureau did this for male recruits or if they still do this for new recruits of either sex, but back then, if a married woman was about to join the FBI, they called in your spouse for a special joint interview to let him know just how an FBI career works and make sure he supported it.

"If Jana makes it through the Academy"—the training threshold for full employment—"there's a pretty good likelihood you will be moving," the interviewer told Doug. "How do you like the sound of that?"

"Well, I have to think about that."

Not a good sign, since I had been prepping Doug for days about what this interview was likely to entail and how he might best respond. It was not the only answer that he prefaced that day with a long and wavering "Well . . ."

A couple evenings later, we were stuck in a colossal traffic jam on one of LA's infamous overcrowded freeways, headed to Hollywood Bowl, when our marital illusions and delusions disappeared for good.

"Why is this so different?" I asked when Doug started in again on why my joining the FBI was a terrible idea.

I'll spare readers the back-and-forth bickering. The gist of it was that Doug had tolerated my dream of joining the FBI only because he never thought I'd make it. Now that I was on the threshold of actually getting a foot in that door, it was time to get real. I had proven myself, he said in so many words. Now my job was to settle down and have our children.

With that, I got out of the car, walked across I don't remember how many lanes to one of the call boxes along the side of the road, and called Doug's father to come get me and take me home.

To this day, I don't know what says more about how upset I was at that moment and how much I was willing to endure to make my dream come true: the fact that I called my soon-to-be ex–father-in-law to rescue me, or the fact that the Hollywood Bowl show I voluntarily missed that night was one I had been looking forward to for months—Willie Nelson and Waylon Jennings, live and together. In any event, our marriage was over. I was headed to the FBI even if I had to break I don't know how many laws prohibiting walking on the freeway to get there.

4.
BREAKING THROUGH

IN MY PREVIOUS LAW ENFORCEMENT work, I learned mostly on the job. Schooling was minimal. Your instructors were mostly the few older colleagues willing to teach you the ropes. Experience might not always be the best teacher, but in many cases it was the only one. The FBI was just the opposite. Your entire career was provisional until you had mastered the basics of the job.

About a month after I received my acceptance letter from the Bureau, a group of forty of us newbies showed up at the FBI Academy at Quantico to begin a four-month training program. (The exact date, never to be forgotten, was July 29, 1985.) Privately, we might have begun thinking of ourselves as "agents," but if we screwed up this training regimen, our tenure with the fabled FBI would be over before it began.

We were all eager, all gung ho, mostly male—I was one of eight women in my class—and, given that this was law enforcement, we were from surprisingly diverse backgrounds. Our class had its fair share of ex-military and former local police officers like me, looking to be part of something bigger. That you might expect. But we also had a fair representation of CPAs, MBAs, and attorneys, people more familiar with white-collar work than kicking in doors. No matter where you were likely to end up in the Bureau

I riddled this target at the FBI Academy in all the right places.

ultimately—white-collar crime, counterintelligence, public corruption, racketeering investigations, bank robbery, government
fraud, you name it—we all started the same place. And for four
solid months, we worked hard to earn our spots.*

At one level, this was like any academic program. We had a
general legal component. We studied elements of specific cases,
learned all about RICO (for Racketeer Influenced and Corrupt
Organizations) violations and the various elements of white-collar
crime, and dove deeply into the sorts of criminal activity more
likely to surface on TV and in the movies: kidnapping, bank robberies, murders for hire, drug trafficking, violent fugitives, and the
like. You had to keep up with the reading and pay attention in

* New agents, I should add, now spend an average of twenty weeks in training. After
9/11, the Bureau added several weeks of counterterrorism and intelligence training.
Other sections are added to the program as domestic and global situations dictate.

class, but there was a host of real-world examples to bring all the legal abstractions home.

At another level, it was kind of like summer camp for young-ish adults. We had firearms training and specialized classes like photography and surveillance—in part so we could learn what we were good at but more to help the instructors place us after the training was all over. It took me only a few hours in photography class—this was before fail-safe cell phone cameras—to figure out that surveillance wasn't in my future. ("What were you trying to do here?" my puzzled instructor asked after I turned in blurry surveil-lance photos, then added before I could answer, "I don't think this is your calling." Roger that!) Like other adult camps, we also got to party some in the after hours. It wasn't all blood, sweat, and tears. There were beers, too, although that was always a bit of a thorn in my side; beer was the beverage of choice for manly LEOs, as law

Beer flowed when we agents-in-training got a chance to party, but I'm more inclined to champagne.

enforcement officers are known, but this LEO is more a fine-wine-and-champagne girl.

Looked at still another way, we were lab rats scurrying (almost literally) through a series of mazes while the grown-ups in the room tried to figure out what to do with us. Skill sets were only a part of that. Temperament, background, performance, and a host of other factors, including need, all figured into the placement calculation. White-collar crime was flourishing in and around the major FBI offices in New York, Chicago, Los Angeles, and the like. The bean counters were pretty sure in general terms where they would land even before future office assignments were handed out about half-way through the four months. The rest of us lived with the suspense.

Back then—I don't think they still do it—the instructors also took time to talk about values: ours and the Bureau's. FBI, we were told, really stood for "Fidelity, Bravery, and Integrity" more than "Federal Bureau of Investigation." I'm admittedly a sucker for this kind of thing: I loved hearing that and I loved our general discussions about ethics. At one point they gave us ten values—honesty, integrity, respect, etc.—and asked us to rank them in order of importance to us. One of the guy trainees, Dale Monroe, and I ended up with identical lists, top to bottom.

The distant odds of that happening led us to explore our other similarities in our off hours at the Academy, and those turned out to be plentiful.

Dale had graduated from the University of Arizona bound and determined to join the Marines. To that end, he took the qualifying test at the Naval Officer Recruiting Center in Tucson. (There was no Marine Officer Recruiting Center, so the Navy handled both.) He passed and was contacted to come in and sign on the dotted line to head off to Marine Officer Candidate School at Quantico, Virginia. However, the Navy handed Dale the paperwork for Naval Officer Training School.

Some young couples pose on tropical islands or ski slopes.
Not Dale and I!

"Wait a minute," he told them. "There's a mistake here. I'm joining the Corps."

"Not as an officer," came the reply. "Your scores weren't high enough. But the Navy—"

"With all due respect, I'm not interested in the Navy," he said. "If I can't get into Marine OCS, I'll enlist and go to Parris Island," which is exactly what Dale did once he got back home to Connecticut.

Dale never got to Parris Island, though. Following his swearing-in ceremony to the USMC and while his enlistment was being processed through the New York City office, Bob Mack, a Marine captain and Vietnam veteran, noticed that a college graduate was headed for boot camp at Parris Island and called Dale in for a talk. As it turned out, the New York City Marine Corps recruiting office handled both enlisted and officer recruitments.

After meeting and confirming the qualifying scores with Marine Corps headquarters, Captain Mack changed the orders from Parris Island to Marine OCS at Quantico, which eventually led to two overseas tours as a Marine helicopter pilot in Japan and Korea.

I should add that I didn't get this full story until almost twenty years later when that same Bob Mack—now an FBI supervisory special agent (SSA)—and I were having dinner in San Francisco and conversation turned to people we knew who were driven by commitment and conviction.

"There was this guy," Bob said, "I don't remember his name, but I at first thought the guy had to be some kind of an idiot. He had qualified for Marine OCS, although the Navy told him he hadn't the scores, so he enlisted in the Marines and—"

"Because he wasn't going to let anything get in the way of what he knew he should do?"

"Well, yeah."

"I think you're talking about my husband, Bob. That's one of the reasons I married him."

Bob was, in fact, talking about Dale, and Dale Monroe and I did get married within the year of first meeting—my second and permanent husband.

A FLOURISHING ROMANCE ASIDE, THE whole four months at the FBI Training Academy was a deep dive into self-awareness. I'm very introspective, and I learned during this time that while I would rather not be confined to prison—having by then already met too many prisoners myself—I could be perfectly happy if I were institutionalized in some other, more benign way. The structure and fast pace fit me just right. I seem to have been constructed to jump from one thing to another to another, doing this and that, against a clock sometimes but more often against my own self-expectations. And I learned I really thrive in that kind of an environment.

Who knew in those balmy early days with the Bureau
that I was destined for the Behavioral Science Unit and
Dale for the Hostage Rescue Team?

I've also always done well in schools—I'm kind of an academic nerd—so that part actually was easy for me, especially since
this wasn't abstract material you had to bang your head against just
to begin to understand what was going on. But what I most loved
about the whole training and got the most out of were the opportunities for practical application. Learning is all well and good, but
there's nothing like operationalizing what you have learned.

The time I had already put in as a LEO gave me a leg up on this
part of the training. I'd made real arrests, in the real world, under
the threat of real violence, but going through one confrontation-
and-arrest scenario after another under the scrutinizing eye of
experienced instructors built memory muscle that I'm sure has
saved my life more than once in the decades since.

I should add that my class of new agents did all this under
relatively primitive conditions. The training site was called Hogan's

Alley—after the crime-ridden New York tenement that was the setting for the 1890s comic strip of the same name—but our urban takedowns took place in basically rural settings, and our surveillance was more peeping around trees than anything cloak-and-dagger. We also were required to play all the parts: a cop one day, a robber the next. Two years later, in 1987, a brand-new Hogan's Alley opened for business on the Quantico campus, and the training took a quantum leap forward.

Officially, this new version of Hogan's Alley is the province of the Practical Applications Unit. The PAU serves as mayor, board of aldermen, clerk of court, and grand impresario of a mock town that includes a bank (the Bank of Hogan), a post office, the All-Meds Drug Store (with rooms for rent in the floors above), and more.

The FBI likes to boast that Hogan's Alley has the highest crime rate in America, maybe in the world, perhaps because it was constructed for the exact purpose of showcasing crime in nearly all its many forms and giving rookie crime busters a chance to hone their skills in more or less real-world situations but before they can do real-world harm. Prowling the streets of this new Hogan's Alley is where everything about the training program comes together: arrest techniques, fire discipline, hostage negotiation, conversations, interviewing skills, interrogation technique, and—not to be underrated—common sense.

Not long after the new Hogan's Alley opened, I happened to be back at Quantico with some time to spare and was allowed to go through several days of training with the current new-agent class. On one occasion the whole group was broken up into smaller groups of three or four people and given a scenario. My group—of which I was as usual the only woman—was told (a) that there was a fugitive down in the dogwood grove at the end of the main street, (b) that we didn't have a warrant for his arrest, and (c) . . . well, that was about it. This, as I already knew from my time in local police work and now two years with the Bureau, was how law enforcement often works in the real world. You are never going to get that ideal two-day briefing beforehand. There will always be things you don't know, which means you are almost always going to need to adjust to some extent on the fly. At some point, it all comes down to instincts, and, at least at this point in their training, the instincts of many of the male trainees were still a little lacking.

"What are you going to do about this fugitive?" our instructor asked, and left the answer to us.

For the most part, the guys knew *just* what to do about this effing fugitive. They charged into the dogwood end of Hogan's Alley ready to mow down anything that moved . . . which was not exactly the right response, given that there had been no indication that the fugitive in the woods was armed and dangerous or holding a hostage. What's more, the federal crime in question for which a warrant had yet to be issued might have been something like interstate flight to avoid alimony payments, which, while annoying, is generally not considered a capital offense. Not to mention, who knows what or who else spraying the woods with gunfire was likely to maim, kill, or impair, just to touch on the obvious flaws in this line of response.

(This was another time—one among many in my early years in this business—when I thought a woman's sensibility was not only called for in law enforcement but absolutely needed.)

The right answer, of course, was to put action on hold while we asked all the questions we needed answered before we could plan a strategy right for the situation. For example:

- **Who is the judge on call so I can get a warrant?**
- **Does he or she take phone calls?**
- **Since he or she is likely to ask me the source of the information that has led me to request this fast-track warrant, what**

am I going to say? Is the source credible? Or is the source the building superintendent who heard it from the boiler repairman who might have heard it from the guy at the front desk who frequently sleeps on the job? All information is not created equal.

• **How long is this process likely to take?** If half a day rather than a few hours, who is going to do surveillance on the dogwood grove to make sure the fugitive doesn't leave? And if that surveillance person is a woman and likely to be on duty for ten hours or more, how in the heck and where is she going to pee? (This is a question I assure you the male agents going through this litany of possibilities were unlikely to have pondered, since behind any tree is bathroom enough for them. Speaking of privacy, there's also the somewhat regular circumstance of female agents being on their "monthly cycle." A few minutes real privacy—not just the cover of a bush—is definitely preferable in that situation, too.)

And on and on.

In short, this was a mental challenge as much as a physical one. It called for judgment. It required the discipline *not* to shoot, the discipline to consider just leaving and coming back another day. If you look at a lot of cases, that's exactly what you should do. You don't escalate the situation into something that it doesn't need to be.

Just to carry this a little further, there was another case thrown at us that involved a bank robbery. The (pretend) bank robbers were literally running down the street in front of us. We were armed with "red-handle" guns—weapons from which the firing pins had been removed to prevent an accidental discharge. Still, the instructors could hear the click of the trigger. What do you do in a situation like that? We didn't have enough information to know if the robbers were armed or unarmed. Given that they were running away from us, should we fire at their backs? Bank robbery is a serious crime, but it's not a capital offense, either, and if they were fleeing, what danger were we in, hypothetically?

Writing all this just now, that scenario sounds so much like contemporary events that have sparked massive protests and unsettled the nation in multiple ways. We were dealing with the issues in an active yet theoretical way. Sometimes, though, play-acting and real world can come awfully close together, and more and more at Hogan's Alley they have. Shortly after my two-day exposure to the program, the scenarios began using real actors from local universities, and the gap between playacting and the real world became significantly narrowed.

When I was back at the Academy a few years later, teaching part of the same course I had gone through, I sat in on one scenario that involved two of these budding actors: a man and a woman who supposedly had gotten drunk the night before. Now it was morning, they were recovering, and the trainees had been instructed to arrest the man. So they did the standard

A few years after graduating from the FBI Academy, I returned as a slightly older but much wiser instructor.

knock-and-announce—"Open up! FBI!"—but the couple didn't answer. Maybe they were there; maybe they weren't. Or maybe the guy was standing behind the door with a gun. The agents in training had no idea what was going on inside that room, just as I had had no clue a few years earlier. But when they finally did push their way into the room, the woman was wearing a bikini so tiny that on first glance she appeared to be nude. The moral being, as I experienced time and again, that when you do these knock-and-announces, anything can be waiting on the other side, and you have to be prepared to be surprised in a dozen different directions, from couples in the thralls of lovemaking to armed combat, and sometimes both.

ADVANCES IN VIDEO GAMING HAVE also made a big difference in the modern FBI training program. Back in the Stone Age of the Bureau, wannabe agents would be sent down the Main Street of an earlier, far more primitive Hogan's Alley while painted metal faces kept popping up at crude windows and doorways. Friend or foe? Dangerous or simply curious? Blast away or hold your fire? Some looked like your great-aunt Sally (assuming Sally wasn't a hired assassin). Others looked like a stereotypical bad guy of the 1920s and '30s: a two-day beard, eyes too close together, and the like. The training was certainly better than nothing. Snap decisions are sometimes called for in certain circumstances; I'll describe some instances later in this book. But gaming-type video makes it far more real, and laser guns give the whole thing an arcade feel.

I took part in one such session maybe a decade ago. I was partnered with someone I didn't know, which isn't all that unusual in the business. Partnerships can be entirely ad hoc sometimes. The video had us stationed in front of a Nordstrom store. The only direct information we got was that a woman in the store who was wanted for a violent crime had just stolen something off a rack and was racing for the front of the store. With that, the video began to roll, and within seconds a mother and her daughter walked out of the front door directly toward us . . . and my partner shot them both—just two everyday customers going about their daily lives.

"Explain yourself," the instructor said, after he shut the video down.

An interesting explanation ensued. My video partner paled noticeably when he was told he had just shot and killed two innocent shoppers, and in retrospect he agreed that the mother and daughter had not been racing out of the store, just walking joyfully along. Soon, though, he was contending that, given the circumstances, it was better to have taken these two lives than risk allowing a woman with a violent criminal history to either escape or endanger the lives of others. Really? From there, he continued further down the rabbit hole of his own illogic, but I was too busy wondering what on earth this man was doing in law enforcement to listen any further.

A few years later, now out of the Bureau and head of security for Southern California Edison, I arranged for our leadership team to go through exactly the same exercise. After all, good judgment matters in business as well as law enforcement. Once again, the instructor—ex–Secret Service and current FBI, where I first met him—paired our leadership group off into two-person squads positioned in front of a department store. Just like before, they received word that a woman with a history of violent crime was racing for the front door with stolen goods in hand. The video rolled. The mother and daughter came happily strolling out, packages in hand, and once again most of the men present cut them down in the prime of their shopping lives.

Six months later, I suggested we go back and do it again, with a fresh video scenario this time. I was trying to be innovative, do something different, find a way to bond with a little more meaning than the usual leadership-team getaway. Let's see what we learned from the first time around, I suggested, and incorporate that into our business practices and outlook.

No, everyone said, this time let's do golf again.

5.
WHAT'S SHE DOING HERE?

I WOULD LIKE TO WRITE that as soon as I joined the FBI in 1985, all my efforts to be taken seriously as a woman in law enforcement came to fruition: doors flew open; opportunity knocked in all directions; it was a lovefest from day one. Trouble is, no one who knows anything about the FBI in those days would believe it.

Part of the initial challenge was geography and location. Having come to the FBI through law enforcement, I knew my first posting was likely to be one of the smaller regional offices, and, at least in that regard, the Bureau didn't disappoint. I graduated from the Academy on November 13, 1985, was given five days to go home and pack, and by Thanksgiving was living and working in Albuquerque, New Mexico.

Albuquerque today is, I'm sure, a bustling and highly livable city, the airport gateway to beautiful Taos and the historic Chaco Canyon. Back then, though, it was a hardship post for someone like me, a Southern California girl who likes to shop and stay abreast of fashion along with taking down crooks. Partly because I was the new kid on the block but mostly because I was a woman, I spent a lot of time on the surrounding Indian reservations, dealing with matters that no one else wanted to handle: crimes that reflected the dismal state of the tribes themselves and their accommodations. Sexual assault, homicide, and incest were a steady diet on that rotation, often deeply complicated by alcoholism. Dealing with the crimes and the criminals often meant overnighting in places like Gallup, where the FBI office was a literal hardship post for families because of subpar schools, inadequate medical facilities, and scarce amenities. My overnights in Gallup were spent at motels that wouldn't violate Bureau expense limits but where I was always wary of the pillows and linens, especially when there was a faint smell of urine emanating from them.

Those problems, in turn, were complicated by gender. As I learned, Native American women can be tough as steel and often held families together on the reservations, but men in that culture like to run the show, and a female law enforcement agent often did not bring out the best in them. This was an issue, I should add, that did not change appreciably with time or as I ascended the ranks of the Bureau. Years later, when I was the FBI special agent in charge at the Denver Office, I had the responsibility of working with a number of Indigenous American tribes through the FBI's Durango resident agency in Colorado. The tribes, though, wouldn't work with me. If I wanted to talk with them, I had to take along my number two, a male agent. Tribal members didn't even look my way during these meetings.

And then there was the land itself, which I found starkly beautiful in a way I've always assumed the surface of the moon must be starkly beautiful. Just like my native Long Beach area, there was plenty of white sand, but there was no ocean lapping up against it. White sand stretched in every direction, nowhere more so than at White Sands Missile Range.

When it comes to driving, I'm a Goody Two-shoes who takes speed limits seriously, but the ride out to the missile range was so mesmerizing, in a kind of negative sensory input way, that I often lost track of my speed. Once, when I was headed to White Sands to see the police chief there on some long-forgotten matter, one of his local deputies clocked my car at 100 miles per hour before pulling me over. Happily, the deputy let me off once he saw my FBI credentials, but on my way back to Albuquerque I had to sit in my car for three hours, waiting for a missile test to be completed before the road opened back up. Believe me, that was punishment enough for what I had done.

How long I might have stayed in Albuquerque is anyone's guess; three years seems possible. The place was shorthanded, and agents weren't lining up to apply for the office. But I had an ace in the hole to play. Dale Monroe and I had headed in separate directions after graduating from the Training Academy. He'd had experience as a Marine helicopter pilot, and the Tampa, Florida, office needed an agent who could help with aerial surveillance, so that was a natural fit. But even though we were almost 1,800 miles apart, Dale and I kept growing closer and closer together until finally we got married on June 18, 1986. That didn't necessarily guarantee a common address, but the Tampa office was down one person, and the FBI does make an effort in these cases to accommodate married agents. So just about the time I thought I couldn't take another day in New Mexico, I found myself relocating to green and sunny seaside Florida.

A new venue, though, didn't solve the larger problems of being a woman in a professional world that had so long been built solely around men. Back then, at least, when you called the FBI, you looked for a beefy guy in a blue suit, white shirt, dull tie, and flat top to show up. That wasn't me, and I got used to that look in people's eyes that said, *What the heck is this petite blonde doing here?*

The societal norms of the day also were not working greatly in my favor. Women had burned a ton of bras during the Vietnam War protests, but they still were too fragile for combat, too ditzy for the C-suite, and too, well, womanly for anything other than a sidebar role in undercover operations, as I found out when I was recruited to help investigate four New York Mafia types who had taken a keen interest in Tampa, Miami, and other Florida crime op zones.

Dave (as I'll call him here) was the front guy for the Bureau on the undercover op. I was supposed to be his window dressing, and in the FBI in those days that meant pretty much one thing: flight attendant. To which, maybe not surprisingly, I balked.

"Why?" asked Dave and the other powers that be.

"Because I don't know anything about being a flight attendant and because these guys fly all the time. All they would have to do is ask me one question I couldn't answer, mention a hub I wasn't familiar with, or use one acronym I couldn't respond to, and they would know immediately we were setting them up. In case you've forgotten, these are mob guys. They take offense at being wrongly used."

The silence that followed was thick and weighty, but finally Dave asked what undercover persona I might be willing to adopt, and for that I was definitely ready.

"Aerobics instructor, for three reasons. Number one, I actually was a part-time aerobics instructor in California for three years before I joined the FBI. Number two, this way I won't have to memorize the codes for 178 different domestic airports. And number three, these guys are going to expect you to drink along with them, which means so much alcohol you can't possibly keep your wits about you. But if your girlfriend is one of these puritanical fitness people . . ."

Dave and the others reluctantly agreed, and for the next eleven months I would caution him about his booze intake whenever the six of us got together, secretly pour out the drinks that Dave had no choice but to accept (if I got a chance), and generally look as if I was ready to break out into three dozen ab crunches, followed by an obscene amount of, say, one-handed push-ups.

Whatever the mob guys thought of me personally, the relationship grew tight enough that the FBI set Dave and his (presumably) main squeeze up in a Clearwater condo packed ceiling-to-wall with audio and video equipment on which our mob friends eventually spilled sufficient secrets to merit an indictment and a long prison vacation.

Near the end of our time together, Dave and I reviewed the audio evidence. I particularly liked the part where Dave and I came into direct comparison.

"There's something about this guy that doesn't seem right," one of the mob guys says. "I don't know; he's too stiff or something."

"Yeah," another one agrees, "but his girlfriend is . . . you know, she's genuine, no question about it."

There's also something to be said for authenticity.

Don't tell the Mafia guys we are chasing, but this woman they think is an aerobics instructor is actually me.

. . .

MAYBE INEVITABLY—SINCE I WAS AN alien creature (i.e., a female) in a virtually all-male ecosystem—there were more than a few occasions when I was assigned a case to embarrass one of my older colleagues and hopefully light a fire under him. Mostly these were penny-ante crimes that just called for more legwork than the assigned agent was willing to put in. One, however, both fascinated me and eventually broke my heart, and it turned out not to be a crime at all.

This was in 1987, a year after I arrived in Tampa. A month or so earlier, nine-year-old Arlena Twigg had died of a heart condition. That was terrible enough for her parents, Ernest and Regina Twigg, but the blood work-ups done in the course of trying to save Arlena's life had revealed something almost worse: Arlena was not Regina Twigg's natural child. Beyond doubt, Regina had given birth to an infant in a Wauchula, Florida, hospital in November 1978, but Arlena could not possibly be that child. What had happened to their natural child?

That question was actually answered fairly quickly. The Wauchula hospital maternity ward had not been overwhelmingly crowded when Regina Twigg gave birth, and blood tests of the now nine-year-old children who had been born at the hospital in that narrow time frame showed incontrovertibly that their daughter had gone home with Barbara and Bob Mays and been raised as Kimberly Mays, while the Mays' daughter had been sent home with the Twiggs and raised as Arlena.

On the surface, this looked to be a horrible mistake, now deepened by Arlena's death, but the possibility that the switch had been somehow intentional—that maybe even money had been involved—brought the FBI into the case. (As I'll get to later, infant theft became a dangerous growth crime in the late 1980s and '90s.)

The case, though, had clearly failed to engage the senior agent assigned to look into it. Hospital records had been barely examined; the interviews he had done with the principals on both sides were cursory at best. Maybe he just figured the stork had picked the wrong chimney, but now that a custody battle was underway between the Twiggs and Bob Mays—Barbara had died of ovarian cancer when Kimberly was only three—the waters had become murkier still.

That was problem one for me: not just the possibility of crime but the human suffering involved in all this. The Twiggs were both grieving and angry. Shortly after learning that his biological daughter was dead, Bob Mays was being asked to give up a daughter he had raised as his own (and on his own) for almost a decade. Problem two was the angry senior agent who had been seconded to me and was now grudgingly following my leads—presumably to teach him a lesson about diligence. But we, or mostly I, did what we had to do.

We pored over the hospital records, checked procedures—were wristbands routinely placed on newborns?—talked with the Twiggs and Bob Mays to the extent that their attorneys would allow and to the extent that they could reveal anything about that stay in the hospital that we ourselves could not learn on our own. In the end, my senior-junior agent and I made peace with one another, and the switched-at-birth girls turned out to be just what it looked like from the very beginning: an honest mistake, if not an entirely excusable one. But the suffering in this case lived on long after the police and FBI had backed out of the picture.

Two years after the switch was discovered, Bob Mays agreed to grant the Twiggs visitation rights with their biological daughter. When he later backed out of that agreement, the Twiggs sued unsuccessfully for full custody of Kimberly or at least expanded visitation privileges. In 1993 a Wauchula circuit court sought to put the matter to rest by declaring Bob Mays to be Kimberly's "psychological father" and permitting her to end all contact with her biological parents, but Kimberly later voted otherwise with her feet and moved in with the Twiggs. That kind of whipsawing can't be good for anyone, and it definitely wasn't good for Kimberly Mays.

Almost twenty years later, I happened to be watching a documentary series called *American Scandals* when I finally saw Kimberly again, this time being interviewed by Barbara Walters about her troubled childhood, how she had lost custody of her first child to her ex-husband, how she had lived in her car with another child and later worked as a stripper to feed herself and her kids. I'm not sure where the "scandal" was in all that. *American Tragedy* sounds like the better title.

MOSTLY, THE CHALLENGES ASSOCIATED WITH being a woman in a male-dominated law enforcement world had to do with biases deeply baked into the Bureau itself, and some of those were flat-out dangerous. One example should suffice.

I was a kid to the Tampa field office when an "old dog" got dumped in my lap. "Old dogs" are cold cases: no new leads were being generated; nothing's happening. The senior agent who had it first had already dumped it on a junior agent, and the junior agent was looking for someone even lower than him to off-load this dog on . . . and when the lowest life form you could find was a female, so much the better. Thus, I inherited the deeply cold (but not uninteresting) case of one James Huntze.

Huntze had a huge appetite for computers and all sorts of related peripherals. In fact, he'd ordered over a million dollars' worth of what was then state-of-the-art equipment, which is no crime in and of itself. But Huntze was also taking delivery of his computers at addresses all over the Tampa area, and the invoices were never quite catching up with him.

So we definitely had a property crime, but the perpetrator kept disappearing. I'd go to one of the addresses, show around a photo of Huntze, and someone would say, "Oh, yeah, I remember him, but you've got the wrong name." Same thing at the next stop, and the next one. All in all, I tallied at least thirty-three names used by Huntze, each backed by a different Social Security account and date of birth.

Tracking all this did eventually lead me to a real address for the actual Huntze—a second-floor apartment—but along the way I also turned up some additional disturbing information. Not only had our man done prison time as an adult in Florida; he'd also pulled a gun during a juvenile hearing in Virginia and shot up the courthouse. Happily, he didn't hit anyone, but between that violent juvenile crime and his adult prison time, Huntze was facing a three-strikes-and-you're-out situation if he went to trial.

"This guy is not going to go peacefully," I told my boss, "I guarantee it. I want the SWAT team along for this arrest."

"Oh, you women," he responded. "You're so emotional! That's absolutely not going to happen. Activate the SWAT team over a property crime? What are you thinking of?"

"I'm thinking that while the classification of this case is a property crime, the offender's consistent historical behavior is that of a violent crime, and I am officially requesting the SWAT team to make entry for this takedown." I didn't back off in my tone, but I was talking to a stone wall.

The next day I got my whole squad—all seven of us—set to go at the apartment complex. We had already cleared the units next door, but I called my boss one final time before we went in.

"This is the last chance," I said. "I still think we need to have this arrest not just augmented by but done by the SWAT team."

"Oh, of course not. For Pete's sake!"

So I knocked on the door and announced "FBI," and he

shouted back, "Fuck you. I'm not going back again. You're going to have to kill me," and began spraying the front door with bullets, one of which went literally right through my hair, and—trust me—my hair was not up in a beehive. One inch lower, and lights out, Jana.

With that, we went into containment mode and waited for the SWAT team, which already would have been in place if a male agent had requested it. When they fired tear gas in through the apartment windows, we heard a shot fired from inside. With that, the SWAT commander made entrance, followed by several SWAT team members, only to discover that James Huntze conveniently had done the justice system the favor of killing himself. And a good thing it was, for several reasons. First, in addition to his firearm, Huntze had knives stored all over the place: in the bathroom, in the ceiling of his closet—everywhere, it seemed. Second, he was wearing a gas mask when he killed himself and so would have a major tactical advantage over us when we burst through the door had he still been alive. And third, his gas mask was a lot better than mine, which was so defective that tear gas permeated my hard contact lenses, which is not exactly what you want to have happen in a potential firefight.

One more outgrowth of the Huntze story, an important one to me: My squad and the SWAT team members were all wearing BPUs—bulletproof undergarments—for this takedown, but in the stress of the moment I couldn't help but notice that, while mine was like a breastplate—they'd even measured my breasts to fit it—it didn't reach down even to my navel. Meanwhile, all the male agents' BPUs stretched way down to their hips and pretty much covered their entire abdomens. Somehow I had always assumed that a woman's abdomen and womb were important, too.

When the deputy director of the FBI called later that day to ask how I was doing, I assured him I was fine but I also mentioned my ill-fitting BPU. He advised me that he would have the head of the Firearms Training Unit contact me ASAP, and to my surprise he called me the next day and invited me to Quantico, where I helped develop a new BPU prototype for female agents.

A second follow-up: A day or two after all this went down, I went to see my optometrist about the continuing misery of my contact lenses.

"Did you put hairspray in here?" he said, after examining the lenses.

"No," I told him. "It's tear gas."

"Why in heaven's name would you put tear gas in your contacts?"

"You had to be there," I explained.

The bean counters back at headquarters were even less sympathetic when I put in for eighty-six dollars to replace the contact lenses ruined by bursting into an apartment full of tear gas wearing a defective gas mask not long after nearly having a hole blown in my forehead.

"No can do," they said.

"No can't do," I told them.

Receiving reimbursement from the federal government takes tenacity, persistence, and determination. I had nearly exhausted my reserves of all three when, eight months later, a check for eighty-six dollars finally arrived.

AS MUCH AS I DISLIKED the idea of getting shot, at that point in my life I disliked spiders even more. Santo Trafficante Jr. got me over that phobia, although I never had the chance to thank him.

This requires a little background. Beautiful, sunny, tranquil Tampa is the seat and economic center of Hillsborough County, Florida, and ever since the early 1940s, Hillsborough County was also the personal fiefdom of the Trafficante crime family—first under Santo Sr., then Santo Jr. after his father died, remarkably of natural causes, in 1954. (Santo Jr. had been training for the job in Cuba, running one of the mob-owned casinos in then wide-open Havana.)

Santo Jr. had a patriotic side, of sorts. On multiple occasions he had helped the CIA try to recruit underworld assassins to rid the world of Fidel Castro. Mostly, though, he was a leading light of the American Mafia and a ruthless mob boss with his hand in any number of highly illegal activities, including drug running. We knew about the drugs at the FBI. On multiple occasions, surveillance pilots, Dale among them, had tracked a light plane leaving his compound out in the county, flying off into the night toward the southwest, then eventually reappearing, looking slightly heavier, landing where it had departed from, and then . . . disappearing. There was a barn on his property, big enough in theory to shelter a light plane, but the barn door was not wide enough to fit a plane through.

Finally, though, we got enough resolution on an aerial photo of the barn to confirm that there were thin slits, maybe six inches wide and no more than a few feet long, on either side of the barn door, just big enough for the plane's wing to slide through. That was enough to secure a warrant, and a few days later a twenty-person FBI drug squad (nineteen guys and yours truly) descended on the Trafficante estate, surprised the bewillickers out of Mrs. Trafficante— who, I couldn't help but notice, was wearing a diamond ring worth at least fifty grand—and confirmed that the barn was indeed the home of a drug-running plane. Since, under existing law, we had the right to seize as evidence any property likely to have come from ill-gotten gains or used to facilitate such gains (the plane, for example), we then set about searching the house for what might reasonably be construed as additional evidence and were completely stymied until one of Santo's lackies saw the writing on the wall and said, "Here, let me show. There's stuff down here."

With that, he pulled back a tarp, and now we're back to my arachnophobia. Beneath the tarp was a narrow hole with a bunch of boards shoved into the top of it. The hole was dark and deep once we pulled the boards out. This was Florida, where spiders grow and breed by the tens of billions in a thousand different varieties, all of which at the moment I assumed were deadly poisonous. And as I looked around at my burly male colleagues, it was perfectly obvious that the only government employee present who could fit down that hole was me.

You can't scream, Jana, I told myself, *and you can't just slip in and out. They're expecting you to bring up something other than spiderwebs. Time to grow up.* So I gave myself over to God, almost literally, slid down into that hole, turned on my flashlight when I hit bottom, and the place was an absolute treasure trove of ill-gotten jewelry, a couple million dollars by the time it was all appraised. And while I would never choose to vacation with them, spiders and I made our peace there and then.

This story has a follow-up, too: Not many months thereafter, Dale nailed Santo's chauffeur selling drugs out of Santo's beautiful Lincoln Continental stretch limousine. That was enough for Dale to secure a second warrant and confront the mob boss directly.

"I'm taking your Lincoln," he told Santo when he answered a knock on the door.

"No you're not."

"Yes I am. Your driver sold drugs out of it. The government owns it now." And thus, what was undoubtedly the most expensive vehicle in Hillsborough County was towed off to the impoundment lot, never to be reclaimed by Santo Trafficante Jr., who died of natural causes not much later, an unlikely end for someone in his line of work.

I thought of that luxurious Lincoln often a few years later when I got to Washington and was begging the FBI motor pool to find me a car to help with my lengthy commute. The motor pool guys eventually came through for me, but it wasn't quite the car of my dreams. The driver's-side door was caved in and wouldn't open. I had to slide across to the passenger's-side door to get in and out. Happily, it was a bench seat without a center console.

6.
WELCOME TO THE SUNSHINE STATE

FLORIDA IS A FUNNY PLACE. You've got your rich Republicans on the Gulf Coast, especially down around Sarasota and Naples, the Tampa Mafia north of them, your rich New York Democrats wintering along the East Coast, families of all sorts hunkered down at Disney World, Cubans and Haitians in Miami, the Beautiful People a few miles and several light-years away on South Beach, native Florida "crackers" hiding out from the tourists and everyone else in the stark interior, and old, old folks everywhere, especially in St. Petersburg. Then you've got your UFAPs, your unlawful-flight-to-avoid-prosecution types, because that's something else that Florida is: a great place for fugitives on the run.

Think about it: the weather is mostly warm if you have to sleep out on the street or in a tent, as folks on the lam often do, and there's a lot of work to be done—day labor, under-the-table type stuff, the kind of jobs where employers never ask for an ID and always pay in cash.

One other part of this nicely balanced ecosystem: Florida, at least back when I was working those streets, was also loaded to the gills with viewers of *America's Most Wanted*. I can't tell you how many times we entrusted some of our most vexing problem cases to host John Walsh, and I still can't believe how many responses those brief notices generated. Sometimes it seemed as if the entire Sunshine State was working overtime for a junior crime-stoppers badge.

Case in point: Not long after I arrived in Tampa, *America's Most Wanted* aired a short segment about a college professor who had gone missing not long after his wife turned up piecemeal, which is to say dismembered in a barrel. The professor's whereabouts were unknown, but not for long. As per custom, Floridians called in by the dozens with tips, and within days the suspected murderer was identified as having recently checked into a hotel operated by the University of Tampa. That's when I got involved, not as the case agent, but as what's known in the Bureau as an auxiliary agent—that is, an agent from an outside FBI office who is asked to cover leads that arise from the case at hand.

I didn't know if the supposed perpetrator taught poetry or podiatry. I had no idea whether he had sectioned his wife with a chain saw or a hacksaw—and as I would soon learn, the mode of dismemberment tells you a lot about the dismemberer. None of that was my need-to-know business. All I knew was that some guy living in a university-owned hotel was violent enough to do something like that and that it was my job to bring him in.

To that end, I first contacted university housing officials even before a search warrant had been issued and secured their cooperation by telling them if they didn't give me the key to the guy's room, we might be forced to bust it down. Fearing liability complications, the university also helped evacuate the rooms adjacent to the professor, which left me once again standing on the outside of a door, about to announce the FBI's presence, and hoping that the response did not involve gunfire, knives, feral dogs, grenades, rabid armadillos, etc. This time, though, I had a partner.

As I suggested earlier, in the culture of the FBI, doing the knock-and-announce is a big deal. It's an honor if you are allowed to assume that risk, and it's a special honor if someone on your team wants to "go through the door" with you—especially if, as happened in this instance, that someone is your own supervisor. Fred Eschweiller always reminds me of the title character in the old *Coach* sitcom, which aired in the late 1980s and through most of the '90s. Fred was truly a sweetheart of a guy and my all-time favorite supervisor. In this instance, he was making a statement; I knew that. He was telling the four backup guys on our team and by extension the entire Tampa Bureau, *This woman's okay*. Fred is also a big hulk of a guy, wide as a truck and in good shape, which made for a comforting physical presence as well under the circumstance.

In any event, with Fred by my side, I knocked loudly on the door and shouted, "FBI! Open up!" Getting no response, I slipped the key in the lock and threw the door open, and then the two of us, pumped with adrenaline, went charging in simultaneously and . . . got stuck. Literally stuck. Fred took up most of the doorway himself. I was wedged into the little space next to him, fairly certain my left shoulder had just been dislocated. Since our arms were wedged in with us, our weapons were useless, and the four guys behind us couldn't exactly shoot through us if they had to return fire, which thank goodness they didn't since our brilliant professor had chosen to hide behind his bed, in plain sight, and gave himself up even as Fred and I were wriggling our way free from our predicament.

Thank goodness that was before body cams and YouTube, because our Keystone Kops routine would have gone viral in a hurry. As it was, the official report of the professor's arrest noted "went without incident." Right.

SOMETIMES YOU GO THROUGH A door the awkward way as Fred Eschweiller and I did and escape without harm by sheer chance. Other times you walk through a door you wish you hadn't opened and have trouble forgetting what you saw. That was the case with another extremely intelligent Florida felon named George Trepal. (For reasons I'll get into later, high IQ sometimes seems to correlate all too well with violent behaviors.)

Trepal was a chemist by training, an ex-con via sentencing for manufacturing and selling amphetamines, and a card-carrying Mensa member (only people with IQs in the top 2 percent need apply). He was also a devotee of Agatha Christie novels, an ardent participant with his orthopedic surgeon wife, Diana, in "Murder Mystery Night" events, and a really, really lousy guy to have the misfortune of living anywhere near. All those qualities coalesced fatally in March of 1988 when Trepal declared war on Peggy and Parearlyn "Pye" Carr, his neighbors in rural Alturas, way up in Polk County.

The combat began almost civilly, with Trepal complaining to the county zoning board that Pye Carr was constructing an illegal apartment on his property. In fact, he was, and the project was abandoned. Trepal upped the stakes considerably, but anonymously, that July, when he sent an unsigned letter to Pye Carr that read: "YOU AND ALL YOUR SO CALLED FAMILY HAVE TWO WEEKS TO MOVE OUT OF FLORIDA FOREVER OR ELSE YOU ALL DIE. THIS IS NO JOKE."

In October, Diana Trepal joined the fray, complaining bitterly to Peggy Carr that Pye's son, Travis Carr, and Duane Dubberly, Peggy's child from a previous marriage, were playing their radios way too loud. And then things started to get serious. Near the end of that month, Peggy was working her waitress job when she thought she had suffered a heart attack. By the time she got to the hospital, she told the doctor, "I feel like I'm on fire." Before long, Travis and Duane were suffering similar symptoms, and Peggy, whose condition had seemed to have improved, was rushed back to a larger hospital in Winter Haven, now in worse shape than ever.

That's where neurologist T. Richard Hostler finally hit on the cause: thallium, a tasteless, odorless chemical that is naturally present in the human body in trace amounts but, in quantity, relentlessly attacks muscles and nerves. Travis and Duane survived the poisoning. Peggy didn't. Testing showed her urine contained twenty thousand times the normal load of thallium—she never had a chance.

With a dead body on its hands and a weapon, at least of sorts, the Polk County Sheriff's Office sent some four hundred objects from the Carr house—everything from ice cubes to homemade pickles—to a private lab for testing. Three of them, all empty Coke bottles, tested positive for thallium. This was a violation of the Federal Anti-Tampering Act of 1982 and brought the FBI into the case. The next step was to have three unopened bottles of Carr family Coca-Cola flown to the FBI lab in Quantico. All of them, it turned out, had had their caps tampered with and were laced with thallium.

And this is where Agatha Christie enters the story, for three reasons: (1) Her 1961 novel *The Pale Horse* is built around a series of murders accomplished with a highly accurate description of thallium and its effects. (Christie had volunteered as an apothecary's assistant in both world wars.) (2) As noted earlier, the Trepals liked to host murder mystery dinners, not infrequently Agatha Christie themed. And (3) a Polk County detective who had gone undercover to check out George Trepal recalled seeing a copy of *The Pale Horse* lying on a table in the Trepal living room. Further lab testing uncovered traces of thallium in several bottles in the Trepals' garage. And with that the case was ready to be brought to a close.

I was involved in the case by this point, too. The sheriff's office had asked the BSU to profile the likely killer—a profile, I should add, that proved uncannily accurate, i.e., "an intelligent white male . . . who liked to resolve conflicts without direct confrontation." I wasn't part of the BSU yet—that was still a year away—but I had been named Behavioral Science Unit coordinator while still serving in the Tampa Division, which gave me a close-up look at how the BSU worked and, of course, gave the people there a first look at me as well. In this instance, I helped liaise between the various law enforcement agencies involved, conducted surveillance, monitored the wiretap involving conversations between the undercover officer and Trepal, and was on hand for the arrest, not in Alturas but at the Trepals' new home in Sebring, about forty miles to the south.

Diana Trepal met us at the door, and to my surprise—since I generally expect doctors to be civil—was profoundly loud and extremely unwelcoming. Summoned by his wife's shouting, George Trepal appeared next, at the top of the stairs, wearing nothing but bikini briefs, in his case not a pretty sight. We suggested he get dressed while we executed our search warrant, and it was in the process of so doing that we discovered a secret room behind a pegboard hung with tools. I was the first to open the door. I no longer remember exactly what I expected to find: vials of poison, a floor littered with human bones—the mind can fly in all sorts of directions at moments like this. But what I actually found was in some ways worse: a bed fitted with manacles, Diana's teddy, various implements of sexual torture, the pleasure-pain principle writ large and ugly. I remember thinking, *When she sets a broken bone, does she give it a little extra twist, just for the sexual thrill of it?*

I should add that George Trepal wasn't the first killer to go to school on *The Pale Horse*. The very first year it appeared in print, a fourteen-year-old English schoolboy and mystery book fan, Graham Young, used thallium to murder his stepmother. But Trepal might have been the first to use it so indiscriminately. The Carrs, down even to their two-year-old granddaughter, were ardent consumers of Coca-Cola, and every single one of them was poisoned to one degree or another by the tainted refreshments George Trepal provided them. Even by the low standards of murderers, he was a truly awful person.

Trepal, by the way, remains on death row in Polk County.

7.
THINKING BIG

IT MIGHT SEEM INSENSITIVE—OR A damning comment on the nature of my work—to call a triple rape-murder my most gratifying case, but please hear me out.

What happened to Joan Rogers and her two daughters, seventeen-year-old Michelle and fourteen-year-old Christe, is the stuff of horror movies, and worse. The three had never traveled out of Ohio until late May of 1989, when Michelle graduated from high school and the three female Rogerses hopped in a car and sped off to Disney World to celebrate, while Hal Rogers tended the family dairy farm back in tiny Willshire. For the complete Florida experience, once they had waved goodbye to Mickey and Minnie, the female Rogerses drove on to Tampa, perhaps to experience salt water for the first time. Or they might have simply taken a wrong turn leaving the Orlando area and decided to make the most of their mistake. There's no way of knowing for sure.

All that's known for certain is that at twelve thirty on the afternoon of June 1, the Rogerses checked into a Days Inn on the outskirts of Tampa, and by seven thirty, they were finishing up dinner in the hotel's restaurant. Two and a half days later, the FBI and local law enforcement agencies got notice that three bodies had floated to the surface in Tampa Bay, and with that, the hunt was on.

I wasn't on the boat that retrieved the bodies, but I was standing on the dock when each of the bodies was brought ashore for examination, and, like everyone around me, I was horrified by the sight, nearly nauseous. All had their hands bound, although Michelle had managed to work one hand free. All were naked from the waist down, and each had a rope tied around her neck, anchored to a heavy-duty cinder block. Their murderer, it seems, had thought of everything except the buoyant effects of decomposition.

Hal Rogers thought his family was homebound. When they didn't show up, he filed a missing-persons report in Ohio, and a few days later the dead females I had watched being fished out of Tampa Bay finally had names. The next day we also received photographs of all three victims, and I could finally begin to get the disfigured, discolored, hideously bloated bodies I had first seen on that dock on Tampa Bay out of my mind. The girls were beautiful, vibrant, and full of life. I could imagine the sheer joy of their visiting Disney World for the first time, of feeling salt water on their skin, of graduating from high school in Michelle's case and having her entire adult life ahead of her—which only made what had been done to them and their mother all the worse, all the more crushing.

By then, we were working backward from the three bodies now in hand to discover where and when they had likely been thrown into the water, or thrown overboard from a boat already on the water. We brought in a whole platoon of experts—on currents, on tides, on the decomposition rate of a submerged human body at various water temperatures, on the type of knots that had bound the bodies to their cinder blocks. (Later on, I would have a somewhat hilarious exchange with a defense attorney deposing me on the case about "whether a knot expert had or had not examined the knots." "Is that 'knot' with a *k*?" we kept saying to each other, just to keep the record clean.)

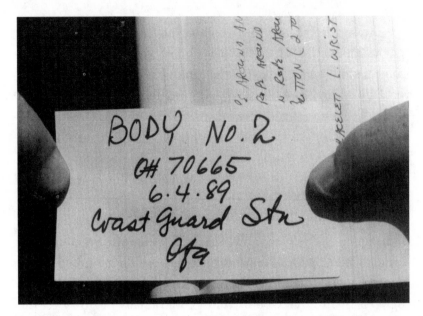

A grim artifact of one of the saddest cases I ever worked on—
a mother and two daughters murdered while on vacation in Tampa.

From the autopsy, we knew that 100 cubic centimeters of car-
rots and either potatoes or pasta had been recovered from Joan's
stomach, three ounces of food particles from Michelle's, and two
ounces of soft food from Christe's. Our tides-and-currents pros
assured us that the three could not have risen to the surface where
and when they did if they had been thrown into the bay from
onshore. We knew that Joan and Christe had been bound with yellow rope and from the Coast Guard that the rope was both very
new and a cheap brand, while Michelle had been bound with a
different rope, but in all three cases the knots had been similarly
tied. Police labs had examined the duct tape used to silence all
three but had found no hair or fiber and had been unable to lift
any fingerprints.

An elderly couple came forward to say that they had seen
the Rogerses' car unoccupied at a boat dock and with a black car

nearby, but in subsequent interviews they kept enhancing their sighting story until it began to fall completely apart. That's not all that unusual in cases like this. Stress, anxiety, the desire to be helpful—even self-aggrandizement—can all be triggered by the publicity given to notorious acts of violence. "Witness typologies," as we referred to them, run the gamut from "reluctant" to "intimidated," "inventive," "distraught," "hostile," and "fraudulent," frequently without the witnesses realizing how they might be skewing small shards of information or investing them with unconscious bias.

In a similar vein, seventeen or more people reported seeing a black Bronco in proximity to a blue-and-white boat that might have been used by the perpetrator—far more promising, but in Tampa Bay blue-and-white boats are almost the rule, not the exception.

The case seemed to take a dramatic turn for the better in October 1989 when two Canadian women reported that they had been physically assaulted while on vacation in the Tampa area, in circumstances similar to those in the Rogers case, but a follow-up visit to Canada by two detectives put an end to that. For all this beehive of activity and expertise, the reported sightings of this and that, the flurry of leads, the only solid clue police had to go on was a scrap of paper with handwritten directions on how to get from the Days Inn where the Rogerses had registered to the parking area off the causeway where their abandoned car had been found.

Like everyone else in the Tampa field office, I shared in the revulsion over what had occurred and the boundless frustration of a stalled investigation into a crime so horrific. We were staring at acts of pure, almost biblical evil, and we seemed powerless to unravel it. A year later I had moved to Quantico and was part of the BSU when detectives from St. Petersburg, which had jurisdiction over the murders, asked if they could come for a consultation. The case hadn't moved an inch.

We agreed to help them reexamine the record and reconsider what was known and could be at least semi-reasonably surmised about the case. Bill Hagmaier, one of the original BSU agents, and I took the lead on our end, and in April 1991 we sent back to St. Pete the results of our collaboration. I include them here in their entirety not because we hit every nail on the head—we were far from that exact—but to give readers a sense of just how our minds worked at the BSU as we tried to bring order and reason out of what was often bloody chaos.

This was all presented under the heading "ARMED AND DANGEROUS":

The behavior exhibited in this crime and the control demonstrated over three victims reflects a probability that more than one assailant may have been involved. Acknowledging the consistency of the manner in which the victims were taped, weighted, and tied further suggests that there were two assailants. They were in a dominant/passive relationship with one assailant directing the act and the other assisting/maintaining control of the victims. For the purpose of this assessment reference will be made to the behavior and personality of the dominant assailant singularly.

Research suggests crimes of violence usually occur along intra-racial lines—i.e., white-on-white and black-on-black. Considering this and the known racial composition of the area of your investigation, especially the boating community, and the absence of forensic or other evidence to the contrary, we would expect your offender to be a white male.

Upon consideration of the offender's age, a number of factors pertinent to the crime are examined. The victim's age, the amount of control exhibited by the offender, the degree of trauma inflicted, how weapons are secured and used, and any evidence taken from or left at the crime scene all become important. Investigators are cautioned that predicting an offender's age is often difficult since what is observed in a crime is a matter of behavior age and not necessarily chronological age. In deliberation of these and other aspects pertinent to this crime, we would expect the offender to be in his thirties to early forties. Investigators are further cautioned that we are evaluating age on the basis of behavior, which is a direct result of emotional and mental maturity. No suspect(s) therefore should be eliminated on the basis of age alone.

As evidenced by the duct tape application over the mouths of the victims and the symmetry of the rope-cutting, as well as other factors, the assailant is neat, meticulous, methodical, and compulsive. We would expect the assailant to have a fantasy life perhaps about ropes and tying up victims and or willing partners. Although the knots used to tie the victims and to secure the cinder blocks are not necessarily demonstrative of a professional regarding knots, this assailant is not a novice in this area and has had some prior experience with knot tying. The ropes and knots used to restrain the victims are excessive and could possibly represent a form of bondage, which would be consistent with the assailant's fantasy life. In further support of the assailant's trait of neatness is the fact that he did not leave a messy crime scene. In essence, there was no crime scene as the water is the ultimate crime scene and disposal site. The assailant's boat, or [the] boat used in this crime, would not have been left in disarray or damaged as the assailant held the victims under his control and chose not to use the knife on them. The victims were not cut or stabbed; therefore, there would be no blood at the scene and very little if any at all to clean up.

The assailant took a cowardly approach toward the murders by choosing the crime scene as he did—i.e., he did not kill the victims, "the water did." He could utilize this form of rationalization to further remove or disassociate himself from the killings. This would allow him to deny and or minimalize any direct responsibility.

People who know the assailant will describe him as controlled and rigid in his own discipline. He is a planner and exhibits confidence almost to the point of arrogance. His discipline and planning can be observed when noting the victims do not have any control marks other than bindings—i.e., no broken fingernails, defense wounds, or hair pulled out. Although the bodies were in a state of decomposition, the autopsy reports did not reveal any signs of bruising, hemorrhage, or cuts consistent with physical pain compliance. [In fact, water in the lungs would later prove that all three were alive when they were thrown overboard. This story kept getting more horrifying the deeper we dug.]

[The assailant] considers himself to be above average intelligence but will not attempt to draw attention to himself, and he will be passively cooperative. As thorough and controlling as the assailant was in this crime, he did not have a comprehension of physics—i.e., the cinder blocks were not of sufficient weight to hold the bodies down. And he was probably surprised when they surfaced so quickly, and this would have offended him.

The assailant possesses some social skills as demonstrated by the fact that he was able to get the victims to accompany him on the boat, apparently on their own volition. It is projected that he obtained their initial cooperation by some con/ruse in which he presented himself in a socially and physically non-threatening manner. As previously mentioned, there is a high probability of multiple assailants in this crime, and in addition to the dominant/ passive relationship between the two, consideration might be given to the *possibility* of a female being involved. She could assist in establishing a "comfort zone" in assuring the victims that it was safe to accompany the assailant. The boat would also be perceived as attractive, neat, and obviously sea-worthy to the victims.

Due to the decomposition of the bodies from being submerged in water approximately 48 to 72 hours, the medical examiner wasn't able to determine if there was evidence of sexual assault on the victims. The only potential sexual indication of the crime is that all three victims were nude from the waist down. They were clothed above the waist, and there was no apparent attention or exploration directed at the victims' breasts. Considering his character traits, it is likely the offender receives his gratification from the "control of and domination over the victims." He placed the tape over the victims' mouths, but there is no evidence to indicate he placed a binding or tape over the victims' eyes. This way he could observe their fear and panic, and he derived pleasure and satisfaction from their suffering. It is not known if the assailant experienced any sexual satisfaction from the victims' suffering, but from the aforementioned scenario, it is highly likely he did. If so, this is a sexually sadistic crime. All sexual desires and sexual crimes begin with fantasy. As contrasted with normal sexual fantasies, however, the sexual sadist's fantasies feature domination, control, humiliation, injury, and violence as a means to elicit suffering. The mixture of these themes varies among sexually sadistic fantasies, as does the degree of violence.

We believe the assailant will kill again if he has not already done so; however, it is likely he will change some method and will alter his manner of disposal as it disturbed him that the bodies were discovered so soon.

At this point in the investigation, the following investigative procedures are offered:

1. Revisit the crime scene through the media—i.e., television and newspaper releases. The effectiveness of this will be enhanced if released on the anniversary-date spectrum of the crime—i.e., June 1–4.

2. Via the assistance of the media, attempt to communicate by appealing to the assailant's ego—i.e., the sophisticated nature of the crime indicates it was committed by an intelligent person, etc.

Should your department require further assistance, please contact SA Jana D. Monroe or SSA William Hagmaier at the FBI Academy . . .

You will soon see just how off base we were on certain aspects of our key suppositions: This was a solo crime, not a group one, for example. But working with Bill to put this together kept reminding me that Joan Rogers's notes on how to get to the causeway remained the only and very slim clue we had to go on, and that somehow loosened or rearranged enough neurons that I finally posed the question we should have been dealing with all along.

"Are you sure these directions are in Joan's handwriting?" I asked the St. Pete detectives who had been working on the case.

"Well, we found it on the seat of her car."

"But have you ever compared it to her known handwriting?"

"I guess not."

"Ever checked with her husband?"

"Uh . . ."

"Maybe, then, someone should ask Hal Rogers if his wife wrote this."

Someone did, and she hadn't. Nor had either of the daughters, but of course that begged the question of who had.

"Let's see if anyone in Tampa Bay recognizes it," I suggested.

"Go door-to-door?"

"No, billboard to billboard."

So we enlarged the directions large enough that you could read them speeding by, pasted them on billboards all around the area, and asked people to contact the St. Petersburg police if they recognized the penmanship. In a way, it was an Amber Alert before near-total cell phone penetration turned whole interstates into all-points bulletins, and it worked. Within forty-eight hours, calls had come in from two unrelated people, both naming Oba Chandler as the writer of the directions.

At age forty-six, Chandler was slightly older than we predicted, but he was big enough (six feet tall, two hundred pounds) to be threatening when the time came. He also had a black Bronco and a blue-and-white boat that he kept on Tampa Bay, and the fact

Bigger is better: To solve the gruesome murder of Joan Rogers and her daughters, I suggested we make a billboard out of our only solid piece of evidence. It worked!

that he had gone under nineteen aliases at various points in his life, from the stately Thomas A. Whiteman Jr. to the racier Juan Kenoble, suggested a desire to stay a step or two ahead of the law.

Most central to the case, Chandler was an aluminum siding contractor who was frequently being hauled into small-claims court. Confident to the point of arrogance in his own abilities, he always wrote out his defense in a very distinctive longhand, which he liked to wave about in the courtroom—the same longhand in which he had scrawled instructions to help lead Joan Rogers to the moonlight cruise from which she and her daughters would never return. This time, though, Chandler had written himself into a death sentence, even though that wouldn't be carried out until November 15, 2011, twenty-two years after the crime had been committed. (I later learned that, during his seventeen years on death row, Oba Chandler, husband and father of three, had not a single visitor.)

WHY WAS THIS MY MOST gratifying case? Not only because justice was done—although, God knows, that's not always the case. Not because my billboard idea helped to turn justice in the right direction—although I'm proud of that inspiration and glad that variations have become commonplace in the years since. Not even because we almost certainly took a serial killer off the streets. Proof is lacking and Chandler never acknowledged even the Rogers murders, but the record strongly suggests the Rogerses were far from his first victims. DNA evidence that emerged in 2014 identified Chandler as the murderer of Ivelisse Berrios-Beguerisse, who was found dead in 1990 in Coral Springs, Florida. The details of that case also suggest that Chandler had been learning on the job, perfecting his bait-and-kill modus operandi and his cinder-block-and-rope disposal tactics on who knows how many actual victims.

I still wonder why the Rogers women simply didn't go

overboard when the threat became apparent, or fight back on the boat itself. They were a farm family. They knew physical labor, and they had numbers on their side. Two perpetrators, as Bill and I hypothesized in our report, would have allowed one to assault the Rogerses individually while the second intimidated the other two into nonaction. Oba Chandler, though, clearly acted alone. Maybe the Rogers women couldn't swim. More likely, Chandler held a knife to each throat as he did whatever he did to them. Most likely, all three Rogerses clung to the hope that everyone has in situations like this: that the nightmare will end.

It didn't, but at least in this case we had a perpetrator, and whether he was ever executed or not, we knew he would never again be at large in the general population. And that gets me to the deepest reason why this was my most satisfying case: In all the years I did this work, this was the sole case I had the luxury of following from the crime itself through conviction. For once, and only this once, I got something close to closure.

8.
THE THIRD DEGREE

AS I MENTIONED EARLIER, I joined the Behavioral Science Unit in the year or so between the Rogers murders and Oba Chandler's arrest, but I didn't go directly from Tampa to the BSU. My initial posting was to the Washington Field Office (WFO), one of the larger offices in the Bureau, and it was there I learned (a) that in the FBI in those days, a bigger office mostly meant the same old problems for female agents, just writ larger, and (b) that, like other big government bureaucracies, the Federal Bureau of Investigation did not always do things according to common sense.

For starters, virtually all my serious experience in law enforcement by the time I arrived at the WFO was in reacting to crimes. I had initially been pigeonholed as another quick-draw female officer, but by then I had built my reputation on murders, bank robberies, drug busts, and the like. I had been shot at and cursed; I'd run robbers down dead-end alleys and pulled them in. I hadn't yet come up with the idea of blowing up Oba Chandler's handwriting for all the world to see, but I figured that my record to date couldn't be ignored when it came to doling out assignments.

However, this was back in the days when working criminal cases was the number one thing almost everybody wanted to do in the FBI, and the half of all humanity most likely to get their number one choice in the Bureau were males. In Tampa, I was a member of an eight-person reactive crime squad; thus, women represented 12.5 percent of the team. At the WFO, women accounted for zero percent of the far larger twenty-person reactive crime squad, which obviously didn't include Jana Monroe.

Instead, I was assigned to a surveillance squad, the majority of whom were (of course) women—which mostly meant sitting in a car or on a park bench or just idly hanging out on a DC corner, logging comings and goings as best we could. Which was, in a word, *boring*, stultifyingly so, like watching grass grow however important the knowledge gained might have been.

Finally—and I admit this was a short "finally"—I went to see the special agent in charge of the WFO, laid out my credentials to him in case he hadn't a good look at them before, then added, "By the way, I've noticed you have zero women on the reactive crime squad, and zero women on the list hoping to join. Can you tell me why this is?"

Tactful, this was not. It might even have been career threatening, but unwittingly, I had taken my case to just the right person. The SAC's wife was also an agent; more than that, she was the only female supervisor in her sector and apparently not shy about expressing to her husband at home opinions such as those I had just saddled him with in the office. That very day, he not only put me on the reactive crime squad but bumped me ahead of almost twenty people, all male, waiting to join, which was either a blessing or a curse in disguise, and probably more of the latter than the former.

To say I was not greeted by the welcome wagon once I joined the squad would be a dangerous understatement. The shoulder I was greeted with wasn't just cold; it was frozen. Conversation was mostly grunts, eye contact rare and angry when achieved. It took all of about a week for this all to come to a head.

FBI agents are not malingerers. If anything, we get to the office early in the morning. But living on an FBI pay scale in an area as expensive as metropolitan Washington generally entails a long commute from cheaper neighborhoods and early alarm clock settings, which is why office days often start grumbly until the coffee kicks in. I've always tried to combat that by being extra chipper in the morning: *Lovely day! Beautiful weather! Great day to be an agent!* and the like. This day, though, it wasn't working.

"I'm sick of your friggin' chirpiness," one agent shouted out from the far end of the squad room, "being happy and all this kind of good stuff. We don't want you on this squad. You jumped ahead of other people, and you only got this because you're a female."

And then he goes, "I should beat your ass or something," which, let's face it, made this somewhat personal.

There might have been only four other people present at the time. The room was just beginning to fill up. But I walked down to his desk and said, not in a whisper but not so any of the others would hear, "You don't know whether you can beat me or I can beat you. So I suggest you not embarrass yourself in front of the guys. And, yeah, if you want to take this outside right now, we can go down to the break room and see what happens."

To this day, I'm so glad he didn't take me up on my challenge. I'm equally glad that I only spent three months on that squad before I was asked to interview for the Behavioral Science Unit because that incident turned distrust and mild enmity into often outright hostility.

Eighteen months later, long after I was settled into the BSU, I was shocked when this same antagonist called me at Quantico and said, "Can you meet me in downtown DC whenever you're coming here next? For a drink?"

My first thought was, *Okay, he's probably going to attack me or lay into me some way. But I have to see this through.* So I met him at a bar down on the Potomac waterfront, and the first thing he said was, "I've seen some of your work at the BSU. I see what you're doing. And

I apologize." And that meant more to me at that point in my career than almost anything else I can ever begin to imagine, even though the Behavioral Science Unit had already ridden to my rescue.

I'D HAD SOME PREVIOUS CONTACT with the BSU when I was with the National Center for the Analysis of Violent Crime as a field coordinator in Tampa, and I had been impressed, and I was both surprised and flattered when Bill Hagmaier asked me to interview for an opening on the BSU team.

Within the FBI, the BSU was one of the truly elite units, dealing with some of the Bureau's showcase crimes. While I was a little tired of being one of the first females at many of my postings, I also thought the BSU might be a little in the dark about the inner workings of fifty-odd percent of the American population and far more than fifty percent of the victims of the violent criminals this unit specialized in.

First, though, I had to make it through the interview, and that, I think, proved to be an instructive experience for both sides of the gender divide.

John Douglas, then the unit chief, and a second agent started off by pitching a series of pro forma queries my way: "What would you consider typical or traditional interview questions?" "Why do you want this position?" "What do you bring to the table?"

Then the conversation got more serious. Without saying a word, John slid five 8 x 10 photographs across the table until they were sitting right in front of me. All of them showed gory crime scene victims. Some had been eviscerated, others decapitated. As I looked at them, the three of us sat in an awkward silence that might have lasted only fifteen seconds but felt closer to several minutes. Finally, I broke the silence.

"I see these," I said. "What are you asking me to do? What do you want?"

"I'm just watching you," John replied.

"Yes, I know you are, but you're making me nervous."

"I wanted to see if you were going to faint—you know, pass out, hyperventilate, squirm."

"And why would I do that?"

"Well," John said, "the few other females we've had in here to interview do that. We wanted to see how you were going to react."

"You know, I've worked on plenty of homicides, seen a lot of brutalized dead bodies in person. Why do you think I would react like that to a bunch of photos?"

Then because I couldn't help myself, I added, "Oh, by the way, I took the liberty of doing some background work on you. I learned you were a tennis instructor in the Air Force before becoming an FBI agent. You want to tell me why that qualifies you to be in this position more than me?"*

In retrospect, I'm quick to acknowledge that attacking your questioner is not a great interview technique, but I hadn't fainted, I hadn't gagged or turned my head away in disgust, and I'd even shown some spunk in the process. Maybe the spunk was what inspired John to ask me to stick around a little longer that day.

"In about an hour, we're going to have a consultation," he said, "and there's going to be myself and five other agents. It's a serial homicide, but"—and on this he was very specific—"you're

---

* John would later tell me that he devised the photograph test after interviewing a woman who had an advanced degree in psychology. His hope was that she would prove a two-fer: adept at psychological analysis and current with the latest research and literature as well as up to the nitty-gritty of the job. She soon disabused him on the latter front. "A lot of our cases involve sexual assault," he told her. "Oh, I can't possibly work those cases," she replied. "I live alone, and if I start thinking about sexual assault, I get very frightened." "Well," John persisted, "a lot of cases are also homicides." "I can't work those either," she said. "Those are *really* scary." The women went on to have a distinguished career in the FBI, but in counterintelligence, not the Behavioral Science Unit.

to say *nothing*. You can sit in the back of the conference room and observe, but you are *not* a part of this. *Got that?*"

I assured him I did, so a few hours later I found myself sitting as quietly as I could in the back of the conference room while the case in question was being presented . . . and presented . . . and presented. The serial killer in this case was presumed to be a male because the victims were all females. (We'll get to the why of that later.) But what was really flummoxing the six males around the table were symmetrical marks under the breasts of the three victims shown in the photographs spread out in front of them.

Were they something the killer had done? A signature maybe that investigators could follow or even a message the killer was sending in some twisted cat-and-mouse game he was playing with his pursuers? Or were the marks perhaps leftovers from some kind of interrupted postmortem activity? A would-be evisceration as in the photos I had been looking at earlier? Something else that was more twisted still? Serial killers don't play within the usual boundaries. But where were the serrations that kind of knife work would have left behind?

Finally, after I can't begin to tell you how long, John looked over at me on the far border of the conference room and said, "Jana, what do you think?"

It took me a little while to get over the shock of being included, but I walked over to the table, had a good look at the photographs I had thus far seen only at a distance, and almost immediately began asking myself exactly how I was going to break this to what might be my new colleagues. Directly, I decided, was best.

"Well," I said, "it looks to me like these are the marks you get after you've been wearing an underwire bra all day. Sometimes your breasts swell and the wire digs in. At least, that's how it affects me."

This was followed by another of those silences that seemed three times as long as it probably was, then a somewhat muted and thankfully brief discussion among themselves until all six agents decided that underwire bra marks were exactly what these were. Two days later John called to say I had the job.

9.
GOD IS IN THE DETAILS

FOR ALL PRACTICAL PURPOSES, THE Behavioral Science Unit was a Washington-area think tank. Just like other, more famous think tanks associated with the nation's capital—the Brookings Institution, the Heritage Foundation, the Cato Institute, the Urban Institute, and the like—we had a room with a big conference table where we frequently convened to discuss topics of mutual interests to ourselves and, as far as we were concerned, the welfare of our country and its citizenry. What's more, like other think tanks, our participants brought a lot of academic degrees and experience to the table. But the analogy runs out of steam just about there.

We met, of course, underground, not above. We had no choice in the matter: that's where we were. No views of the Capitol or the White House through our (nonexistent) windows. No policy issues to hash over, either, or grand schemes to present to the House or Senate or the relevant offices of the executive branch. Our bible wasn't the *Congressional Record*. It was the *Diagnostic and Statistical Manual of Mental Disorders*, or *DSM*, a thick compendium of mental disorders and the behaviors associated with them because so many of the people we studied seemed to be stepping right out of the manual's pages. Nor were our mentors seasoned lobbyists or the old pols Washington is famous for. Often we learned from medical examiners, and our classrooms were morgues.

I can't begin to tell you how many autopsies I witnessed up close during the eighteen months when I was officially a BSU trainee, essentially performing the full duties of a unit member but not yet receiving the GS-14 pay that was supposed to come with the job. One of those autopsy sessions involved an entire family that had died of carbon monoxide poisoning. The point was to show us how the adipose tissue, which stores fat, differs in poisoning cases versus other kinds of homicides. I've never forgotten that, or the dead mother and her three children at the center of our tutorial. Sessions with other experts were devoted to analyzing pronoun usage in confessions, to different forms of applied linguistics, and even to handwriting analysis. The BSU left few stones unturned.

Like think tanks elsewhere, we analyzed constantly, but our work was mostly link analysis, and what we were trying to connect were battered and maimed corpses, first to assure that they had been murdered and were not the victims of horrible accidents, then to determine whether the murders were the work of a single hand—one-off violence, a drive-by shooting, a copycat murder— or our particular sphere of interest, serial homicide, which the FBI itself defines as "the unlawful killing of three or more victims in separate events."

Serial homicide is not to be confused with mass homicide (three or more murders that occur in one event, with no defined time lapse between them) or with spree-killing (murders that occur at two or more locations but are driven by the same burst of anger, rage, or whatever the motivation might be). Serial killing is a world unto itself, and not a pretty one. Serial killers murder, then walk away from it, then murder again, and often again and again. (When they are caught, they almost invariably say they couldn't stop.) Our job, first, was to link the murders when we could—so we knew we were looking for one killer, not two or more unrelated killers; then to tease out what we could learn about the murderer, often from scant threads of evidence; and then, if the murderer was identified and apprehended, to analyze him—or on rare occasions her—and find out as best we could what made that person tick.

Generally, we would start with proximity. Did the murders occur in the same neighborhood, broadly speaking? Did the victims appear to be murdered at roughly the same time of day? If so, you could begin to speculate that the killer might be local and perhaps that he had a day job if all the crimes took place in the evening or night hours. That was comparatively easy work, but proximity could take you only so far. We had several serial killers who were cross-country truck drivers. They would carry the bodies with them and dump them in different states half a continent or more apart. Proximity was meaningless in those cases.

One particular cross-country trucker was convicted on only two murder charges, but my colleague Roy Hazelwood and I learned about another five victims when we interviewed his wife and learned that she had found Polaroids of seven women, including the two known victims, hidden in the heating ducts in their house.

From proximity, we would move on to modus operandi. Did the killer leave a signature that would help tie victims together? Did he sever their heads? Open up their chest cavities and examine the organs? Did he keep a particular body part or similar body parts as souvenirs of his crimes? Given the danger of discovery, doing so is far more common than you might expect. When Roy and I interviewed the aforementioned truck driver about his Polaroids, he told us that he would look at the photos as he masturbated, to help him relive the crime.

"I can't kill as many women as I need to, to get that excitement," he told us. "The photos are the next best thing," which might be the only argument for therapeutic pornography I've ever heard.

• • •

NONLETHAL SERIAL CRIMINALS OFTEN LEAVE all sorts of unintentional clues that can aid law enforcement in finding them. We took on fewer serial rapist than serial-killer cases—not for lack of interest or caring but because we were overwhelmed with homicides—but occasionally the suspected victims were so numerous that we were asked to sift through the evidence and determine if we were dealing with one rapist or multiple perpetrators.

In one case, my colleague Stan Jacobsen and I sifted through eighteen rapes that had occurred in a fairly confined territory over a two-year period and were eventually able to say with reasonable authority—based on physical evidence and the victims' own accounts—that at least fourteen of those had been the work of one man. Another prolific rapist I tracked seemed to be compulsively clean. He always smelled as if he had just showered and doused himself with cologne. His victims invariably remembered a specific soap and scent. We could assure the police who brought the case to us at BSU that they were looking for one rapist and what he was likely to smell like when they found him. Whether they ever did apprehend him and he did smell as predicted, I don't know. That was part of the frustration of the work: We saw only the human misery, seldom the reward of following a case to closure and seeing justice done in the end.

Serial killers are not so helpful. Their prey can help us only indirectly, but dead and mutilated bodies are not silent. Victimology—the science of unwrapping those mute secrets—was also a big part of our calculations. Did the dead lead high-risk lives—most often prostitutes and the unhoused—or were they low-risk, everyday people who had been chosen at random or had somehow placed themselves in the metaphorical crosshairs of someone with a broken moral compass? That could lead us to how the killer preyed on his victims and where. Were they violated before or after death? What was in their stomachs? Food stays in the body far longer than you might think: It takes about six to eight hours for food to pass through the stomach and small intestine and approximately thirty-six hours to move through the entire colon. Very often, the process of answering such questions will lead investigators to motive, which will lead to the offender, but you can't get there without doing a complete history of the victim, whether he or she is living or dead, including lifestyle, marital status, employment, personality traits, and more.

Eventually, if this truly is the work of a single serial killer, the crime scene, the victims and their locations of discovery, the time of day, the modus operandi, and any signatures will start to gel, and a pattern will begin to emerge. But few things in life tie up neatly, and, generally, finding a pattern is only the beginning of the job. Sure, the victims and the locations match up, but why did this murder take place at noon and that one at midnight? Why did the killer take a souvenir in one instance but leave, say, all the fingers attached in another? Was he scared off by a passing vehicle whose driver might remember something useful? Or was this one killer really two?

IN PONDERING THE CASES PRESENTED to us, we had two constant challenges. The first was to not rationalize away solid evidence that argued for a single killer. Simultaneously, we had to guard against talking ourselves out of a serial-killer match just because every *i* wasn't dotted, every *t* crossed. Murder is messy. Crime scenes are often chaotic. To the extent it's humanly possible, we had to control our own emotions. It's impossible at some level not to feel revulsion at the sight of an obviously tortured and battered body, and very challenging not to feel hatred for whoever committed this and sympathy for the victim. But emotions almost invariably cloud reasoning. In a sense, we had to stand outside of our own humanity while we were doing our job. This is where the "think tank" part of our BSU work became so valuable.

Time and again, I and others who worked on individual cases would gather our colleagues with relevant expertise around the conference table and lay out the story we had assembled about a serial killer who might or might not exist—the argument for, any arguments against—and then we would sit back and let fresh perspectives confirm our theories, sidestep our assumptions, or maybe rain all over our parade.

In the white heat of the investigation into the Rogers murders, it was taken as a given that the handwritten directions found in Joan Rogers's car were in her hand. A year later, after I had joined the BSU and the St. Petersburg police brought the case to us in Quantico, that assumption jumped out of the record and practically slapped me in the face. Sometimes you are too close to see the obvious. That was a big part of our think tank work: to spot the obvious hiding in plain sight—oftentimes hiding behind an assumption just as those handwritten directions were.

Sometimes we would stay at it for two or three hours, pounding our heads against a single mystery; those marks from the underwire bra that I mentioned earlier are one example. Sometimes we would go on for two or three days, depending on the case, the factors in aggregate and individually, and what agency had brought the case to our attention and how much staying power it had. On multiple occasions we were working at the behest of foreign law enforcement agencies taking advantage of our unique talents in probing the deeply macabre. Having flown in from abroad, the agents from Scotland Yard, France's Sûreté nationale, and elsewhere were reluctant to go home without some likely answers in hand.

Our "think tank" for any particular case might be as few as two people. I found that the ideal number was three or four— enough for a variety of experiences and opinions, without being overwhelmed by input—but for some of the higher-profile, more complex cases we dealt with, there could be seven or eight of us around the table.

In a perfect world, we would have been sent in advance all the materials we had requested—homework to assure that when we sat down to play our instruments, we weren't sight reading the sheet music. In the world we lived in, though, there were always gaps, even with very large and sophisticated agencies, and we would end up twiddling our thumbs while the people in ultimate charge of the cases scrambled for whatever information we were missing, or thought we might be missing, or just needed to get as complete a picture as possible before we dove into the crime scene and picked the autopsies apart for the little data points that often lead to the biggest answers.

God is in the details; that's what I really learned from all those round-table think tank sessions at the BSU. In our work, details were almost holy, and it is absolutely amazing how many details there are at most crime scenes and how the details multiply and take on new meaning with each fresh look.

Whether you are studying a live crime scene or photographs of one, the first tour through gives you the big picture, an overall comprehension of what happened. Maybe there's a dead body on the floor in the middle of a room. You register that fact, register signs of a struggle. Then, on the second look, you notice one lamp in the room has a crooked shade; another, an undisturbed shade, despite the fact that the struggle seems to have engulfed the entire room. On the third look, you start to ask yourself why and if that has any significance or is simply an anomaly. And on the fourth look, you start to wonder if even an anomalous undisturbed lampshade has meaning.

When you are dealing with people unmoored enough to murder multiple people in cold blood, you have to remember that what is odd to you might be a telling aspect of the perpetrator's character, a side door into discovering who this person might be and how he did what he did. So you begin to construct a narrative in your mind about how this happened and why one lampshade is crooked and another undisturbed, and then you look again and again. At a crime scene, I came to understand, you never stop learning, you never stop turning over rocks, because you never know what you will discover beneath them.

Surveying a crime scene is like those spy-in-the-sky satellites: The first images show you a microscopic car speeding down what looks to be a dusty road in some arid landscape, and then each new image has greater and greater resolution until the view from halfway to outer space has narrowed to ten feet above the car and you are reading the license plate and watching the driver flip a cigarette out his window just before the drone strikes. That was the thrilling part: when you get down to that level of resolution and suddenly all these disparate data points, these loose pixels in your head, pull together into a coherent whole, and the mayhem you have been studying alone and in groups for weeks or maybe months on end finally makes sense.

I COULD CITE HUNDREDS OF examples of how God is in the details, but none drives the point home more effectively than the case of Jeffrey MacDonald. I was still in high school when the story of the MacDonald murders broke, and I was gone from the FBI by the time the last litigation in the case was adjudicated, but we studied the case closely at the BSU as it was crawling at a snail's pace through the courts, and I frequently used it to model the need for microscopic attention to detail when I was teaching investigative technique at the FBI Academy in Quantico. The MacDonald case has also been the subject of enough television and movie attention to fill multiple nights of creepy binge-watching, but here's the basic story for readers who need a refresher:

In the very early morning of February 17, 1970, dispatchers at the U.S. Army base at Fort Bragg, North Carolina, received an emergency call from Jeffrey MacDonald, an Army doctor assigned to the Green Beret unit at the base. "Help!" MacDonald said in a weak voice. He then gave his address on the base and managed to add, "Stabbing! Hurry!" before the phone dropped to the floor.

Military police responded within ten minutes, circled the house until they found the back door wide open, and walked into a scene of appalling violence. Colette MacDonald, Jeffrey's wife, lay dead on the floor of the master bedroom with thirty-seven stab wounds in all—twenty-one from an ice pick, sixteen more from a knife, including two that had severed her trachea. She had also been battered repeatedly with a club, so hard that both forearms had been fractured.

MacDonald's five-year-old daughter, Kimberly, was dead in her bed, also stabbed repeatedly and clubbed hard enough to fracture her skull and splatter the wall and ceiling with blood. A post-mortem examination suggested that one of the blows had bruised her brain sufficiently that death probably came quickly after the attack—maybe the only blessing in the entire family holocaust. Kimberly's two-year-old sister, Kristen, was dead in her own bed, stabbed thirty-three times with a knife and fifteen with an ice pick. Two of the knife wounds had penetrated her heart.

Jeffrey MacDonald was the only family member to survive the mayhem. He was found lying facedown beside his wife in the master bedroom with cuts and bruises to his face and a single ice pick wound between ribs in the right torso, deep enough to collapse a lung but not life-threatening.

Across the headboard of Jeffrey and Colette's bed, someone had scrawled in red the single word "PIG," written with what later proved to be Colette's blood. MacDonald's first words upon seeing the graffiti were "Jesus Christ! Look at my wife! I'm gonna kill those goddamn acidheads!" And thus was established MacDonald's own story line, an account he has been clinging to now for more than half a century.

According to MacDonald, at about 2:00 a.m. that night, he had finished washing the family dinner dishes, moved two-year-old Kristen from beside her mother—where she had fallen asleep and wet the sheets—to her own bed, then settled on the living room couch rather than risk waking Colette. At some later point he heard Colette yelling, "Jeff! Jeff! Help! Why are they doing this to me?" But when he bolted up from the couch, he was immediately attacked by three males—two Black, one white—wielding a club and an ice pick, while a fourth intruder, a woman with long blonde hair wearing a floppy white hat that obscured her face, held a candle and chanted, "Acid is groovy. Kill the pigs!"

MacDonald said that he fought off the intruders as best he could before being overcome and knocked unconscious near the bedroom end of the family living room. When he came to, the intruders were gone. Still unsure on his feet, he lurched from bedroom to bedroom, first trying unsuccessfully to resuscitate his daughters, then pulling a small paring knife from his dead wife's chest, calling for help, and collapsing again by Colette's side.

Because the crimes took place on a U.S. Army installation, military investigators immediately took over the case, sealing Fort Bragg's gates in an effort to nab the four intruders before they could get off the base. That failed, but in the first light of morning, investigators found the murder weapons wiped clean of prints and lying on the ground just outside the house. The kitchen knife, ice pick, and "club"—a two-and-a-half-foot piece of finished hardwood lumber—had all come from the house itself, although, in the case of the club, that took a while to figure out.

Doubts arose in short order about some parts of Jeffrey MacDonald's story, but the crime scene was so grim and messy that confusion about what MacDonald saw and did that late night seemed almost inevitable. Also, MacDonald's account of events, even with its holes, fit the mood of the times. The Charles Manson murders had occurred only half a year earlier, and the specter of drug-fueled cult killings, once the province of horror movies, had gone mainstream in the American consciousness.

It helped, too, that the "PIG" scrawled in blood on the Mac-Donalds' headboard was a direct evocation of the "PIG" scrawled on Sharon Tate and Roman Polanski's front door after Tate had been murdered at Manson's direction. The fear of Manson imitators was widespread, and in the three-month military hearing that followed, MacDonald's attorney was able to produce a seventeen-year-old female drug addict, Helena Stoeckley, who vaguely fit the description of the chanting girl in the floppy hat and could recall being out with her boyfriend that night, riding around somewhere on the base, but she testified that she was too far gone on mescaline to remember where.

All that seemed to be enough for Colonel Warren Rock, who was in charge of the hearing, and on October 17, 1970, he recommended dismissing all the charges against MacDonald, adding his opinion that the perpetrators of the murders must have been either insane or completely flipped out on drugs. Within weeks the charges had been formally dropped. That December, MacDonald was honorably discharged from the Army and by the next summer he had relocated to Long Beach, California—my hometown—and was practicing as an emergency room physician at the St. Mary Medical Center. There the story might have ended, but investigators continued to pick apart the crime scene and examine the victims and the known facts of the case, and with every new pass Jeffrey MacDonald's story crumbled a little more.

Start with the crime scene. While gore was everywhere, the pivotal scene MacDonald had described—where he fought off the swarm of intruders in the living room after being alerted by Colette's screams—had produced something that looked curiously like a staged disruption. A top-heavy coffee table seemed to have been tipped carefully onto its side. A plant had ended up on the floor, but the pot itself was still upright. Additionally, the dining room, which was an extension of the living room, displayed no signs of a struggle. Plates remained balanced on edge in an unstable china cabinet, and Valentine cards stood upright on the dining room table.

In the cold light of further investigation, MacDonald's account of his wife's last words—"Why are they doing this to me?"—also merited further thought. Do people who are being bludgeoned and stabbed to death really say such things, other than in Shakespeare's tragedies and eighth graders' crime stories? The same applied to MacDonald's own first words to the military police who arrived shortly after his call: "Look at my wife! I'm going to kill those acidheads!" seemed almost rehearsed, in both its stilted outrage and its Manson echo. The echo part of that became more understandable when it was established that MacDonald had recently read an *Esquire* magazine article on the Manson murders.

Then there were MacDonald's own wounds. The attacks on his family had been vicious beyond description. It's hard to imagine there's enough space on a two-year-old's body to stab and puncture it forty-eight times. And these were ugly wounds: slashes, gouges, thrusts. By contrast, MacDonald's single ice pick wound was done with near-surgical precision, cleanly between the ribs.

From there, MacDonald's account fell apart even more completely. The "club" that inflicted such damage on everyone but him turned out to be a slat from under one of his daughter's mattresses. Surely it was a stretch to imagine a mescaline-crazed intruder going to so much trouble to find such a weapon for his or her murder spree.

The more microscopic the forensic evidence, the more it also shifted the narrative of what had happened that night. MacDonald had told investigators that his pajama top had been torn in his struggle with the intruders, but no fibers from the blue top could be found in the living room. However, fibers were found in both his daughters' bedrooms and under the younger one's fingernail. He'd also claimed he was not wearing the top when he tried to revive his daughters, but Kimberly's blood was nonetheless found on it. That list goes on for pages.

The kicker, though, was a genetic anomaly: All four Mac-Donalds had different blood types. "Follow the money," goes the old investigative axiom. Following the blood led investigators to a hypothesis that made a lot more sense than those "goddamn acidheads."

I'll spare readers the details of that. It's too gory to repeat, but the CliffsNotes version is that Jeffrey and Colette got into a shouting match in their bedroom, maybe because Kristen wet the bed; that in turn might have been magnified by Jeffrey's alleged infidelities and by the psychologically explosive effects of the amphetamines he was taking to lose weight so he could conform to Green Beret standards required even of the unit doctor. From there, the increasingly violent battle between the parents came to include Kristen, who was still in the room, and Kimberly, who was drawn in by the screaming. By this reasoning, the outcome was a bloodbath and horror show entirely of Jeffrey MacDonald's making and perhaps driven at least in part by his own massive vanity. Fourteen years later, when *Fatal Vision*, a TV miniseries based on Joe McGinniss's 1983 book of the same name, first aired, MacDonald was said to be upset not by painful memories of the horrific murder of his entire nuclear family but by the fact that his character was played by a then virtual unknown, Gary Cole. Robert Redford, he told friends, would have been a far more suitable choice.

I will also spare readers the endless details of the nearly five-decade legal circus all this gore let loose. Suffice it here to say that in August 1979, more than nine years after the murders, a North Carolina jury conferred for less than seven hours before finding Jeffrey MacDonald guilty of one count of first-degree murder in the death of Kristen and two counts of second-degree murder in the deaths of Colette and Kimberly. Appeals followed appeals as surely as winter follows fall, but Jeffrey MacDonald as of this writing is a resident of the Federal Correctional Institution in Cumberland, Maryland, and still a valuable lesson to people like me in never forgetting that the deeper you mine in every violent crime, the more you know and the more justice is served.

MAYBE HARDEST OF ALL FOR me, I had to accommodate myself to the fact that sometimes there is no answer to cases that cause survivors so much pain and that you try so hard to help untangle and solve. Melissa Witt first came to my attention in a consultation with the Fort Smith, Arkansas, police department. Nineteen years old, white, five-foot-six, and 130 pounds, Missy (as she was known) shared an apartment with her mother and attended the local community college. She dated occasionally but had no serious boyfriend at the time, and was described as very religious and proud of her virginity.

About 5:55 p.m. on the afternoon of December 1, 1994, Missy left her job as a part-time dental assistant and drove to Bowling World, intending to watch her mother roll some games and have dinner with her afterward, a regular ritual with the two of them. Instead, Missy's nude body was found six weeks later by a hunter tracking deer through the Ozark National Forest, forty-five miles from where she had been seen last and about seven miles from a Job Corps camp. Missy's clothes and purse were never recovered.

Those were the bones of the case. By the time it got to my

attention, a month later, Fort Smith police had identified three people of interest in the investigation: a white male in his mid-thirties; another white male and convicted sex offender who left town the day after Missy went missing; and a nineteen-year-old former boyfriend. But there was little solid evidence to go on. Blood found on Missy's car keys proved a dead end. An eleven-year-old boy in the bowling alley parking lot told police that he heard a woman screaming for help at approximately 6:35 p.m. on the day she went missing, roughly where her car had been parked, and two women leaving Bowling World at the same time said they had seen a white woman and a large Black man arguing at the same location. But as promising as they sounded, those leads proved fruitless, too.

The one item that caught my attention as I reviewed the case was that the body had clearly been moved from a more remote location deeper in the woods to a site visible from the road where the hunter found it. To me, this suggested that whoever had done this liked to revisit his crime, perhaps on foot but at least via a drive-by. Why bother moving the body otherwise? My suggestion to the Fort Smith police was to plant a story in the local *Southwest Times Record* featuring Missy's photo and mentioning that friends had set up a memorial to her at the disposal site without stating what the memorial site might look like. Even if the murderer was suspicious, I thought, he would have trouble resisting a look, and surveillance cameras might capture his license plate or, best case, his actual image.

Simultaneously, Fort Smith police and the Bureau were working with NBC's *Unsolved Mysteries* and Fox's *America's Most Wanted* to bring Missy's story to a larger world and unleash what has often proved the awesome investigative power of group awareness.

Was my suggested story ever planted? Did *Unsolved Mysteries* or *America's Most Wanted* turn up any useful leads or even air

Missy's story? Honestly, I have no idea. There was so little time for follow-up at the BSU and so many grief-filled stories like hers begging for our attention. But in preparing for this book, I did due diligence online and discovered (a) that Melissa Witt's murderer is still at large almost three decades later, and (b) that those seeking to solve this long-cold case have turned to an idea I pioneered. In late 2021, four large billboards around Fort Smith were outfitted with oversized photos of a very lovely Missy—an 800 number to call, a web address to consult, and a message that reads simply, "WHO KILLED MISSY WITT? Someone Knows."

Here's hoping that someone comes forward.

10.
BEWARE WHAT YOU WISH FOR

JOINING THE BEHAVIORAL SCIENCE UNIT meant living daily with depravity on an industrial scale. My skin literally crawled when Bill Hagmaier first described for me the series of interviews he was then conducting with Ted Bundy, who would eventually confess to thirty homicides, after years of denial and with almost certainly far more to his credit.

Bundy's arrogance, the way he claimed to have chosen only "worthy victims" (no "ugly" women, no prostitutes), his contempt for the women he killed, the cold-blooded way in which he would often select a remote pre-burial site and sometimes partially excavate it before even approaching his victims for the first time—all that filled the room as Bill talked on. Maybe no serial killer had ever been more premeditated in his actions.

I never was in the same interview room with Ted Bundy. He and Bill were a world unto themselves, and after their first meeting, it was all murderer's rules: no recording device, absolutely no females in the room, while Bundy doled out just enough information to keep himself out of the electric chair, or so he hoped. But there were plenty of nights in those early months with the BSU when I lay in bed imagining myself in that situation: just the two of us, with nothing more than a plexiglass divider between us, with Bundy refusing to look at me and with my knowing that the man across from me had twice before managed to break out of prisons while under heavy guard. Bundy sometimes seemed half human, half wraith, able to walk through walls, or maybe plexiglass dividers. Sometimes, I even wondered if he wouldn't find me "worthy" enough to bother with.

This is what I mean by living with depravity. It burrows into you. Jeffrey Dahmer is another example.

Dahmer's serial-killer credentials are impeccable: seventeen men and boys known to have been murdered over thirteen years, beginning in 1978. His depravity is impeccable, too. Dahmer dismembered his victims but not before having sex with their dead bodies. Going deeper into his story—as I did in preparation for a prison interview with him—was a tour through darkness that is hard to shake.

The local police officers who came to Quantico to consult with us on Jeffrey Dahmer were a talkative crew, and they left us with details of his story that I've never seen in subsequent accounts: that his first victim, for example, had been a bicycling mailman who survived the attack but barely. Jeffrey, then fifteen, laid in wait for him in the bushes, slammed the mailman with a heavy piece of lumber as he rode past, then had anal intercourse with the man as he lay unconscious on the side of the road. The officers also told us that Dahmer had progressed from there to breaking into funeral homes late at night and having intercourse with the corpses awaiting burial. From there, the officers' account segued into the better-known parts of the story: how Dahmer used sex to lure men to their deaths, the necrophilia that followed, how he sectioned their remains, and on and on, almost literally ad nauseam.

I should add that all my homework on Jeffrey Dahmer was for naught. He was bludgeoned to death in November 1994 by a fellow inmate at the Columbia Correctional Institution in Portage, Wisconsin, two days before our interview was to take place—"prison justice" being a fairly common outcome when an inmate population has even limited access to a serial killer, especially one who preys on young males.

Finally, no account of depravity would be complete without mention of a third member of this unholy trinity, Edmund Kemper, who combined in some ways the worst traits of Ted Bundy and Jeffrey Dahmer. Like Bundy, he preyed on coeds. Like Dahmer, he was a necrophile (although with females, not males) with a penchant for dismemberment and an obvious bad seed from his early teens on.

Kemper was so destructive as a child growing up in Santa Cruz, California, and his relationship with his mother, Clarnell Strandberg, so contentious that she sent him to live with his grandparents in a rural area a day's drive from Santa Cruz when he was still shy of fifteen, thinking the country air would do him good. It didn't. A few months later he called his mother with a message no parent ever wants to hear: "You better come and get me: I just shot Grandma and Grandpa." Shot *and* killed them both, to be exact.

Too young for a "fit and proper hearing" in adult court, Kemper was diagnosed as paranoid schizophrenic and institutionalized until he was twenty-one, then was released on the condition that he not live with his mother. That didn't happen, either. His mother took him in, and the two resumed a toxic relationship.

Kemper was said to have a near-genius level IQ—perhaps as high as 180—and at six feet, nine inches, he was an imposing physical specimen, but gainful employment was not in his wheelhouse. Every weekday he would drive his mother to her job as a secretary to one of the deans at University of California, Santa Cruz. Then he would use the parking sticker on her car to cruise the campus, pick up hitchhiking coeds who assumed from the parking sticker he was a fellow student or maybe graduate student or younger faculty member, and kill them. (The correlation between hitchhiking and serial murders, by the way, is frightening to contemplate. Mothers, don't let your children thumb a ride!)

At first, Kemper focused on one victim at a time. Then, emboldened, as serial killers frequently become, he started killing by twos, severing both their heads and all four hands and burying them together. In time, Kemper became convinced he would never be caught: The police, he told me, "were too ignorant and incompetent." To prove his point, he started walking around Santa Cruz with a severed head in a clear plastic bag. By then, people on California's Central Coast must have become completely immunized to weirdness, because no one seemed to have found it odd.

To end the killing, Kemper finally turned himself in, but not before administering a dramatic coup de grâce of sorts to his life to date. On the night of April 20, 1973, Kemper attacked his sleeping mother with a claw hammer, slit her throat, severed her head and engaged in sex acts with it, then placed her head on a shelf and screamed at it for an hour while throwing darts at it. Downstairs in the kitchen, he placed Clarnell's severed tongue and larynx in the garbage disposal—presumably to silence her really for good— but the disposal rejected the tough tissue. After downing multiple drinks at an area bar, Kemper returned home, invited his mother's best friend, Sally Hallett, over for dinner and a movie, murdered her when she arrived, stuffed that corpse in another closet, then drove a thousand miles nonstop to Pueblo, Colorado, and called the police back in Santa Cruz to report his crimes.

"Yeah, right," the duty officer seems to have said. So Kemper called another officer he knew personally, re-reported his tale of gore and horror, then waited to be arrested.

Some years later, my colleagues John Douglas and Bob Ressler interviewed Kemper prior to his appearance before a board charged with determining whether he should be allowed to transfer to a different psychiatric prison to finish out his life sentence.

The part of that interview recorded on film lasts only ninety seconds, but it's horrible to watch in its own way.

Clearly, Kemper had been told by a psychiatrist somewhere along the line how heinous a crime matricide is, especially in the manner in which he did it. "Tell them you're filled with regret for killing your mother," he must have been coached. "Conjure up a tear." Kemper did manage to say "I regret," and he struggled mightily to produce a single tear, but he just couldn't do it. Watching his cold, dead eyes as he tried to express an emotion he had never felt and didn't understand was both painful and as eerie as anything I've ever witnessed.

A few years later, I was doing link analysis on a widely publicized series of murders in Philadelphia—Was there a single killer? Were they related or not?—when I got an actual phone call from Kemper, offering his help. (The call was filtered through FBI headquarters and sent my way. BSU didn't advertise its number.)

I spoke with him somewhat reluctantly. Serial killers grab so much media attention that they often have an exaggerated sense of their own self-importance. Those who welcome probing have also talked with so many psychiatrists and other researchers and therapists along the way that they have a ready store of psychobabble to regurgitate for interviewers and the media. But on the theory that it takes one to know one, I took Ed Kemper's call and described the murders and all the bodily mayhem that followed, and he kept replying, "That's for control, the enjoyment. It's knowing that you are totally in control, and they are totally petrified of you."

Kemper spoke in the same flat monotone he uses in prison interviews readily available on YouTube, but there was something about the implied intimacy of our telephonic tête-à-tête that left me frankly shaken when it was over.

If all that calls to mind Hannibal Lecter, there's a reason.

11.
THE SILENCE OF THE LAMBS

HANNIBAL LECTER CAME TO BROAD public attention with *The Silence of the Lambs*, both the 1988 novel and the 1991 film, but Thomas Harris had been refining Hannibal ever since he first appeared in his novel *Red Dragon* in 1981, and he continued to fill in his backstory through another two novels, giving him aristocratic Lithuanian and Italian heritage and a traumatized childhood. His parents, we learn in *Hannibal Rising* (2006), were killed by a Nazi bomber, his sister murdered and eaten by Nazi collaborators right before his eyes. Unknown to himself at the time, Lecter is fed his sister's remains.

Broadly speaking, Lecter was apparently inspired by a well-born Mexican doctor, Alfredo Ballí Treviño, who murdered his friend and lover and mutilated his body and later is thought to have killed and dismembered an unknown number of hitchhikers back in the late 1950s and early '60s. (I'll say it again: Don't hitchhike!) Out of that seed eventually grew, in Thomas Harris's hands, a genius-monster who turned his victims into gourmet meals and played nonstop mind games with anyone who tried to engage him.

To be sure, Lecter is a brilliant creation, but if we had Harris's rich imagination and literary skills and an actor of Anthony Hopkins's talent to bring him to life, any one of us with the Behavioral Science Unit could have come up with something similar.

Hannibal Lecters were our daily diet (no pun intended). We saw echoes of him constantly—through in-person interviews we conducted, by studying their victims' remains, and by poring over case studies of earlier serial killers to hone our understanding. Most of us had seen our own Hannibal Lecter face-to-face in one form or another, often in unforgettable circumstances.

Once, John Douglas and another agent, Bob Ressler, were interviewing Edmund Kemper at one of the prisons for the criminally insane where he is still spending the rest of his life when, by accident, all three of them got into the same elevator during a lunch break. In the interview room, correctional guards were right outside the door, looking in. Now John, who was a little over six feet, and Bob, who was shorter, were in an enclosed container with a ruthless six-foot-nine-inch serial killer.

This is how John described the moment to me:

" 'You know,' Kemper said to us, in his almost robotic voice, 'I could kill you both right now if I wanted to.' And we both knew he probably could do just that and not feel a moment's guilt or remorse about doing so."

It was, John would later tell me, the longest elevator ride of his life, but Kemper, I'm certain, enjoyed it immensely.

This was after the book and movie versions of *The Silence of the Lambs* had appeared. Kemper would have at least read the former if not seen the latter. It's not inconceivable that he was consciously channeling his inner Hannibal at that moment, but by then Edmund Kemper had been evil incarnate for decades—real evil, not the fictional version; our very own evil at BSU.

Maybe inevitably, since I had something to do with how she was portrayed on-screen, however, Clarice Starling remains the more interesting character to me.

Patricia Kirby had been briefly with the BSU back when Harris was writing *The Silence of the Lambs*. The two had met then, and I'm sure some of Pat can be found in the written version of Clarice. By the time the film crew came to the FBI Quantico campus several years later to shoot scenes there, I was the only female and thus naturally assigned to be the handler for Jodie Foster, who would play Clarice in the movie.

Jodie and I met regularly down in my dismal subterranean office (minus the gory photo wallpaper) and in the conference room with John Douglas to talk over just what the job was like and how the BSU worked. I also worked daily on the set with the crew and director, fine-tuning exactly how an agent might phrase something, how she would carry herself in certain situations, excising any give-aways that this was a made-for-the-big-screen version of the BSU.

One morning Jodie and I were out walking the Yellow Brick Road, as the Marine Corps base obstacle course is known, when she said to her assistant, "Get my double to do this."

"Wait a minute," I said, "why can't you do this?"

"I've never done an obstacle course."

"Well," I told her, "there's a first time for everything. You're a few years younger than I am [eight, in fact]. You look like you're in good shape. Why don't you do it yourself?"

So Jodie took me up on the challenge, worked with our physical trainer, Larry Bonney, and eventually ended up conquering an obstacle course that involved, among other feats, bounding over low logs, clearing an eight-foot-high steel bar, doing a wall climb, weaving through a series of high logs, clearing more high bars (two this time), then sprinting to a twenty-foot-high rope climb. The obstacle course scene is a relatively brief moment in an almost two-hour movie, but Jodie did it all herself. And to me, at least, the movie feels more real because of it.

MORE IMPORTANT TO THE SUCCESS of the movie—and the legitimacy of Jodie's character, at least in my estimation—were the hours I spent schooling her in just what it was like to be a woman in the male-driven and male-defined world of the FBI.

Part of that was sheer girl-talk fun. Jodie shared some tales about the famous "casting-couch" culture of Hollywood and the "industry" generally. (Think Harvey Weinstein.) I told her about my earliest days in law enforcement, at that youth training facility in Chino, California, and the slimeball guards who were forever telling me to go get 'em some coffee and about where I told 'em I would put their coffee if I got it.

The FBI was never that nakedly male piggish in my experience, but to call it an inclusive culture when I first arrived at the Tampa office in 1986 would be very, very wrong. Take clothing. I don't think of myself as a fashionista, but I do like to dress professionally and I don't mind making a fashion statement or two when I show up in the office. And that's exactly what I did one day early on in my time with the Tampa office.

The black-and-white wool suit might not have been entirely appropriate for Florida weather, but I did wear it in winter. And, frankly, I thought the suit looked sharp. I had a little black-and-white polka-dot scarf for the pocket and set the whole outfit off perfectly with four-inch polka-dot high heels. Then, twenty minutes into the workday, my boss called me into his office and said I had to go home and change.

"Why?" I asked.

"Because no FBI agent dresses like that."

"Well, of course not. Most FBI agents are men."

"Look," he said, "I'm not kidding. You need to go home and change—and, oh, by the way, I'm going to dock your pay for the time out of the office while you're doing that."

That last part, I have to admit, got my attention—and my dander up.

"With all due respect," I told my boss, "I'm not going to do that. There's nothing in the *Manual of Administrative Procedures* or in the *Manual of Investigative Guidelines* that addresses how I must dress. I read them carefully. They do not address polka-dot, high-heeled shoes. And, respectfully, I'm not going home and I'm not changing my shoes."

There were eight of us on the squad, seven men and me. Two of them already knew our boss was going to send me home, and they were all snickering when I came back from my showdown.

"See you later," they said. "Hurry back, and be sure to wear sensible shoes."

I told them I was absolutely not doing that, and only a week later two of those guys and I responded to a bank robbery in progress in time to see the robber fleeing, covered in red from the dye pack that exploded inside his sack of money. Both my partners were in their early fifties by then and not exactly fleet of foot, so I slipped off those same four-inch polka-dot heels, took off running after that bank robber, and finally caught him trying to scale a fence at the back side of a dead-end alley.

It was only when we had the felon safely behind bars at the sheriff's lockup that I realized I was barefoot. My partners did agree to run me back by the spot where I had shed my shoes, but they were no longer there, so I returned barefoot to the office, only to find the high heels waiting on my desk and my colleagues in high good humor about the whole incident. But no one ever bothered me about my footwear again.

Fingernails were part of the same all-male mindset. The Bureau operated on the unwritten assumption that fingernails had to be kept carefully trimmed and even created a rationale to justify the assumption: Nails that look the least bit feminine are an impediment when using firearms. Granted, I gave them some small evidence to that effect during a firing-range test when I chipped off a piece of a fingernail while trying to slam the cylinder shut on my gun and the instructor had to shut the whole test down while he helped me pry the fingernail piece loose so the cylinder would actually close. Embarrassing? Yes, of course, but I didn't see them harassing male agents about their beer guts, and I was damned if I was going to give up the two things that define my femininity: high heels and eye-catching fingernails.

Jodie and I also had a good sisterhood laugh about another incident down in Tampa—in 1988 if I'm remembering correctly. Along with Fred Eschweiller and several other agents, I was sitting in on a very large meeting of multiple law enforcement agencies all working together on a major crime. One of the regional police captains was chairing the meeting, doling out assignments, when he happened to ask—and I'm *not* making this up—if anyone had brought along a "female unit."

Female unit? I thought. *What in creation is that?* Then I realized that in all that big room, I alone was the "female unit," and so, with Fred and the others choking back their laughter, I raised my hand, stood up, and said "Right here, Captain."

"'Female unit' sounds sort of like *Barbarella*," Jodie said, referring to the 1968 cult classic sci-fi film starring Jane Fonda.

"Precisely," I replied. "Just shows what an extra Y chromosome will get you."

It all sounds like silliness now—remnants from the dinosaur age of the American workplace—but I thought it was important background information for Jodie Foster if she was going to play on the screen the role I played every day: the lone feminine presence in what was pretty much an alpha male world—and, in the case of the BSU, a mostly underground world at that. Jodie was the consummate professional when it came to soaking it all up.

I ALSO SPENT TIME EDUCATING Jodie Foster in the ultimate test of female survival in an alpha male world, one that involved a feral environment where all the rules of the civilized world are off: prison interviews. The basics are pretty simple: You have to know, going in, that a hundred hungry male eyes are staring at you, all at the same time, boring holes in you, tearing your clothes off with their eyes. You have to expect hooting, whistling, lewd comments, all that, and you can't expect the guards in most prisons to do a lot to help you. I've known more than a few who seemed to take sadistic pleasure in the whole scene.

You're not in danger, though it might feel that way. Those bars the guys are shouting from behind are real. But you are uncomfortable and it is awkward, and sometimes truly disgusting things do happen. By way of example, I told Jodie about the time I was walking down a prison hallway, between two rows of cells, when a guy threw something on me that I soon realized was his own ejaculate. Whether he produced it on the spur of the moment or had been holding it in his hand for who knows how long, waiting for just the right moment, I can't say.

An almost identical scene, by the way, appears in *The Silence of the Lambs*, to great effect. Watching this same thing happen to Jodie's character, Clarice Starling, was almost as repulsive as it was when it happened in real life to me, but the masturbatory prisoner and I didn't get into a discussion about the matter because that's cardinal rule no. 1 for this kind of work: You absolutely cannot show any emotion; you can't reveal anger. That's what they want, of course, and rule no. 2 is you've got to fight like hell as you're going through this to keep an open mind about the person you are going to interview.

"I'm never going to interview Hannibal Lecter," I told Jodie one afternoon, down in my BSU crypt. "There is only one Hannibal Lecter, and he's yours to worry about. But if I'm going to interview a man—or, occasionally, a woman—in prison, odds are pretty much one hundred percent that he or she has done unspeakable things. That's a given, but if I go into that interview room thinking this is an awful person who is likely to lie to me with every word that comes out of his mouth, I'm not going to hear and follow up on those moments when the truth is just sitting there, waiting to be spoken and explored, and if I'm not going to do that, I might as well stay home and find another line of work. You've got to rid yourself of prejudice and any form of preconceived notion to do your job the right way."

I've always taken extensive notes about seemingly trivial items when I've interviewed someone—"has triple chin," "teeth are crooked," "sits very erect," "slouches," that kind of thing. Then, when I'm through and reading over the transcript, I ask myself at every key moment if I let those items color my understanding or interpretation of what was being said. I do this still, even now that I'm in the private sector and less likely to encounter serial killers in my professional life.

Most central to the compelling authenticity of *The Silence of the Lambs* were the further hours Jodie and I spent dissecting the critical scene where she first interviews Hannibal Lecter in prison. By then, I had done so many of those interviews—some, as I just suggested, with people only thinly removed from Hannibal Lecter—and those long hours and their many nuances and twisted contours were so deeply embedded in my psyche, that I actually found myself wanting to pour out my experience for Jodie to examine. It was a kind of purging for me as we hashed over time and again how a character like Hannibal Lecter would try to manipulate his interviewer in such a situation and how she should best react to counter him.

Honestly, too, I think we got it just right. Watching that scene in a darkened theater a year or so later, I realized I was leaning forward in my seat, gripping the chair arms, almost ready to burst into the screen if something went wrong. The public must have liked it, too, because, weirdly enough, *The Silence of the Lambs* was one of the best recruiting tools the FBI ever had as far as women were concerned. We had a significant spike in applications for at least two years after the movie first came out.

Only two things struck me as particularly off-key about the film. First, Clarice is still portrayed as a trainee. That's how the novel had it, and I guess the movie had to be true to that. But a trainee would never be handed that much responsibility, or a gun, or be exposed to that much horrible risk, or expose the FBI to so much risk. They didn't take my advice there. Second, and more dramatic, is the scene very near the end when Hannibal passes a dossier out between his cell bars to Clarice and briefly but poignantly slides his finger along hers as the handoff takes place. That's pure Hollywood: Agents and serial killers don't touch. But in her review of *The Silence of the Lambs* for *Film Comment*, Kathleen Murphy got the import of that moment just right: "It was an image of purest frisson, more terrifyingly intimate than any full-out assault. . . . That whisper of flesh on flesh marked Clarice Starling as Lecter's own."

The filmmakers were using that moment not just to bring this movie to a close but to set up for its sequel, but I knew just what was happening in that scene—the way Hannibal kept trying to plant his malicious seeds in Clarice's psyche. I've experienced that, too, from people almost as evil as Lecter himself. A few must have taken root and grown in there, because sometimes I hear them still.

12.
STARSTRUCK

JUST TO BE CLEAR: THE FBI campus at Quantico, Virginia, is not the kind of place you can show up, knock on the door, and join the next sightseeing tram ride. Tour buses were not disgorging passengers regularly outside the BSU. There's no serial-killer gift shop, although that could probably turn a fortune. Even international celebrities must have some kind of connection to get inside the belly of the beast.

Thomas Harris had already established his creds with John Douglas, who ran our shop, and with FBI higher-ups before Jodie Foster and *The Silence of the Lambs* film crew descended on us, and Jodie also did her best to assimilate our culture. Demi Moore, another famous visitor during my time with the BSU, was almost Jodie's polar opposite.

Like Jodie, Demi had come to us to prep for a movie role: as Medical Examiner Kay Scarpetta in a film version of one of Patricia Cornwell's wildly popular crime novels. Cornwell had had the brilliant idea of installing her medical examiner at the single spot in the nation where the weirdest crimes and most demented criminals happen to gather: our BSU. In fact, we never had a resident medical examiner, but the FBI generally cooperated with such requests even knowing in advance that the Bureau portrayed in the movie was likely to be no more like the real Bureau than an Eggo waffle is like a real waffle.

Since I was still the only woman in the BSU, coaching duties again fell my way, but the two experiences could not have been more different. Demi Moore fought our BSU culture and ethos at just about every turn.

Example: To get in the groove for her role as a medical examiner—for a film that was never made, incidentally—Demi wanted to sit in on one of our BSU consultations. That made sense, but the request was almost unprecedented in my experience, and we had to jump through a bunch of hoops to make this happen, including securing the approval of the law enforcement agency with jurisdiction over the case being brought to our attention.

"How long is this going to take?" Demi asked me as we were walking into the meeting.

"Probably five or six hours. It's a triple homicide. But don't worry: We'll take a lunch break."

The way she rolled her eyes at that prospect alarmed me, but at least I wasn't surprised when she walked out of the meeting forty-five minutes after it began. Naturally, I had to leave, too. On the FBI campus, outsiders have to be accompanied everywhere, for their own security—wandering onto a shooting range, for example, is a very bad idea—and for the security of our operations. Most celebs understand that; it's not rocket science. But Demi danced to the beat of a different drummer.

Another example: Dale had joined the Hostage Rescue Team, also based out of Quantico, about the same time I signed on with the BSU, and he kindly agreed to show Demi around, which should have been a big deal even for a gold-plated Hollywood star.

The HRT, as it's known in Bureau shorthand, is patterned after the U.S. Army's Delta Force. It's the go-to group for extreme moments. Out of roughly 13,000 FBI agents in total, forty might be invited in any given year to try out for the HRT, and far fewer will be called back and actually offered a slot. I explained this to Demi: She was being given a rare inside look at some of the best of the FBI's best. Demi, though, had other concerns. She insisted Dale not introduce her by name. She even wore a baseball cap pulled low down her forehead to keep the masses away—all of which proved unnecessary because no one seemed to give her a second look. The next day Demi actually did divulge her identity to a small group and seemed to enjoy the flurry of attention that followed.

Then there was the firearms range. Demi, it turned out, had little or no experience with firearms, so Cathy Schroeder, who was our instructor, a national champion pistol shooter, and an all-around phenomenal shot herself, took Demi under her wing while I snapped some photographs to memorialize the event, which (little did I know) was a big mistake. Like a lot of Hollywood stars, Demi was fiercely protective of her image and threatened to sue if any of images I had just taken ever saw the light of day. Actually, she didn't put it quite that nicely. Miss Congeniality, Demi was not.

All good things come to an end, and Demi's and my time together was no exception. I was walking her back to her room, after a fourth and final day of coaching (which felt more like babysitting), when either she called her equally famous husband, Bruce Willis, or he called her—I can't remember which—and they launched into what sounded like a normal discussion and I did my best not to eavesdrop. Then, when we got to her door, Demi took out her key, opened it, and tossed the phone to me.

"Here, you talk to him," she said as she hotfooted it to the bathroom.

And so I introduced myself and told Bruce I was the FBI special agent who had been taking care of his wife.

"Oh, yeah?" he goes. "How's it going?"

"Fine," I told him, which probably qualified as a white lie, and then added, "By the way, I really liked *Die Hard*," which was the absolute truth. It's kick-ass entertainment!

We talked for a few minutes. Bruce sounded like a nice guy.

One last celebrity hand-holding tale, just because it was so much fun. Maybe a year after *The Silence of the Lambs* was released in 1991, who should show up on our doorstep but Geena Davis and Gavin de Becker. Gavin de Becker is well-known today; his 1997 book, *The Gift of Fear*, was a runaway bestseller and established him as a regular on the major talk and news show circuit. Oprah Winfrey devoted two full hours to de Becker and *The Gift of Fear* on the tenth anniversary of its publication. Back in the early 1990s, though, Geena Davis was far and away the star attraction of the two. She and Susan Sarandon had paired up memorably in *Thelma & Louise*, released the same year as *The Silence of the Lambs* and every bit as popular. (Davis and Sarandon were both nominated for the Best Actress Oscar that Jodie Foster won.)

Gavin de Becker was the original reason for the visit. He was just launching his own security firm and had enlisted the Bureau's help with some of the fine points of protecting the rich and famous. Geena, meanwhile, had let it be known that she could think of no better birthday present than touring the newly famous Behavioral Science Unit, and Geena naturally was entrusted to the care of the only woman the BSU had to offer up: me.

Fortunately, I had seen her movie and loved it—unlike any of my colleagues.

"Go see it!" I urged them, even before I knew she was coming to see us.

"Right," they said. "Sad housewife and headstrong waitress set off on road trip. Housewife almost gets raped in some honky-tonk. Waitress plugs the creep with a handy .38 and the chase is on until—that is, Thelma and Louise floor it off a cliff into the Grand

Canyon and ruin a perfectly good vintage T-Bird convertible. Very believable. We're not wasting money on that!"

Which, of course, filled me with delight when Geena and I were having lunch in the Quantico cafeteria, and this same group of leading cinema experts spotted us and started tripping over each other trying to sit as close to Geena as they could get.

"Oh, Miss Davis," they kept saying, "you were so good! Just magnificent!" Et cetera.

"Well," I said, once I couldn't stand to hear this any longer, "let's get more specific. Why don't we go around the table, and everyone can tell Geena *exactly* what they loved *most* about *Thelma & Louise*?"

This led to a chorus of "Ums" and looks that would have killed me if looks could, and finally a round of confessions that, while no one had actually *seen* the movie, they certainly were intending to as soon as they could spring the little woman free from her household responsibilities, which by then was amusing Geena as much as it was me.

IN RETROSPECT, I CAN'T BLAME Demi Moore for being bored by her half-week tutorial on the secret life of BSU special agents. She stars in movies in which the dialogue is witty, the action moves swiftly along, and everything is solved—or at least over—in two hours max. Nor can I blame directors or scriptwriters for compressing consultations that can last a complete day into a single scene full of quick cuts and anguished faces. Demi walked out of the crime consult I took her to in forty-five minutes. Moviegoers probably would have walked out of the theater after five minutes.

What Hollywood and television and Bureau-themed crime books almost never get right is that none of that is the way things go in the FBI, even in gore-filled redoubts like the BSU. I understand the need for time compression, but evidence doesn't return from the lab fully analyzed in nine minutes—or fifteen pages, for that matter. Sometimes it can take years, depending on how you prioritize the cases and how much publicity is focused on the matter, and the volume is always so great that you must prioritize . . . and, yes, public clamor can move that needle.

Again for obvious reasons, the entertainment industry favors interdepartmental and interagency warfare and free-spirited cops who cut through all the crap and get the job done, rules and regs be damned. My childhood movie mentor Dirty Harry, for example, or good old Starsky and Hutch. People love that stuff, but I hope they realize it's not real. Law enforcement thrives on command and control, and it should. Too much is at stake to have everyone going rogue.

There can be a lot of drama in an FBI special agent's life, but a dramatic bent is rarely baked into our character. A professional stoicism sits over everything. Take us out of our natural setting, and we often come across as bland. In my new private-sector life, I've had to counsel retired special agents looking for a position to frankly lighten up.

Speaking of life's personal side, that, too, is rarely as neat and tidy in the real world of law enforcement as it is in the "industry's" version of that world. The hours are too chaotic and unpredictable, and the salary doesn't allow for even a part-time housekeeper.

That's the reason I really liked *The Closer*, which ran on TNT from 2005 to 2012. Deputy Police Chief Brenda Leigh Johnson (played by Kyra Sedgwick) was attractive, as you might expect from someone who in real life is married to Kevin Bacon. She was also very good at her work—smart, sharp, a winning personality, all that—but then she would go back to her apartment and it was a hot mess. Lampshades sat crooked; bras, underwear, and shoes were all over the place . . .

The irony is that Sedgwick herself is descended from

generations of New England money that probably traces their roots back to the *Mayflower*—a background better suited to the Ivy League and vintage wines of the CIA, not the beer-and-kick-the-door-in culture of everyday law enforcement—but darned if she and her scriptwriters didn't get our world right!

EVENTUALLY, ALL THE ATTENTION SHOWERED on the BSU by the movie industry and elsewhere introduced a little pixie dust into our own lives in the musty bowels of our Quantico fortress. John Douglas, our unit chief, would move on to a prolific and highly successful writing career. Bill Hagmaier would take over as chief of the FBI's National Center for the Analysis of Violent Crime. I even had my own small brushes with the high life thanks in large part to the celebrity that settled upon us following the huge success of *The Silence of the Lambs*.

At Quantico, Demi Moore had been a royal pain and major celebrity-sitting problem, but when Patsy Cornwell invited us to her home in Richmond to celebrate her birthday, then whisked us in a limousine to dinner at some off-beat restaurant with a beautiful outdoor patio, Demi's harshness fell away, and the three of us had a great time yakking away and puffing fine Cuban cigars afterward—although the yakking was largely Hollywood insider stuff that flew over my head, and my cigar-smoking amounted to a single courtesy puff on what must have been a hundred-dollar stogie.

A few years later, Patsy celebrated my birthday with a party at her house (Dale was included this time) and a cake that some-one had iced with an exact copy of the FBI seal. The crowning moment of her generosity, though, came in November 1993 when Patsy asked me to accompany her to London, where she was being feted at a formal dinner of the Crime Writers' Association. (And, yes, I vetted that one thoroughly with my superiors before I accepted.)

Anonymous crime fighter and famous crime writer:
That's me on the left, during my time with the FBI's Behavioral
Science Unit, and on the right is Patricia Cornwell, who turned our
often gruesome daily lives into best-selling novels.

Amidst all this reflected glory, I even had a chance to get famous on my own—well, sort of. The FBI wasn't alone in noticing that the Behavioral Science Unit was suddenly red-hot. The advertising gurus on Madison Avenue are always looking for ways to tie their clients in with newly popular cultural icons and powerful social movements like feminism, which is how I happened to be approached by a major national manufacturer of women's hosiery about becoming their pantyhose model.

This wasn't anything tawdry, mind you. The message was going to be (a) that a woman could succeed in even perilous, once all-male roles such as tracking serial killers and bringing them to justice while (b) still looking her best—in this particular brand of pantyhose, for example, which in the ad would be visible only below the knee-length hem of my well-tailored woman's business suit. (Yes, the miniskirt was popular in the nineties; no, I wasn't wearing one to the office.)

My first thought once the project was explained to me was *Oh, shoot me!* But I've always been a good soldier, so I took the prospect to my BSU boss, John Douglas, and it wasn't long before we had expanded the possible tie-ins between pantyhose and law enforcement generally to far more epic dimensions. As John suggested, in a pinch an agent could easily use pantyhose for handcuffs or leg restraints. From the other side of the law enforcement aisle, bank robbers were already commonly pulling pantyhose down over their heads to distort their facial features while still being able to breathe. If they were about to be caught after a multistate bank-robbing spree and couldn't stand the thought of doing prison time, they could always hang themselves with it, too. Talk about an all-purpose product!

"Your problem," I told the manufacturer's liaison when I finally got back to him, "is you're being too myopic. This is a much bigger idea than you realize." I was just getting started on pantyhose's many virtues in addition to covering buttocks and legs when I heard him easing the phone back into its cradle. He never called again, but, really, fame and fortune aside, did I want to be known for the rest of my career as the FBI's "Pantyhose Girl"? No.

It was just about this same time I also passed up a chance to throw back melon shooters—or maybe just sip Chardonnay—with the first lady. This was yet another spin-off of our new-won fame at BSU. CNBC had launched a political talk show called *Equal Time* that featured two female co-hosts—one Republican, one Democrat—gently kicking back and forth subjects of contemporary interest, often with a single guest joining them and with viewers calling in questions as the show went along. The cohosts were Mary Matalin on the GOP side and Jane Wallace weighing in from the left.

I had met Mary a couple of times previously, in one venue or another, so when the producer called and asked if I would be the guest for one of a series of shows on women who had succeeded in the workplace against long odds, I was inclined to accept, and when I put the matter to the Bureau public relations and media people, they gave it their blessing. And thus it was that on August 13, 1993—I remember the date exactly because it happened to be my birthday—at about 9:30 in the evening, the "On Air" sign lit up at the CNBC studio in downtown DC, I perked up in my seat, and after the usual introduction Mary Matalin looked over at Jane Wallace and said in a very upbeat voice: "This evening, we're here to talk about serial killers!"

And Jane Wallace looked back at Mary and replied: "Oh, I *hate* serial killers! I don't want to talk about that!"

And that's just about as deep as we dug into the subject for the entire hour despite my faltering efforts to add a little texture and insight to the conversation. The only comfort was that a number of the callers asked insightful questions and none of my BSU colleagues, who were lined up at their own phones to throw Whac-A-Mole questions my way, got past the phone-in gatekeepers.

Afterward, perhaps aware this hadn't gone exactly as I had hoped, Mary and Jane asked if I didn't want to join them for drinks.

"No, thanks," I said as we stepped out on the street.

"But it's not just us," they said. "We're going with a friend."

And there, believe it or not, standing curbside beside the back door of her limousine and tastefully surrounded by Secret Service agents, was Hillary Clinton.

"We're taking her car," Mary whispered to me, not quite sotto voce.

Was I tempted? Who wouldn't be, all politics aside? For all I knew, we were headed back to the White House to throw a few down. There aren't many chances to do that in life. But I was also dead tired and wanted to spend the remaining moments of my birthday with Dale, back in our smaller, not-white house, with a soothing glass of wine. So I thanked Mary and Jane, nodded respectfully to Mrs. Clinton—who was probably wondering what the heck I was doing in this picture—climbed in our somewhat dated Pontiac Bonneville, started for home, and . . .

Just as I was about to clear the DC streets, some kids stepped out of the shadows, splashed goop on my windshield, and offered to clean it off for ten bucks hard cash. Give me credit: I didn't go for the .38 I'm always supposed to carry. But I didn't pay the money, either, and by running my wipers on high and exhausting my entire reservoir of windshield washer fluid, I was finally able to clear just enough glass to make it home safely and very, very slowly. Dale was waiting for me, wineglass in hand, when I got there just after midnight. Meanwhile, Mary, Jane, and Hillary were probably having a hell of a good time.

13.
FOR BETTER OR FOR WORSE

RUBY RIDGE WAS A BOILING pot just waiting to spill over. For eighteen months beginning in early 1990, the U.S. Marshals Service had been conducting surveillance in and around the remote Idaho property, looking for the safest and most reliable way to conduct an arrest of Randy Weaver on illegal firearms charges and his continuing failure to appear in court to answer those charges. On August 21, 1992, the cat-and-mouse game finally came to a head, with disastrous results for both sides. Weaver's dog detected the marshals approaching the property and gave warning that brought the armed Weaver clan running, and the firefight was on. By the time it ended, Deputy U.S. Marshal William Degan lay dead, as did the dog, Striker. Only later was it discovered that another combatant, Weaver's fourteen-year-old son, Sammy, had also been killed and carried back to the family compound.

As dawn broke the next morning, August 22, the remaining U.S. marshals appeared to be pinned down by Weaver and his friend Kevin Harris, and that's when the FBI's Hostage Rescue Team was summoned to action. In short order, eight HRT members were flown from their base at Quantico, Virginia, to Idaho and briefed at a local National Guard armory, but by then their mission had changed dramatically. The surviving U.S. marshals were no longer pinned down. Instead of rescuing them, the HRT was charged with surveilling and somehow effecting the arrest (now on additional and more serious charges) of Weaver and Harris, who were both holed up in Weaver's cabin, which presented a whole new set of problems.

"Rugged terrain" hardly does Ruby Ridge justice. The HRT's ascent, necessarily by foot, from the U.S. marshals' base camp to the top of the ridge took most of the late afternoon. By the time they arrived, evening was coming on, and the closest observation positions they could safely set up—four two-man teams each— were more than two football fields away from the cabin's front door, in fading light.

Back east, 2,400 miles away from the action, I found myself following events in Idaho compulsively, for two reasons. First, if as expected the Ruby Ridge confrontation matured into a standoff, I knew I would be a part of a small Behavioral Science Unit contingent charged with trying to read the mind of a man about whom we knew very little. Could Randy Weaver be reasoned with after the opening hostilities? (The question had to be asked, even if we did not yet know his son had been killed.) Was he the sort of man who would want to go out in a blaze of glory? Should we act now or wait him out? Time is always of the essence in such situations, and I like to hit the ground running.

Within twenty-four hours, I was facing those questions in earnest at the Strategic Information and Operations Center (SIOC) in FBI headquarters—a round-the-clock exercise in educated best-guessing. But I also had a second, far more personal reason for honing in laser-like on Randy Weaver and Kevin Harris. My husband, Dale, was one of the eight Hostage Rescue Team members sent to Ruby Ridge, and as I would soon find out, he was in the forward position, paired with team leader Lon Horiuchi. While we kicked around best- and worst-case scenarios on Pennsylvania Avenue in downtown DC, Dale was lying prone on the ground using a bipod for his weapon while Lon Horiuchi stood with his rifle, steadied by the branch of a pine tree. Both could hear the *thump-thump-thump* of an FBI helicopter approaching the site when all hell broke loose.

Here is how Dale described subsequent events in his 1995 testimony before the Senate Judiciary Committee—and the fact that he was testifying about all this more than three years later in front of some of the most powerful senators in the nation says tons about the blowback that followed.*

"Forty-five or fifty minutes after selecting our position, I was trying to determine who and what individuals were inside the cabin or out and where they were when I briefly saw three individuals, two adult males and a woman, all carrying rifles. A few minutes prior, I had heard the helicopter sounding like it was approaching our area, and when the individuals came out, it coincided with the arrival of the helicopter. They had rifles and they moved towards the birthing shed across the front area of the cabin. I had an intermittent view because of the trees, the vegetation, and rock outcroppings. I never saw the three individuals at all times, but I did see them going towards that area. I asked Mr. Horiuchi if he could locate them and give me directions, being that his position was somewhat elevated from mine, and he did give me directions and told me to stay on the front door of the cabin. Given the darkness, I was not exactly sure where that was, but I changed my view back to the cabin, then swung back and forth between there and the people with the rifles because I was concerned for the helicopter crew and wanted to be sure that if a threat action was going to be delivered to it, I could respond to that as well.

---

* Literal testimony transcripts are often hard to follow. I've smoothed out the bumpy moments for ease of reading and understanding.

"As I did that, I saw an adult male come around the back side of the birthing shed with a rifle and stop at the corner. At that time his rifle was pointed skyward, and that is when I heard the first shot, and I knew it had come from Mr. Horiuchi's rifle."

That individual Dale saw was Randy Weaver, now shot clean through the shoulder. The drama, though, was far from over.

"I never saw the female again after she initially came out of the cabin, but following that first shot, the two adult males began to return to the cabin at a fast rate. They still had their rifles, [pointing them in our direction], but they were hurtling towards the cabin. And again, because of the trees and the vegetation, they were in and out of my view, but just as they were reaching the porch of the cabin, I saw one adult male disappear behind what I now saw was an open door, and I saw the second adult male stepping onto the porch. At that time, the second shot went off, and I saw him bending forward as if diving out of sight, and he just disappeared. I did not know for sure if either of the individuals had been hit."

The anguished, high-pitched screams that quickly emerged from the cabin left little question about outcome. Not until three days later was it determined that Vicki Weaver, Randy's wife, had been killed by the same round that hit Kevin Harris, although he would recover. The outcome was terrible, of course, but the optics were almost worse. In the original firefight, Sammy Weaver had been shot in the back. (By which side wouldn't be known for years, but it was eventually determined to have been a U.S. marshal's round.) Dogs can be vicious killers, but shooting one is rarely a winner with the general public, and how could you not grieve for a mother killed even if she had been seen moments earlier pointing a rifle menacingly?

The optics would eventually get even worse when Weaver's grandstanding lawyer, Gerry Spence, claimed that Vicki Weaver had died with her infant daughter in her arms. The Weavers' ten-month-old daughter was in the cabin when all this went down, but there is absolutely no evidence that Vicki Weaver had put down her rifle and picked up her daughter in the brief interlude between the dash to the house and the round that killed her.

Dale and I could imagine the headlines before they started to appear—"Brutal FBI Snipers Savage Idaho Family"—and we both knew that a shitstorm was sure to follow. The storm was still raging on September 15, 1995, when Dale and eight of the nine other HRT members who had been at Ruby Ridge that day were sworn in before the Senate Judiciary Committee. If anything, it had gotten worse in the intervening years.

The Department of Justice, in its infinite (and deeply flawed) wisdom, had found the shootings at the Weaver cabin to be a violation of the victims' constitutional rights. Lon Horiuchi, who had fired the two shots, had been so frequently and anonymously threatened that he was in the U.S. Marshals Service witness protection program. Randy Weaver had been successfully defended on murder, assault, conspiracy, and gun charges by the publicity-hungry Gerry Spence, who had painted the Hostage Rescue Team as murderous thugs. The press for the most part seemed to agree, and so, it turned out, did the bulk of senators present in the committee room. Along the way, the press and the politicians seemed to forget that the original charges brought against Randy Weaver—the ones for which he had refused to appear in court—were for trying to sell a pair of illegal sawed-off shotguns to a federal informant within the white supremacist Aryan Nations movement, a group for which Weaver was known to have an affinity.

Lon Horiuchi was the missing team member at the Senate hearing: He was facing civil litigation and had repeatedly pled the Fifth Amendment when he appeared at previous closed hearings. That left Dale, Lon's partner, as the point man for the questioning and the whipping boy for a torrent of high political dudgeon.

Dale, at least, got the first word. He was the only one of the eight witnesses with a prepared opening statement, and he used it to defend the Hostage Rescue Team's honor against Gerry Spence's broadsides:

"Mr. Spence said we were trained killers. We are not. We are trained to save lives. In fact, this Congress gave us a commendation for a rescue of hostages at the Talladega, Alabama, Federal Penitentiary, where hundreds of rioting inmates held nine Bureau of Prisons employees hostage with zip guns, machetes, and knives for ten days until HRT entered and secured every inmate without a single shot being fired. That's how we are trained.

"We were created in 1983 to protect the 1984 Los Angeles Olympic athletes because of concern that never again should athletes be massacred as the Israelis were in 1972. In my ten years as an agent, I have never shot or killed anyone. And in the twelve years of HRT's existence, and the dozens of operations responding to violent crises, a firearm was discharged on only four occasions. The trained-killer accusation is unfair to all dedicated agents and to the widow of United States Marshal William Degan."

Watching all this on C-SPAN—I couldn't stand to be in the chamber that day—I was as proud of Dale as I could be . . . and then the pummeling began, led by committee chairman Arlen Specter of Pennsylvania, who never failed to remind listeners he was a former district attorney in Philadelphia. Specter's major point seemed to concern the second shot. People running into a cabin couldn't possibly be a threat to a helicopter flying overhead. Dale countered that with the obvious:

"I believe [the threat was real] as long as the helicopter was airborne and it contained people who could be harmed. These are individuals who have exhibited a propensity for violence. And I also believe that the threat existed whether the individuals were outside or inside the cabin. Actually, in my opinion, the threat was heightened with the individuals inside the cabin. . . . They could fire at any point from inside."

By then, though—and this was early in the hearing—an Abraham Lincoln or Martin Luther King Jr. or even Demosthenes on his best day could not have turned the tide. Specter had some lackeys drag in the very door of the Weaver cabin to exhibit a point I could never understand—nor Dale, either, although he was required to come forward and be part of the farce.

Senator Herbert Kohl of Wisconsin followed, gently at first, before painting Randy Weaver as a virtually flawless citizen, despite his failure to show up in court to answer charges that precipitated the entire sequence of events and his chummy links with the Aryan Nations. Senator Kohl was trailed in turn by Tennessee's Fred Thompson, who—despite having played tough guys, military men, and DAs in multiple movies and TV shows—had no actual experience in this field but nonetheless droned in at length about faulty rules of engagement without ever acknowledging that the situation on the ground that early evening three years earlier was dynamic, ever changing, and deeply complicated by the presence of a helicopter whose pilot and passengers would be sitting ducks if the Weavers or Kevin Harris opened fire on them. There's a reason all eight hostage team members who testified that day said they thought the second shot was justified and why two of them, Dale included, said they were about to take the same shot when Lon Horiuchi fired his rifle. They were there—in the heat and fog of the moment—not sweating it out in a well-lit U.S. Senate chamber. Later the microphone was passed to Idaho senator Larry Craig, who seemed to think the FBI had acted much as an invading army on Idaho's sacred soil where nary a citizen had ever committed a crime.

In retrospect, how to choose the worst of the lot is impossible, but since Senator Specter led off and concluded the nearly four-hour verbal waterboarding, he was the only one Dale and I rewarded privately with a permanent nickname: Arlen Sphincter. Somehow it seemed appropriate. All kidding aside, though, watching Dale getting beat around like that was one of the low moments of my life, and the after-echo has never really gone away, for either of us.

AS NOTED EARLIER, MY OFFICIAL involvement in Ruby Ridge came after the shooting was over and the standoff had begun. The bitter court battles, the stacked Senate hearings, the demonization of Lon Horiuchi (and, to a lesser extent, Dale)—all that was to follow. The question we faced at the Strategic Information and Operations Center in the immediate aftermath of the gunfire was straightforward: Storm the cabin or wait it out? To me, the answer—or, more accurately, best guess—was fairly simple. There was no evidence Weaver was a survivalist; nor did he have numbers on his side. Inside that cabin were two wounded men and a child less than a year old.

I counseled a quiet siege, and eleven days after the standoff had begun, Randy Weaver surrendered, but not before Bo Gritz, an ex–Green Beret and headline-grabbing fringe presidential candidate (Populist Party; slogan: "God, Guns and Gritz") inserted himself in the process and laid claim to ending a standoff that was about to conclude on its own. Either way, the American militia movement had been given a major boost.

Six months later, in an eerily similar incident, agents of the Bureau of Alcohol, Tobacco and Firearms down in Texas tried to execute an arrest warrant on Branch Davidian leader David Koresh. The firefight that ensued killed four government agents and six of Koresh's followers and left another sixteen government agents injured. That was on February 28, 1993. Dale and the Hostage Rescue Team were immediately deployed again, this time for a siege that would last fifty-one days and be the subject of intense media scrutiny the entire time—and, as things turned out, for years to come. For my part, I was back at FBI headquarters in downtown DC, hunkered down in the SIOC, reprising my role as one of the chief interpreters of the leader's actions and intentions as the siege wore on.

This time, though, things were radically different. The Branch Davidian compound at Waco was packed with months' worth of food. David Koresh also had a small army at his command, and he himself was a deeply unstable man with media savvy and a hard-core group of followers who gave every indication of having been brainwashed. The horror of Jonestown kept echoing in my brain as I parsed his communiqués for meaning. I particularly remember one video he sent us in answer to charges that he had been sexually abusing the children in his compound. The girls on the video looked to be early teenagers or younger, and they swore that Koresh had never touched them, but their eyes kept flickering up and to the right. Either they were reading from placards as they spoke or they were being directly coached. Whichever the case, their performance was creepily robotic. More than creepy, actually: It deeply concerned me, both for the people inside the compound and for those outside, Dale among them.

Mind you, I had complete confidence in Dale and his abilities. He was on the ground in Waco, and I always deferred from an operational standpoint to those who were on-site. What's more, I trusted his judgment—that he wouldn't go running into harm's way unnecessarily. But, yes, I was worried. Who wouldn't be?

Koresh had more than enough foot soldiers at his command to do enormous harm both inside and outside the compound, and more than enough firepower, too, including a large cache of .50-caliber rifles accurate to almost 2,000 yards out and with an enough muzzle velocity to pierce armor. To keep an eye on the compound, the HRT took over two houses and split into two teams. Dale's was directly in line with the front gate; the other, at the rear gate. Each house took ten days to set up ten final firing positions, each of the positions protected by a thickness of ten sandbags because field testing showed that while a .50-caliber cartridge might penetrate nine bags, it wouldn't make it through the tenth. (The weight of the bags would eventually buckle the floors, and both houses would have to be razed.) And then the HRT members sat and waited—one day on, one day off, for a hotel bed, a shower, and a decent meal—for forty-five straight days, Groundhog Day after Groundhog Day, until April 19, when everyone was called in for duty and this time all hell broke loose on an industrial scale. I had known that was going to happen, too, and that there wasn't a damn thing I could do from all the way across the country to protect anyone except provide the best behavioral analysis I was capable of.

I also became a kind of a den mother as the first weeks stretched into a month and longer. In addition to the sheer danger involved, hostage rescue can be hard physical work. A lot of the HRT "operators," as we called them, were a decade or two younger than Dale and me, with equally younger wives and often starter families but without the experience either of us brought to this kind of ordeal.

In our dual professional capacities, Dale and I talked on a fairly regular basis, but for the younger operators a radio silence had been imposed. This left their wives and loved ones with the challenge of trying to tease out the situation from overwrought media reports and rampant speculation. I barely knew most of the wives, but Dale began passing along messages for home from a few of his operators, and word soon got out that if you wanted to know what was going on, you should call Jana. More than once in the increasingly dangerous closing days of the siege, I found myself saying soothing words to women whose husbands I was sure would soon be challenged—women I feared might even soon be widows.

Then there was the perspective from the Strategic Information and Operations Center itself. The SIOC today is state-of-the-art, but back then it was more like a giant classroom. Everyone sat in a big, open bay area divided by departments: Operational, Counter-Intelligence (basically, the CIA), Communications, etc. I was part of a rotation of three representatives from Behavioral Science. Next to me sat the negotiators and the legal team, and over to the side, behind a glass partition that created a smaller room, loomed the director, the deputy director, and other top brass. We circulated in and out all day, every day, but the place was fully staffed 24/7, which meant that generally you could count on about sixteen people in the SIOC whatever the hour.

Much of my time was spent picking apart the calls Koresh made to our on-the-scene negotiators—What did he really mean? How would he likely interpret this or that response?—plus the videos and other communiqués he fired our way (with copies to the media of course), all complicated by the micromanaging of the lawyers among us, who had become even more picky than usual thanks to the growing legal storm from Ruby Ridge. On top of all this sat Director William S. Sessions and his top aides responding to pressures from higher up that we couldn't begin to imagine or sometimes understand.

As the standoff wore on, for example, Sessions came to believe that he alone could best negotiate an outcome, one-on-one with Koresh himself. Because Sessions had practiced law in Waco for eleven years earlier in his career, he felt he could relate to Koresh as a "fellow Texan." His plan was to go to Waco and speak with Koresh while sipping Texas sweet tea, as I found out when Deputy Director Floyd I. Clarke came to my tiny desk area scrunched between the legal team and the negotiator representatives and asked to speak with me privately. We huddled in the stark, sterile FBI hallway outside of SIOC as he related Sessions's idea.

"The director," he told me, "wants to speak with a behavioralist, so you're it, and I hope you give the right response to him."

I felt tremendous pressure as I entered the small anteroom in which the director waited, but I managed to summon my common sense when Sessions asked for my opinion.

"I don't think a meeting with Koresh is a good idea for two reasons," I told him. "One, you will be undermining your on-scene hostage negotiators and the HRT by not allowing these exceptionally well-trained agents to do their job. And two, you will be setting precedent by personally negotiating with offenders. From now on, all of the up-and-coming crazies will demand to deal with the FBI director personally."

I was unceremoniously dismissed and returned to my tiny desk in SIOC. But I still had a job the next day, and Director Sessions never went to Waco to have sweet tea with Koresh. And a good thing that was, because I'm still certain that had he gone to Waco, the director might well have become yet another pawn in whatever crazy, vainglorious, apocalyptic scheme Koresh was hatching from day to day and hour to hour—a danger to himself and a danger to the law enforcement officers who would have felt obligated to protect and shield him.

Koresh's many pronouncements, his frequent phone calls, his rambling musings on the book of Revelations and its Seven Seals—sometimes broadcast on the PA system so our negotiators could listen in along with his Branch Davidian followers—and everything else, I became convinced, were pure theater, a way to buy time while he plotted or perfected in his own mind whatever the final act would be. The glacial silence that soon settled over the compound suggested to me that the end days were near.

"He's not doing anything, not saying anything, not talking at all to the hostage negotiators any longer," people kept saying to me. "What do you think he's doing? Is this a situation where he might be aggressive? What should we try next?"

All I could offer in response was yet another educated guesstimate. The compound was a fortress, still packed with food, water, weapons, and ammunition so far as we knew even after almost seven weeks of siege, certainly still protected by those .50-caliber rifles. I had no doubt that Koresh and his lieutenants had contingency plans galore. But the more I thought about it, the more the name "Jim Jones" kept sounding in the back of my head. I doubted it would be suicide by poisoning as at Jonestown; Koresh would want something more visible, a bigger splash for the cameras and newsreels.

The scenario that really scared me was suicide by cop: over one hundred Branch Davidians armed with weapons they had been trained to use, charging out of the compound straight at the heavily fortified HRT positions. They had no chance of getting there. For our operators, it would be like shooting ducks in a pond, only infinitely more horrible, but imagine what those headlines would read like the next day. Imagine the footage that would lead newscasts for days and weeks to come.

In the end, a little bit of everything went down. Fearing as I did that mass suicide was imminent, the HRT dispensed tear gas into the compound starting at 6:00 a.m. on April 19. Then the Branch Davidian firepower went on display for the next six hours with constant gunfire pouring out of the compound. Just about noon, fires sprang up simultaneously at three specific locations inside, and a few Branch Davidians came out, and with that, the media—or at least the worst and laziest part of it—had its story line. The fascist FBI had done it again, just like at Ruby Ridge, just like everywhere. The seventy-five dead when it was over, including Koresh himself, were all the proof that was needed.

Even the genuine heroes of those final minutes of the siege found themselves pilloried in the press. When Jim McGee, one of our HRT operators, spotted a woman in the flames engulfing a ground-floor bedroom inside the burning compound, he jumped from the safety of his armored vehicle, raced to her aid, smothered the flames, and saved her life. None of that was mentioned in the media when he received a Medal of Valor from the FBI. Instead, the story line was *Oh my God, these jackbooted thugs were all killing people, and now they're getting awards for it.*

They didn't know what the award was for, and they didn't know what I already knew from my unique perspective on the mass tragedy. First, nearly all of the dead inside the compound had bullet holes in their skulls or had been stabbed—victims of murder before the flames ever touched them. Of the nine Branch Davidians who survived the conflagration, including the woman Jim McGee saved, at least several exited the compound as the murders began and before the fires took hold. One man was found in the water tower afterward, probably the safest place to be in the entire compound. Another man climbed out on the roof and slid down to the ground, where he had to be told to drop his gun. Second, the FBI insertion of tear gas didn't start the fires as widely reported. From the scope of his sniper's rifle, Dale watched Koresh's lieutenants set the fires shortly after the canisters exploded. The fire was a conflagration of opportunity, a last attempt by David Koresh to write history in his favor, and for more than one person it worked like a charm.

Three years to the day later, on April 19, 1995, Timothy McVeigh "avenged" the Branch Davidian deaths by shearing the front off the Alfred P. Murrah Federal Building in Oklahoma City, killing 168 people and injuring 680 others. Had he bothered to look in the local phone book, McVeigh would have known that the FBI, his primary target, had their office elsewhere in Oklahoma City.

14.
HEARTS OF DARKNESS

WHY DO THEY DO IT? Why do children born normal to all appearances grow up to commit unspeakable acts, sometimes again and again? That was always the billion-dollar question at the Behavioral Science Unit—the pot of gold at the end of the rainbow. *Why* was the big reason we got up in the morning, the big question that hung in our minds as we lay down at night. *Why* was what sustained us as we spent mind-numbing hours cozied up in prison interview rooms with murderous psychopaths.

We had a forty-two-page protocol to follow during these interviews, but the FBI had nothing to offer in return for the insight we sought—no shortened prison sentences, no upgraded cells, no wide-screen TVs for the solitarily confined. At one level, also, we had very little objective to learn. Yes, we always wanted to know if there were unrecorded victims, more bodies somewhere—not so we could extend sentences that were often already life in prison with no chance of parole, but for the sake of the victims' families, to bring closure to their endless wondering if not to their grief. But the crimes for which they had been convicted were heavily documented. Often there were folders full of grisly photos of the victims and what remained of the crime scenes. Voluminous medical examiner reports detailed how and where and when (to the extent it could be estimated) the crimes had been committed.

What we didn't have was the question I posed above: Why? All we really had to offer to that end was our ignorance, our desire to be educated—but, surprisingly, that was often enough to crack the doors open.

"Tell me the story of why you are here?" I would ask one of these hearts of darkness, and then I would sit back and listen for the lies, the delusions, the self-justifications, and the magical thinking that allowed these epitomes of evil to go on living with what they had done. Time and again, that's where the real answer waited, or as close as we were going to get to it.

An example: I was never in the same room with Timothy McVeigh, but while I was still with the BSU I was given a large packet of letters he had written to his younger sister and asked to prepare an assessment. The entire time I worked on those letters, McVeigh wouldn't stop telling me the story of himself—or, more accurately, *his* story of himself, which wasn't at all the same.

The Oklahoma City bomber clearly doted on his little sister and liked playing the role of big brother. As I was later to learn, his sister, five years younger, also worshipped him, and little wonder. Far from the overt sociopath I expected to encounter in the letters—enraged at the government generally and the FBI, the ATF, and the U.S. Marshals Service in particular, and hell-bent on repaying blood with blood—McVeigh's account of himself was full of success stories. He had wowed them in the Special Forces, stood out as a leader among men until an injury cut short his military career, but nonetheless piled triumph upon triumph until it seemed the world was surely his oyster.

Was any of it real? I shared the content of those letters with his older sister—the one who had first cast suspicion on McVeigh after the Oklahoma City attack and who deeply feared him.

"Not true . . . not true . . . not true," she said as she paged through the letters. "He tried out for Special Forces but was rejected. He never did this. He wouldn't even know how to do that."

Obviously, you have to discount for sibling rivalry in situations like this, but as she tore apart the story her brother had been telling their younger sister, I began for the first time to form a picture of Timothy McVeigh that I'm convinced is far closer to the truth if not the whole truth. He wasn't avenging the Weaver deaths at Ruby Ridge or the Branch Davidians who had died at Waco. He was taking revenge on all the wrongs he conceived had been done to him personally, including the failure to appreciate his unique qualifications to be a member of the Special Forces, a leader among not just men but *he-men*!

At another level, McVeigh reminds me of David Koresh: Both staged a slaughter to enshrine themselves in history. And at least according to his own terms, McVeigh succeeded brilliantly. Many current-day historians date the rise of the modern militia movement in America to the standoff at Ruby Ridge, but Timothy McVeigh was the movement's first stone-cold hero and remains that way to this day, almost two decades after he was executed by lethal injection on June 11, 2001, at age thirty-three.

McVeigh, it should also be noted, provided the template for phase one of perhaps the most notorious mass murder in modern European history. On July 22, 2011, Anders Behring Breivik parked a McVeigh-inspired truck bomb outside a federal building in downtown Oslo, Norway, lit the fuse, and walked away from an explosion that killed eight people. While that dominated the news and police attention, Breivik hopped a ferry to the island of Utøya, home to an annual summer camp for the Workers' Youth League, affiliated with the ruling Labour Party. There, disguised as a police officer and heavily armed, he methodically hunted down and killed in cold blood sixty-nine defenseless people, most of them teenagers. His goal, he said, was to save Europe from Muslims and multiculturalism. Like McVeigh, he didn't have the guts to face his victims on equal terms.

SOME MURDERERS, I LEARNED, LIKE to hide behind specific words. For whatever reason, there was a big spate of infant abductions while I was at BSU. All across America, it seemed, women were telling boyfriends they were with child, racing to the altar, then scrambling six or seven months later to secure the infant that had supposedly necessitated the marriage. (Leave aside the issue of the new husbands who never seemed to notice the soon-to-be moms showed barely a bump in the proper place.)

Mostly, these abductions took the form of staking out hospital maternity wards, looking for a chance to snatch a newborn— a fearsome possibility for the real mother and the infant, and one that required a lot of expenditure to increase maternity ward surveillance and security. But the workarounds the infant-nappers found were often far scarier.

One New Mexico woman got around the challenges of maternity ward security by identifying a pregnant woman clearly within a week or so of delivery, tailing her until an opportunity presented itself, then whacking her unconscious with a board, and—skip ahead two lines if you can't handle this—basically sawing the fetus out of the womb with her car keys. The infant survived. The mother didn't. Maybe you have to be a woman to appreciate just how horrible that is, at so many levels. My male colleagues gave me some space after that case landed in our laps.

Another woman—the daughter of a retired police officer, as it turned out—stalked a very expectant mother closely for several weeks and was waiting in the hospital parking lot when the woman, her husband, and her mother arrived and headed for the maternity ward. The next morning—this was back when delivery meant an overnight stay—the would-be abductor was still waiting alertly when the dad reappeared in the parking lot and picked up the grandmother, new mother, and infant at the front door, then headed home with them.

This story could have had a happier ending. The stalker lost the car on the way home. Moving surveillance clearly wasn't her long suit—but no problem. She knew the general neighborhood if not the exact house and simply drove around and around until she saw one of those big pink storks out in a front yard with a sign that said, "Congratulations on Your Delivery." Bingo! (And a good reason to *never* put out a sign like that again.)

Once more, the stalker waited until the husband left for work, then knocked on the front door, patted her own artificially padded belly to acknowledge a common bond, and asked if she could use the phone. Being naturally sympathetic to pregnant women at this point, the mother and grandmother let her in, and, once inside, the stalker stabbed them both to death, grabbed the baby, and ran.

I tell the story more or less as the woman who committed the murders told it to me, with one exception: When she got to the actual murder, she never said, *I did this . . . I did that.* It was always *The knife did this . . . the knife did that,* as if the knife had a life of its own, as if it hadn't even been connected to her hand, her arm, her mission to steal another woman's infant.

I suppose that's an understandable deflection when someone has committed an act so heinous, but I found it worse than eerie. The devil, or whatever force was behind that disembodied knife in her mind, has never made anyone do anything. The devil just applauds when it happens.

SERIAL KILLERS TEND TO PICK broader reasons than one-off killers or mass murderers to hide behind, or to justify themselves to themselves and the world. After all, they have repeated the act time and again, often with months, even years, in between. Specific rage or revenge dissipates or is slaked by the act itself. Serial killers' demons need to have legs, stamina. They're marathon runners, not sprinters.

Ted Bundy was executed the year before I joined the BSU, but had he still been living, he almost certainly would not have talked to me or even looked my way. With Bill Hagmaier, though, Bundy morphed into an absolute Chatty Cathy as the years wore on, the prison interviews mounted, and his day of reckoning loomed ever closer. Bill, in turn, packaged those sessions into a crash course on twisted psyches as he mentored me during my first year with the unit.

After years of coy silence, Bundy also began carefully doling out information on where his many victims were buried. He seemed to believe each revelation would earn him yet another stay of execution even though that was the Florida governor's decision, not the FBI's, but at another level I think he simply wanted us to appreciate just how thoroughly he had outsmarted us all. Bundy had to accept responsibility for his crimes so that we could all proclaim him the evil genius he longed to be considered.

But as to *why* he had murdered the thirty women he would ultimately confess to slaying and the many others he is suspected of having killed—and *what process* had brought him to that point—Bundy would never budge from the same pat answer: Pornography made him do it. He was still beating that drum on his last day on earth, January 24, 1989, in an interview with a Florida prison psychologist, using diction that is at best weirdly formal or perhaps carefully rehearsed:

"As a young boy, and I mean as a boy of twelve or thirteen, I encountered outside the home in the local grocery store or the local drugstore, the pornography that people call softcore, but as young boys do, we explored the back roads and byways of our neighborhood. Oftentimes people would dump the garbage and whatever when they were cleaning their house, and from time to time we came across pornographic books of a harder nature—a more explicit nature than we would encounter in say your local grocery store. That also included such things as detective magazines that featured violence. This is something I want to emphasize: The most damaging kinds of pornography—and I'm talking from hard, personal experience—are those that involve sexual violence. Because the wedding of those two—sex and violence—brings about behavior that is just too terrible to describe."

The psychologist interrupted at this point to ask Bundy to describe what went on in his mind at that point.

"In the beginning," Bundy answered after some delays, "it fuels this kind of thought process. Then at a certain time, it crystallizes into something which is almost like a separate entity inside you, and you're at the verge—or I was on the verge—of acting out on these kinds of things now. . . .

"My experience with pornography that deals on a violent level with sexuality is that once you become addicted to it, like other kinds of addiction I would keep looking for more potent, more explicit material, something that gives you a greater sense of excitement, until you reach the point where the pornography only goes so far. You reach that jumping off point where you begin to wonder if maybe actually doing it will give you that which is beyond just reading about."

And thus, the thirty known murders and the many others he frequently hinted at. Strip that pornography out of Ted Bundy's childhood, and none of this ever would have happened. Who knows: This handsome, scholarly, carefully spoken man might have become a professor, a family man with sweet daughters bouncing on his knee, maybe even an accomplished lawyer, as Bundy's sentencing judge had suggested. Instead, the Ted we never got to know was taken over by that "separate entity" he mentions above, and the rest is bloody history.

To which I have one response: Bullshit!

Pornography is a big problem globally, especially the sexual exploitation of minors that fuels it, and of course pornography consumption is not confined to men. But most pornography consumers, thank God, carry their urges into a dark room and relieve them in the traditional fashion. Unlike Ted Bundy, they don't dig graves, then go looking for someone "worthy" enough to fill them after torture, forced sex, and God knows what else. Either Bundy didn't have the guts to dive deep enough into his own psyche to find out what had twisted him so terribly, or he did and was so horrified by what he found that he couldn't say the words. Whatever the case was, it's lost to time. Less than twenty-four hours after that interview, at 7:16 a.m. the next morning, Ted Bundy was strapped to an electric chair and executed.

LIKE TED BUNDY, ED KEMPER became very polished in talking about his crimes as his prison years rolled on. Both men spoke in flat tones sometimes wildly at odds with their subject matter. As I mentioned earlier, Kemper was incapable of showing genuine contrition for his acts, but he had no trouble talking about the emotions that drove him.

"For much of my upbringing, my mother was sick and angry—a very sad woman," he said in a 1984 interview for a documentary. "I hated her. But I wanted to love my mother. And I watched the alcohol increase. I watched her social life drop off. I watched her get bizarre. She had terrible pain from her earlier life, her upbringing, a failed marriage with my father. I'm a constant reminder of that failure."

In other interviews, Kemper talked at length about his mother's alcohol consumption, how she frequently drove drunk with no regard for the safety of others on the road. He even seemed to suggest at one point that he had murdered his mother for the public good—in essence, to protect the world from her.

In fact, it's not hard to see how Ed Kemper's mother might have been a burden, or worse, to him. But none of that explains why he had to kill her so brutally or abuse her dead body quite so thoroughly once he got around to murdering her—by cutting out her tongue and larynx, sexually abusing the corpse, using her head for a dartboard, etc. That would require a depth of self-understanding that Kemper seems unwilling to plumb—and a reservoir of emotion as well.

The same can be said of the coeds Kemper killed. His self-analysis was seemingly thorough in that interview broadcast in 1984. His words even veered occasionally toward emotional awareness, but his tone varied hardly at all. The tears of regret, if they exist at all, seem to be permanently frozen inside him.

"Why did you actually kill the girls?" the off-camera interviewer asked.

"My frustration, my inability to communicate socially, sexually. I wasn't impotent. But emotionally, I was impotent. I was scared to death of failing in male-female relationships. I knew absolutely nothing about that whole area. Ironically enough, that's why I began picking people up. I'm picking up young women, and

I'm going a little bit farther each time—a daring kind of a thing. At first, there wasn't a gun. I'm driving along, we'd go to a vulnerable place where there aren't people watching and where I could act out, but I would say no, I can't. And then a gun is in the car hidden. And this craving, this awful raging, eating, feeling—I could feel it consuming my insides. This fantastic passion was overwhelming me. It was like drugs. It was like alcohol. A little isn't enough. At first it is. And as you adjust to that psychologically and physically, you take more and more and more, so it finally came down to the thing of 'Do I dare bring this gun out?'—already realizing if that gun comes out, something has to happen. It was going to happen. I didn't see it then, but it was going to happen. I was playing a dangerous game with a loaded gun, and it got us all."

From the heart, right? Except it isn't. Look at how the account slides back and forth between the present and past tenses and how suddenly "a gun is in the car hidden." How did *that* happen? It's like the knife that killed the new mother and grandmother. The gun had *a life of its own*, which is how people like Ed Kemper manage to go on living inside their own skins—unless the rigors of prison justice intervene, as they did with Jeffrey Dahmer.

DAHMER'S OWN JAILHOUSE MUSINGS FEEL somehow more honest, less rehearsed and carefully constructed than those of Ted Bundy and Ed Kemper—maybe because Dahmer was himself murdered within three years of his arrest, half a year shy of his thirty-fifth birthday, before he had time to craft a way of portraying himself. Asked by NBC interviewer Stone Phillips to describe the roots of a thirteen-year serial-killing spree that resulted in the deaths and dismemberment of seventeen boys and men, Dahmer got right to it.

"In ninth-grade biology class, we had the usual dissection of fetal pigs. I took the remains of my pig home and kept the skeleton, and I just started branching out from there. Dogs, cats—I suppose it could have turned into a normal hobby like taxidermy. All I know is that I wanted to see what the insides of these animals looked like. There may have been some violence involved, some underlying subconscious feelings of violence, but it just became a compulsion. I'd take them back in the woods, skin them sometimes, split them all the way up, look at the organs, feel them. It was just mystifying to me how the insides of the animal looked. There was a sort of general excitement for me. I don't know why, but it was so exciting to see.

As Dahmer described it, that general excitement increasingly resolved itself into specific and ever more violent fantasies. Finally, he said, "I acted on my fantasies, and that's where everything went wrong . . . I started buying sleeping pills and using them on various guys in the bath clubs. It just escalated slowly but surely. But then it felt like it was out of control. The compulsion was too strong to stop."

"Were you relieved to be arrested?" Phillips asked.

"It was a relief not to have to keep such a gigantic secret that I'd kept for so many years, and once I saw that I had no choice with the facts, I decided to face it head-on and make a full confession. So I am glad that the secrets are gone."

Sounds like normal regret—for admittedly heinous acts—but that was the rule, not the exception, among this interview cohort: minimize the crimes themselves, maximize the agony of carrying the secret of what they had actually done, and say it all in a tone so without affect that you might think they were ordering a BLT to go from the neighborhood deli. The only time I ever saw anyone break down in one of these sessions was in a taped interview a colleague had done with a serial child molester who targeted young boys. For once, all the walls came down, the excuses evaporated, and the man utterly broke down. It was horrible to witness, but what makes the video memorable is its complete rarity, like spotting an albino tiger slinking through the underbrush in some Southeast Asian bamboo jungle.

That's the tension I lived inside for those five years in the BSU: the evasions of everyday human behavior juxtaposed by the horrendous things we human beings are capable of. In truth, I live with it still.

AILEEN CAROL WUORNOS, TO HER credit and by sharp contrast, hid behind nothing at all.

I still have in my possession a "Behavioral Science Services Accomplishment Report" that reduces to bureaucratic shorthand the consultation that Bill Hagmaier and I undertook on the Wuornos case over the course of three days in late March 1991. The report notes that the consultation was done on site in Marion County, Florida, and included National Center for the Analysis of Violent Crime coordinators from nearby Jacksonville. It confirms that Aileen Carol Wuornos has been from the beginning the only suspect in the seven murders with which she was ultimately charged. The summary section on the back of the form gets into the difficulties encountered in interagency cooperation on the case and notes for the record that the Bureau was requested to attempt enhancement of three tapes that contained Wuornos's confession.

In all, the report credits Bill and me each with twenty-four hours of labor—not an inflated number. We worked hard during those three days. We always did in situations like this. These consultations were anything but fly-bys. By the time we returned to Quantico, we knew the Wuornos case inside out. But if there can ever be a truly straightforward, utterly uncomplicated instance of something as horrible as serial murder, this case was it.

Aileen Wuornos, simply put, hated men. She had been abandoned by her mother at age four, sexually abused by her older brother and the grandfather who took her in, and raped by one of her grandfather's friends. At age fifteen—a year after she had given birth to a son she put up for adoption—Wuornos was thrown out of the house and forced to earn her living as a sex worker.

A tortured life, in short, and on the last day of November 1989, now thirty-three and after eighteen years of turning tricks to put food on the table and alcohol in her system, Wuornos began taking her revenge. Over the next year, she murdered seven men who either sought her services or demanded sex from her. The seven were all shot at point-blank range, two to nine times each. (See Charlize Theron's Oscar-winning portrayal of Wuornos in the 2003 biographical film *Monster* for what struck me as a dead-accurate capture of a horrible life.) A decade later, in a petition to the Florida Supreme Court, Wuornos explained her motivation as nakedly as it could possibly be stated: "I have hate crawling through my system."

It's the rare serial killer who has ever admitted to that level of self-awareness, but Aileen Wuornos is unique among serial killers in another key way as well: She was a woman.

Women do commit murder. (See the earlier discussion of women who murdered other women to steal their infants, either in utero or after childbirth.) Typically, though, when a woman kills, the victim is a husband, a significant other, a male they know personally. Maybe the woman is just sick of him, or he has been beating her up and she can't think of any other way to get him out of her life. Unlike men, women also rarely kill serially. With the exception of Aileen Wuornos, who was totally consumed by hate, it's virtually unheard-of.

Why? I think it has to do with control, with wanting power. Yes, a sexual component often accompanies serial killing, but that's about domination, too: *I'm having sex with you against your will because I can, because I'm in charge and you're not, because you are under my control and at my mercy.* Ed Kemper mentioned control specifically when he called to "counsel" me on the unsolved case I described earlier. Jeffrey Dahmer, who kept physical souvenirs of his victims, talked about it even more hauntingly in the Stone Phillips interview:

"The only motive that there ever was was to completely control the person, a person that I found physically attractive, and keep them listening as long as possible. Even if it meant just keeping a part of them."

Women mostly aren't wired to think that way. If someone is posing an existential threat to them and they have no other recourse, they'll take care of the situation themselves—with a knife, a gun, poison, a hatchet, whatever else will get the job done—but that's the end of it. Necrophilia is not uncommon among male serial killers, as we've seen, but necrophilia is rare among female murderers generally. And, of course, male anatomy, unlike female anatomy, is better suited to violating the dead.

FOR MANY YEARS, WOMEN WHO fall in love with serial killers were a greater mystery to me than the Aileen Wuornoses of this world. Love is said to be blind, but can it be that blind? The answer, I now think, is yes, but for overlapping and conflicting reasons.

Several decades back, my BSU colleague Roy Hazelwood and I set out to interview a broad sampling of women who were either married to or significant others of serial killers. We were unable to secure adequate funding to complete the project, but the few interviews we conducted were eye-opening. My expectation was that these would be people at the margins of society—downtrodden in one way or another, ready to marry or hook up with anyone who could provide material support, no matter his proclivities. But the first woman we met with held a master's degree in nursing and was perfectly capable of sustaining herself financially. Instead, she had at first endured her husband's erotic and increasingly violent desires and then, to free herself, had begun recruiting other women to be his playthings and ultimately his victims.

"Why didn't you divorce him?" I asked.

The answer, of course, was "I love him," which is basically the same answer you get in nearly all these unsettling cases where a fascination with a famous serial killer turns into a pen pal relationship and then into a jailhouse marriage with someone who might have confessed to a dozen or more murders and will never, ever see the light of day outside of a prison again.

Nuts? Yes, but the more I've looked into these cases and thought back to my own experience with serial killers and my own perspective as a woman, the more I'm convinced that what is at work here is a fatal chemistry of low self-esteem and masterful manipulation. The former can be far more crippling than poverty and leave women, especially, more vulnerable as well. And as I and others have mentioned before and will again, manipulation and control are the mother's milk of those who murder in quantity. Manipulation and control are why they get up in the morning, why they go to bed at night, and why they do the horrible things they do in the hours in between.

AMERICA IS NOT ONLY AWASH in murders; it's awash in unsolved murders as well. Less than two-thirds of reported homicides get solved annually. Total homicide cold cases—murders on the books but with unknown perpetrators—is somewhere over 260,000, or one unsolved homicide for every 1,300 Americans.

How much of that is accounted for by serial killers still at large? Who knows? But Ed Kemper—he of the genius IQ—willingly answered that question for one of his interviewers:

"It would be a guess, but it's far more than thirty-five. I came in out of the cold. And what I'm saying is there are some people who prefer it in the cold."

Maybe it takes one to know just how many more like himself there might be. But as hard as it can sometimes be to identify serial killers, run them to ground, and bring them to justice, it's harder still to predict who the next Ed Kemper might be.

A number of studies built on the profiling we did at the BSU and other sources have worked backward from the serial homicides themselves to the early years of the perpetrators, searching for what if any developmental experiences might have influenced their later acts of savagery. One of the most interesting—"A Behaviour Sequence Analysis of Serial Killers' Lives: From Childhood Abuse to Methods of Murder," authored by Abbie Jean Marono, Sasha Reid, Enzo Yaksic, and David Adam Keatley—creates what seems like a solid link between specific types of early abuse (physical, psychological, or sexual), later motivations (lust, anger, power, or financial gain), and murder methodology.

Serial killers who had been physically abused as children, for example, were more likely to "overkill" their victims—that is, "kill" them again and again after they are already dead—while those who had been sexually abused were likely to mutilate, torture, and bind their victims but not prolong the act of murder itself, perhaps because, according to the authors, "those who have experienced sexual abuse suffer from deep-seated anger and self-blame, leading them to lash out and kill their victims quickly, and they are more likely to feel guilt or remorse afterward and thus are unlikely to show evidence of overkill." Killers motivated by power uniformly murdered their victims quickly and generally efficiently, with little or no unnecessary pain, no overkill, and no evidence of enjoying the act itself. Again, by way of contrast, those driven by lust commonly engaged in postmortem sex.

The connections and delineations are far more sophisticated than when I joined the BSU in 1990. Back then, we tended to classify serial murders mostly as either "organized" (carried out by someone who planned the crime, preselected the victim, and displayed at least some measure of self-control in the act) or "disorganized" (little or no planning, chance victims, and the like). By the time I left the BSU, newer studies had proposed various typologies of serial killers: visionaries, missionaries, hedonists, and power freaks; thrill seekers, murderers for profit, and family slayers; traveling, local, and place-specific serial murderers. All of the distinctions were helpful, but those researchers didn't make the extensive linkages found in "A Behaviour Sequence Analysis of Serial Killers' Lives."

The numbers behind this newer study are also impressive: the database included 233 serial killers, all males. And the study points to a critical issue in serial homicide: lousy nurturing. Roughly half of all serial killers claim to have experienced psychological abuse as children, more than a third say they were physically abused, and a quarter claim to have been sexually abused. While horrible, those figures need qualification: Serial killers are often quick to assign their actions to forces other than themselves. Think of the pretend-pregnant woman who contended "the knife," not she, had murdered the new mother and grandmother, or of Ted Bundy's claiming he was powerless in the face of pornography. That list goes on and on, too.

Even if the numbers are accurate, though, they address the past far more than the future. They get to the why and how of a serial killer, not to who might become one. Of the 100 percent of children who are sexually abused, only a tiny, tiny percentage will take revenge on humanity the way the minuscule few sometimes do. How to identify those very few headed that way before it was too late was our holy grail at the BSU, but, hard as we tried, we could never pin down an exact "type" that was more predisposed to serial murder than any other "types."

Males of the species, yes—but that's almost 50 percent of the total population. Ed Kemper himself described the challenge: "I was raging inside. There were just incredible energies, positive and negative, depending on my mood, which would trigger one or the other. And outside? Outside, I looked troubled at times. Other times I looked moody. There were times I was perfectly serene. Not very sane, maybe, but people weren't even aware of what was happening."

If moodiness, mood swings, and incredible energies positive and negative were the criteria for placing someone on a serial-killer watch list, we would probably have to include every third teenager in America. And that gets to the larger problem of trying to typecast and predict where the next hearts of darkness might be hiding. To one extent or another, every case I worked on during my three decades in law enforcement broadened my horizon of the possible, and not always in the most comforting way. Under certain conditions, I came to learn, a lot of people can do a lot of things that no one would have thought possible of them: heroic feats, incredible acts of generosity, and horrific crimes that everyone around them would have sworn on a stack of Bibles or Korans or whatever you use that this individual absolutely, positively, no way in a thousand years could have done any such thing.

AS STATE'S EVIDENCE, I OFFER you John List. Born in Michigan in 1925, List served briefly in the U.S. Army after graduating from high school in 1943, then attended the University of Michigan in Ann Arbor, where he took part in the Army ROTC program while earning his bachelor's degree in business administration and a master's in accounting. Commissioned a second lieutenant, he did a two-year tour of duty, mostly with the Finance Corps, and married the widow of an infantry officer killed in Korea. Late in 1952, List returned to the private sector, and he and his new wife, Helen, began living the American dream.

Over the next two decades, John List moved steadily up the career ladder—from a Detroit accounting firm, to general supervisor of accounting for a Kalamazoo paper company, to Xerox in Rochester, New York, where he eventually became director of accounting services, and finally to vice president and comptroller of a bank in Jersey City, New Jersey. By then, the Lists had three children of their own as well as Helen's daughter by her earlier marriage and were living in nearby Westfield, in a nineteen-room Victorian mansion known as Breeze Knoll with a ballroom topped by a stained glass skylight thought to be by Louis Comfort Tiffany and worth more than half a million dollars in current terms.

As the years went on, Helen developed a drinking problem, which might have accounted for the Lists' disinclination to socialize much with their neighbors, but John was a pillar of the community: a devout Christian, a Sunday school teacher at his Lutheran church, a man wholly above reproach. And then, on November 9, 1971, the wheels came off. While the children were at school, List shot Helen in the back of her head and then his own eighty-four-year-old mother, Alma, in the forehead. Later, as sixteen-year-old Patricia and thirteen-year-old Frederick arrived home from school, he shot each in the back of the head, made lunch, drove to the bank and closed out his own and his mother's accounts, went from there to Westfield High to watch his oldest son, John Frederick, compete in a soccer game, then drove John Frederick home and shot him—repeatedly, since John Frederick, unlike the others, apparently had a chance to resist.

With that, the killing was over, and List's inner accountant took over, seeing to virtually every last detail. His mother's body was left in her attic apartment where she had been killed, but the other four bodies were zipped into sleeping bags and dragged to the basement. Afterward, List scrubbed the crime scenes, clipped himself out of every family photograph in the house to make identifying him more difficult, stopped all deliveries (milk, mail, newspapers), and wrote notes to his children's schools and part-time employers explaining that they would be away for an indefinite time, visiting Helen's sick mother in North Carolina. (Helen's mother was, in fact, sick and had had to cancel a visit to Westfield. Otherwise, List later admitted, she would have been victim six. Helen's daughter, Brenda, escaped the massacre because she was away at college.) Then List turned on every last light in the house, set the radio to a religious station, walked out, and locked the door behind him.

Neighbors noticed that the List house glowed day and night, but it wasn't until individual lights began to burn out one by one that anyone thought to alert the police, and thus, almost a month after the five murders, police entered Breeze Knoll through an unlocked basement window and found all that remained of what had once seemed to everyone a model American family.

As for motive, financial reversals had played a role. Rather than tell his wife that the Jersey City bank had gone under, List dressed for the office every morning, then spent the day interviewing for new jobs and reading newspapers at the local train station. To keep ends meeting, he had begun siphoning funds from his mother's account. But the deeper motive was found in a five-page letter to his pastor that List left behind in his study: The world had become so evil that List was compelled to kill his family to save their souls. He looked forward to eventually being reunited with them in heaven, which apparently has a pretty lenient admission policy.

In the meantime, John List simply disappeared—or, more accurately, he re-created himself as "Bob Clark," a person remarkably similar to his old self. Bob Clark was controller of a paper box manufacturer in greater Denver. He joined a Lutheran church and started driving shut-in church members to medical appointments and the like. In 1988, with new wife, Delores, a former Army PX clerk, Bob moved to the Richmond, Virginia, area and went to work for a small accounting firm. That's where he was in May 1989 when *America's Most Wanted* aired a segment on an eighteen-year-old multiple murder in Westfield, New Jersey, including a clay bust by forensic artist Frank Bender suggesting how the fugitive killer, John List, might have aged. Bender, it turned out, was right on the money. Within days a former Denver neighbor had made the connection between the fugitive and Bob Clark, and less than two weeks later John List was under arrest. (Not surprisingly, friends of Bob Clark recalled after his unmasking that *America's Most Wanted* had been his favorite TV show.)

I wasn't involved in the List case, but I was about to join the BSU in April 1990 when John List was convicted on five counts of first-degree murder and sentenced to five consecutive life imprisonment terms, and I couldn't have agreed more with the judge when he declared that "after eighteen years, five months, and twenty-days, it is now time for the voices of Helen, Alma, Patricia, Frederick, and John F. List to rise from the graves." (John List died in a New Jersey prison another eighteen years later, at age eighty-two.)

A few years later, I spoke with John Walsh, the creator and host of *America's Most Wanted*, about the case. John List, he told me, was the show's biggest win ever.

To me, the takeaway from the John List case is twofold. First, without succumbing to total paranoia, we have to recognize that there is evil in the world and that it does not always look ugly or frightening. John List was thick with admirers: *Oh, those kids are so polite and well-groomed, Mr. List must be a wonderful guy. And his church work—my gosh!*

Trouble is, assumptions like that have no basis in actual experience, no depth, nothing behind them. They're an expectation based on often casual observation and sometimes the triumph of hope over experience—nothing more—but with things like dating apps, we can easily place ourselves in a precarious position and get in dangerously over our heads before we have any real idea what or who we are dealing with. It's speculation on my part, but when Ted Bundy boasted about choosing only "worthy" girls as his victims, I think he might have really meant "trusting" girls—coeds whose appearances, achievements, and general experiences in life had failed to arm them with reasonable caution.

Don't get me wrong: Those nice young women did nothing to cause their own deaths. But for someone like Bundy, they were sitting ducks. He would study them from afar, make his choices, often predetermine their burial sites as earlier noted. Then he might park next to their car or run into them by chance in the student union or a favorite coffee bar. His arm might be in a sling or he might be on crutches. Props are cheap. The point is he couldn't quite complete some task: get an object into or out of the trunk, juggle his coffee and his books at the same time.

"I'm so sorry to ask," he would say, "but could you give me a hand?"

Maybe the coeds would give him a once-over, casually examine him and find a pleasant-looking guy temporarily in need of a little help and—who knows?—fun to have a beer or wine with afterward. What could go wrong? Answer: Everything. And once that hook was set, it went wrong time and time and time again, because evil has a thousand faces and endless doors to pass through.

The second takeaway from John List and Ted Bundy and many others is closely related: Stone-cold, blackhearted killers— people capable of shooting family members one at a time in the back of the head and going right on with their lives—can emerge from anywhere and surprise the pants off us every time. John List is just an extreme example of an inescapable truth that will always handcuff any effort to predict where the next heart of darkness might emerge from.

WHAT CAN BE SAID WITH certainty about serial killers is that with early intervention some of their murders, maybe many more than some, might well have been prevented. Just consider Ed Kemper. As we've already seen, he murdered his grandparents at age fifteen and did no more time than any inner-city kid might have drawn for playing *Grand Theft Auto* on the real mean streets of LA or New York, but he had displayed sadistic traits for years before that. At a very young age, he had methodically cut off the heads and hands of his sister's dolls—presaging what would become one of the signatures of his adult-age murders.

Released from his juvenile hospital incarceration at age twenty-one, Kemper went to live with his mother despite unvarnished warnings that doing so would reawaken a toxic relationship, and ultimately it did so, with highly predictable results. And then when coeds started turning up murdered on the campus where his mother worked, his mother apparently never suspected that the son who cruised the campus in her car and who had already murdered his grandparents might have had something to do with the nine-year killing spree. Or if she did have suspicions, she never acted on them. Clearly, there was justification for an intervention that was never attempted and a need for far better decision-making on all fronts, going back decades.

Every little boy who mutilates his sister's dolls is not going to grow up a serial killer. Nor will every little boy (or girl—not to forget Aileen Wuornos) who is cruelly abused physically, sexually, or psychologically go down that dark path, but a few always will. Failing to adequately identify, treat, and prevent such abuse is not good citizenship or good stewardship of the sacred trust of our young. We can do better, and we must.

15.
VICTIMOLOGY 101

INTENTIONALLY OR NOT, ACCOUNTS OF serial killings almost without exception spotlight the killer, not the killed. It's the rare person who doesn't recall Ted Bundy, but it's an even rarer person who knows the names of even three of the twenty or thirty or maybe a hundred victims he confessed to or hinted at before his execution.*

Similarly, at the FBI, just about the biggest reward you can have is being the case agent and applying the handcuffs on a major offender—and few offenders are more major than the serial killers among us. There you are, maybe in your FBI jacket or a monogrammed Kevlar vest, and walking right beside you, grim-faced and handcuffed, is Public Enemy No. 1, or 2, 3, 4, 5, etc. It's reflected glory in a way. You are momentarily famous only because

---

* To give them their due, the twenty Ted Bundy murder victims for whom identifiable remains have been recovered are: Lynda Ann Healy (age twenty-one), Donna Gail Manson (nineteen), Susan Elaine Rancourt (eighteen), Roberta Kathleen Parks (twenty), Brenda Carol Ball (twenty-two), Georgeann Hawkins (eighteen), Janice Ann Ott (twenty-three), Denise Marie Naslund (eighteen), Nancy Wilcox (sixteen), Melissa Anne Smith (seventeen), Laura Ann Aime (seventeen), Debra Jean Kent (seventeen), Caryn Eileen Campbell (twenty-three), Julie Cunningham (twenty-six), Denise Lynn Oliverson (twenty-five), Lynette Dawn Culver (twelve), Susan Curtis (fifteen), Margaret Elizabeth Bowman (twenty-one), Lisa Levy (twenty), and Kimberly Dianne Leach (twelve).

the perp is more lastingly infamous, but in a bureaucracy as gargantuan as the FBI, you can go through a dozen careers without getting that kind of spotlight.

At the Behavioral Science Unit, we toiled at the other end of that food chain. We were victimologists, sifting through the debris of often barbarous acts in search of method, motive, and pattern.

Case agents can tell you stories that have a beginning, a middle, and an end. They know the names of those involved, what the victims looked like in happier times, where they came from, their spouses, maybe their children and parents, whether the victims were born into poverty or wealth, educated or untrained. The people in case agents' professional purview have texture, depth, and nuance, even when none of that still exists any longer. They can imagine a life that preceded whatever tragedy or horror or gross misjudgment has brought them to the Bureau's attention.

Victimologists almost never have that luxury. The murdered, the brutalized, the violated, rush by us—here today, gone tomorrow, with a seemingly endless line waiting for our attention. In preparing for this memoir, I found an old spiral-bound notebook in which I had jotted down quick notes about more than 250 cases I consulted on in my five years at BSU—less than a third of the total caseload I handled during that time. Paging through the notebook was like a flash card documentary of half a decade of my life.

09/25/90: Victim Lisa Pruett—multiple stab wounds, found with clothes partially removed in grassy area near boyfriend's house.

09/26/90: Suspect shot two kids, ages 11 and 14, at their home and attempted to rape a woman two days later in Tennessee.

10/10/90: Deposition of Trepal case [the thallium murderer described earlier].

10/24/90: 9-year-old boy abducted and assaulted in Norman, Oklahoma.

01/14/91: Senator [Joseph] Lieberman threat.

02/06/91: Prostitute killings.

03/26/91: 18 rapes.

03/27/91: Child abduction.

04/22/91: Female prostitute, legs cut off.

06/10/91: Kidnap out of New Jersey. Victim Timmy. Suspect mom.

10/13/91: Homosexual shootings in Ramble Area of Central Park.

11/25/91: Kastanis family murders.

01/10/92: Bomb Pete Wilson's office [governor of California].

03/20/92: 2 family homicides, Charlotte County, FL.

There were ten Canadian cases to consult on in April 1992 and cases from Amsterdam the following month. Murders cluttered my spiral-bound notebook through that summer; one note reads, "Homicide—baseball bat insertion." From this distance in time, I can assume only the worst about what that possibly means. The year 1993 was notable for a spate of stalkings and shootings, a serial rape involving six victims and one homicide, two filicides (when someone kills a son or daughter), a threatening letter to Barbara Walters, and an Alabama case in which a husband and wife were suspected of burning down their house with their son inside to collect on a $25,000 insurance policy they had taken out on the son six months earlier. The year 1994 got off to a bang with five unsolved homicides, all women. The year 1995 brought Major Case 111: abortion clinic murders and shootings.

The very last entry in the notebook, dated 4/5/95, reads simply "V [for "victim"] Bonnie Haim," but the few words mask a world of hurt. "Victim," in this case, was speculation. Bonnie went missing in 1993, just about the time her troubled, preschool-age son began suggesting to a therapist that a "monster" had sexually abused him. Aaron later told his aunt, with whom he lived after his mother's disappearance, that the monster "lived inside" his father, Michael. By summer, he was adding further details, including that "the monster" had shot and killed his mother, along with accompanying details.

Those revelations were enough to launch a court hearing, which found in October 1993 that Michael Haim had caused Bonnie's disappearance, but that was about as much as the justice system could do in the absence of a body or any evidence of physical harm other than Aaron's word. The court refused to intervene in Michael's twice-weekly visitations with his son, but Aaron's behavior became increasingly aggressive, and over the next half year he moved from his aunt's home to his grandparents' and finally was placed in foster care and allowed to cut off all contact with family members. In the fall of 1994, much improved, he started kindergarten and recorded five statements to be made, via video, to his grandparents:

1. "The monster sticked his finger in my butt."
2. "It's real important because it shouldn't happen to nobody."
3. "The monster shot my mom."
4. "The monster lives on Dolphin Avenue in a cage."
5. "The monster lives in my dad."

That's where the story stood in April 1995, when I entered Bonnie's name in my spiral notebook, and it's where the story still stood in 2014 when then-teenage Aaron found his mother's skull and other remains while demolishing an outdoor shower at the house where the family had once lived. In May 2021, twenty-eight years after Bonnie's disappearance, a Florida appeals court upheld Michael Haim's murder conviction and the life sentence imposed on him.

Beside each one of these entries, I wrote down the time involved. Sometimes it's as little as an hour; more often, it would be half a day or more. Consulting on the Haim case gobbled up ten hours of my time. If the case made it to one of our roundtable discussions, the total staff hours expended would mount accordingly. But however much time we devoted individually and collectively at BSU, these were lives caught on the fly, lives most often seen at their worst possible moment, not complete human beings, too often not living or whole ones, either.

We knew bodies mostly in a state of advanced decay. We were piecing together a biography from shards of grisly evidence, trying to decide if enough pieces fit together to call something an ongoing pattern that might suggest another serial killer on the prowl. Sometimes, just to break the ice, we would give the perpetrator a nickname. The "Vampire Killer," for example, removed the organs from his victims, put them in a bowl, then (or so he confessed after he was in jail) drank their blood as it drained from the organs. But the dead themselves almost never got actual names. They were Victim One/Case 522, or whatever. The investigation into their deaths had to be assigned numbers from among 320 choices in the official FBI classification list—at least, that was the number when I left the BSU in 1995. Many of those classification numbers, in turn, had multiple subsets. Serial killings were bureaucratically uncomplicated—always number 306—but the government guidelines for "Victim Risk Assessment" ran six pages of sometimes nuanced distinctions:

- Did the victim's injuries include stabbing, slashing, gunshot, blunt trauma, burns, ligature, broken bones, defense wounds, dismemberment, disembowelment or evisceration, and/or postmortem activity (most often necrophilia)?
- Was the cause of death asphyxiation, strangulation (manual or ligature), blunt trauma, sharp instrument, gunshot, or burns?

- Had the forensic examination shown the presence of blood, semen/seminal fluid, other body fluids, stomach content, foreign object insertion, or hairs fibers?
- Did the crime scene suggest rape, rape/murder, homicide (anger/hostility, contract/hit, burglary, robbery), sexual homicide, autoerotic death, or suicide?

And all that was before we even got to the "characteristics and traits" of the supposed offender, his "stressors and pressures" (conflict/problems with a significant female, family conflicts, financial troubles, marital problems, employment problems, death of a family member or close associate, birth of a child, drug or alcohol issue) and the suspect's "post-offense behavior," which could include everything from "need for seclusion" to "leave community," "get married," and "become more religious."

As mentioned earlier, we also had to account for our own time on a "Behavioral Science Service Accomplishment Report" with eighty-four boxes to choose from, including origin of case (foreign, domestic, Bureau, or other); type of investigation (consultation, profile, personality assessment, trial strategy, etc.); number of victims, subjects, and suspects; and on and on. There was room for notes, and if the reports were particularly thorough, they might give us a hint of the people involved.

One such document from 1991—written by Bill Hagmaier, circulated to me, and still in my possession—tells of an Alabama high school principal who confessed to strangling his wife with her own belt on the back porch of their house, placing her body and a teenage daughter's bicycle in his pickup truck, and driving several miles to a bridge over a creek near a truck stop. At the bridge, he stripped his wife's body naked, threw it into the water, hid the bike in the woods nearby, and drove to another bridge, where he threw his wife's clothes into the same creek. The principal then returned home in the truck, took the family car to the site where he had disposed of the body, dumped her purse out on the car floor, took the cash, and bicycled back home to establish his alibi.

"Subject," Hagmaier writes, "gets along exceptionally well with victim's family." But that's where it all ends—with that last great mystery and a hundred questions, because this is government shorthand, not biography or history. The detail work was important, and big agencies always tend toward codification and bureaucracy, but the impersonality and incompleteness of it all was disconcerting, in a way even deadening.

AT THE START OF THE book, I mentioned the photos I had taped to my office wall—the images that caused the Senate aide to faint. They were black-and-white glossies of eight women in Philadelphia, mostly homeless and with most of the high-risk factors that come with prostitution. (Multiple murders of prostitutes and the homeless, female and male, were particularly hard to link because they had so many angles of exposure to danger.) The Philadelphia victims all had names, of course, as well as histories, a few triumphs to boast about, maybe, but mostly sorrows that had left them washed up on the edge of society. For us, they were case studies in behavior almost too aberrant to contemplate.

As noted earlier, all the women had been eviscerated from below the navel all the way up to the neck. Their organs hadn't been totally removed, but they were all sitting outside the body cavity as if awaiting examination. Some of the heads had been severed, but most were still attached, if only barely. From that evidence, it was probably safe to deduce that the crimes and the subsequent knife work had taken place very late at night or in the predawn hours, when the surrounding streets were deserted. This wasn't a hack-and-slice job. That sort of activity takes a lot of time and privacy.

We were also able to determine that the cuts had been made with something scalpel-like but perhaps not a scalpel itself. The tool was obviously razor-sharp, but the cuts had a slightly jagged edge. The killer, it seemed likely, had held or still held some position in the medical field—maybe an actual surgeon, or a surgeon's assistant, or somebody who had once studied to be a surgeon. The killer had been doing the kind of exploratory work in the body cavity that you can't learn about solely from books. There was no semen found at any of the crime scenes, so we knew it had been all business, and we knew beyond any reasonable doubt that all the women had been done in by the same killer. He had left too many signatures for there to be any doubt of that.

(If these murders bring to mind the Jack the Ripper slayings that terrorized London in the late 1880s, it's with good cause. An ocean and a century separate the two murder sprees, but the modi operandi of the two anonymous killers are remarkably similar.)

My own theory about the Philadelphia murders was that the killer had flunked out of medical school and never gotten over the insult, but why he should take that out on homeless women escapes me still. Maybe they were simply easier to get hold of than cadavers so he could further hone his surgical skills outside of the classroom, or maybe the homeless women were substituting for the medical school professors who had dared to send him packing. Or maybe none of that is anywhere near correct. The killer has never been identified. Educated speculation is all we can do.

This was the most frustrating part of the BSU, for me and for others of my colleagues. We were brought in for a specific purpose: the methodology, the victimology, the link analysis to determine if this was a serial killer. All we saw was the house of horrors that had been left behind, human suffering divorced almost entirely from the humans themselves. It was if we had walked into the movie *Psycho* just as the shower scene was ending and walked out again before Alfred Hitchcock had the camera pan away—and done so again and again and again.

THAT SAID, THE OPPOSITE WAS almost worse. While I was at the Behavioral Science Unit, the crime writer Mark Olshaker brought the parents of one of the victims we had studied to Quantico, introduced them around, and asked me to join them for lunch. The meal was awkward for all of us. I remembered the case: Their daughter had been brutally murdered and left in a shallow grave by what we at the BSU had determined was a serial killer, but this killer, too, had never been captured (and by now, more than a quarter century later, almost certainly never will be). A situation like that left little room for small talk anywhere around the table.

Later, after I moved to Colorado to become the assistant special agent in charge of the Denver office, Mark again asked me to lunch with the woman's parents, and this time the guard-rails fell completely away. She had been their only child and they were still reeling from her loss. For them, their daughter's murder would always be an open case, a festering wound that would never heal. As we sat there talking, her mother and father's devastation became my devastation, and I found myself thinking for the first and maybe only time in my professional life that there are worse things than living with body-part photos taped to the office walls.

I also realized at that moment just how much of my own humanity I had been required to put in cold storage while I was part of the BSU. Unless we are true psychopaths, we are all emotional beings; we naturally feel empathy for those who suffer, who go through horrendous ordeals, who lose loved ones to illness or accidents or violence. But at the BSU our job was to understand why people did the awful things they did, not to empathize with their reasons, or their victims, or their victims' families. The more we allowed ourselves to become washed in the emotions of the case, the less effective we would ultimately be.

True, Aileen Wuornos had been treated horribly by the men in her life. Their abuse had undoubtedly helped to turn her into the monster she became. Psychologists, psychiatrists, even movie directors and scriptwriters can mine that territory all they want. In the same vein, the woman who sawed the fetus out of the mother's womb with her car keys undoubtedly considered herself in a terrible, maybe even an existential bind. For seven months she had been telling her boyfriend she was pregnant; now she had to deliver or face his wrath. But to feel sadness or pity in the first case, or disgust in the second one, almost inevitably clouds the essential analysis to follow: the what, why, when, and where of the crime; the body of solid knowledge we can build upon to understand more broadly these hearts of darkness and their actions.

Our answers were rarely found in confessional sessions in a jailhouse interrogation room despite how hard serial killers like Ted Bundy and Edmund Kemper tried to play their interviewers. Our answers were far more likely to be found at the morgue, or on a coroner's examining table, or in those grisly crime photos that were my office décor for half a decade. And, yes, there is a price to be paid for that knowledge.

16.
WHEN THE ABNORMAL BECOMES NORMAL . . .

EVERY JOB HAS ITS COMMONPLACES: the office clown, lunch-room banter, all the office rituals and experiences that develop in a collective work life. The BSU was no different, but—thank God—our commonplaces were not everyone's middle ground.

One example: Toward the end of my time with the BSU, I went up to New York City with three colleagues as part of a study of how the police in different jurisdictions handle crime scenes. We were looking for best practices, especially in homicide cases, and we had already seen a bunch of very good ones in Los Angeles.

Eventually, of course, you've got to remove a dead body from the street or wherever it has ended up, but what you do before then is important. The LAPD would cordon off enough space to preserve any evidence that might be associated with the crime, even if that meant rerouting impatient drivers every which way. Everything would be photographed. Medical examiners called to the scene were invariably professional from what we could see.

New York was a different story. For one thing, it was a partic-ularly murderous night in Gotham. As I remember, we were riding in two police cars—four to a car, with two NYPD officers up front in each—racing from crime scene to crime scene. A third police car in our entourage was for Robert De Niro, who was prepping for a movie role, or so we were told, but we never saw him. What we did see, though, was a consistently minimal effort to seal off the crime scenes. Avoiding public disruption seemed more important than preserving evidence. Nor was there much effort to preserve the dignity of the dead—or just follow basic hygiene. The medical examiner who showed up at a number of the homicide scenes we visited seemed never to stop smoking his cigar. Worse, he performed his preliminary examinations at the crime scene without putting on medical gloves. At one point I saw him shove his naked finger into a wound to measure its depth. I was mortified. Gloves were standard practice by then. If I'd had a full stomach at that moment, I might have lost it.

Speaking of food, we did finally take a dinner break, back at one of the station houses. We were just digging into some Styrofoam containers of spaghetti when in came the report of yet another homicide, so we closed the lids on dinner and off we went racing again. This time the body was inside, a guy with a bullet wound and a broken neck lying at the bottom of a flight of stairs. A gay couple had apparently gotten into a big argument while they were cooking dinner. A shot got fired, and the victim fell backward down the steps. Whether that amounted to murder one or voluntary manslaughter or a crime of passion or whatever, I never found out, but I remember the kitchen scene to this day. Dinner was going to be Italian that night. Spaghetti was everywhere—on the floor, the walls, the counter, the shooter, and the victim.

Back at the station house forty-five minutes later or so, we nuked our abandoned Styrofoam containers and tried to resume our dinner. Law enforcement officers are used to meals that have gone cold, but my colleague Steve Mardigian looked at that congealing pasta and spoke for all of us when he said, "No way am I going on that diet!"

We laughed about it—what else are you going to do?—but I think at some level we all knew we were living in a world where abnormality was commonplace, and I, at least, was becoming increasingly aware of how few resources I had to combat that. My schedule was too hectic and unpredictable for daily meditation. I had neither the vacation time nor the salary to enjoy restorative long weekends at Canyon Ranch or one of the Miraval Resorts. And my professional background reading wasn't exactly *How to Be a Better Boss* or *Finding the Inner Workplace You*. My professional reading included learned pamphlets like *The Serial Rapist: His Characteristics and Victims*, coauthored by my colleague Robert Hazelwood and Janet Warren. (Of the forty-one serial rapists interviewed about a third collected pornography; slightly more than half had served in the armed forces, scored above average on intelligence tests, were raised in average or above-average socioeconomic environments, and held stable jobs; seven in ten had been married at least once; and 76 percent had been sexually abused as children. Also, the number of sexual assaults committed by these same rapists ranged from ten to seventy-eight.)

Further on the reading list: three-inch-thick three-ring binders with titles like *Detection and Recovery of Human Remains*, with fourteen separate interior binders ranging from "Found Human Remains" to "Field Manual for the Recovery of the Human Skeleton," "Training and Utilization of Cadaver Dogs," "Animal Artifacts: Postmortem Injuries Due to Terrestrial and Aquatic Wildlife," and finally "Skeletal Charts and Diagrams." This was no exception. Over the course of my five years at BSU, I must have pored through at least eighty of these binders. On the subject of violent death, I was a walking encyclopedia.

I could reel off the types of injuries caused by edged weapons—chopping, stabbing, and incising (i.e., marking with a series of cuts, sometimes in an intentional pattern, which is more common than you might think)—and tell you that the most common weapon used to inflict edged-weapon wounds is a screwdriver. (Ninety-two percent of police officer injuries are caused by edged weapons.) I knew that blunt-force wounds were marked by abrasions of the skin and undermining (or shelving) of the tissue and that with undermined wounds, the tissue splits and rises in the direction of blow.

We had coroner reports to give us the fine points of death, but I didn't have to see them to predict that most of the people we studied had died of exsanguination (i.e., they bled to death, usually internally), cardiac tamponade (compression of the heart by the accumulation of fluid in the pericardial sac), embolism caused by an air bubble, or asphyxia due to blood aspiration (i.e., they choked to death on their own blood). I could look at a bruise in a four-color crime scene photograph and pinpoint with reasonable accuracy when the trauma to the subcutaneous tissue had been inflicted: red (shortly before the photo was taken), blue (one to four hours after the trauma), green (four to seven hours), or yellow (seven to ten hours). I knew that hesitation wounds often indicate suicide.

All this information crammed into me was vital to doing my job to the best of my ability, but it was not necessarily designed to elevate one's spirits.

The same could be said for the people I studied in what little free time I could find—Ed Gein, for instance. A mid-twentieth-century murderer and grave desecrator from Plainfield, Wisconsin, Gein decorated his house with knickknacks made from the body parts of his all-female victims: chairs covered with their skin, human-skin lampshades, bowls made from skulls and bedposts decorated with them, a belt made from nipples, a pair of lips tied to a window shade drawstring. The list goes on, including six vulvas from teenage girls for which he apparently had not yet concocted a use. For good measure, the decapitated body of hardware store owner Bernice Worden was hanging upside down in Gein's shed when police raided his house. She was the sort of portly woman Gein favored: more skin.

Ed Gein is frequently described as having been mentally deficient. To me, he was just another ghoul who expanded my knowledge of the awful darkness that surrounds us.

Then there was this man—a victim not of murder but of his own insatiable appetites—who I came across while reading through back copies of the *American Journal of Forensic Medicine and Pathology*. To quote from the article:

> *The body of a 57-year-old white man was discovered by a neighbor who responded to the sound of "a vacuum cleaner running continuously for a long time" coming from the decedent's trailer home. Upon entry, he found the decedent slumped over a vacuum cleaner and proceeded to notify the police. A medical examiner was requested at the scene for a possible case of "electrocution." The decedent was naked, leaning against a dining room table with his feet on the floor. His testicles, thighs, and buttocks were tightly wound with panty hose. Areas in direct contact with the beater bar (his abdomen, parts of his chest and arms) showed some burn marks. His tongue, which protruded, was dry and cyanotic. A bottle of wine, some food items, jars of lubricant, a glass of urine, and a wooden table leg laden with fecal material were seen on the dining room table. The decedent had had a history of heart disease. No electrical defect was detected in the vacuum cleaner.*

A horrible scene, in short. Why do I include it here? To show in this tale of man's inhumanity to others how inhumane we can sometimes be to ourselves. Also because the case history obviously stuck with me. I've held on to this article for more than forty years. Life in the BSU was not for the faint of heart.

• • •

EVEN WHAT SHOULD HAVE BEEN the lighter moments of such a vocation were ultimately unsettling in the extreme. We weren't "all killers, all the time" at the BSU. Sometimes diverting cases (at least, by our standards) dropped on our desks because of shortfalls elsewhere in the criminal justice system. Thus it was with a case of extreme scatophilia that was plaguing the National Parks in the western mountains of Virginia.*

Normally, park rangers would have taken care of the problem, but they were overworked and understaffed, and the problem was becoming so noxious that the National Park Service got word to John Douglas, and John agreed to hear the rangers out at one of our famous think tank sessions.

At the root of the problem—at least the physical root—were the latrines in the more remote parts of the parks, where plumbing is just a pipe dream. In those places, hikers and campers do their business the way our great-grandparents used to do it: in an outhouse, seated over a hole that has been dug out and is generally limed to keep the odor down until the hole fills up and has to be dug out again or the latrine moved to another location.

For dedicated scatophiliacs, though, this is also an opportunity. By stealth of night, they can dig their way into the latrine from the bottom, stick their head in, and wait for their prey—and that, the rangers told us, was exactly what had been happening, almost under their noses, so to speak. Woman after woman had told the same story: They had been doing their business when they started to hear a strange collection of grunts and groans coming from down below them. Invariably, they would jump to their feet,

---

* The American Psychological Association's *Dictionary of Psychology* defines "scatophilia" as "sexual interest and arousal derived from talking about excrement and using obscene language." Some people, though, go beyond just talking about it.

have a look through the hole, and there would be a face deep down in the shadows, staring back up at them even as the women started to scream. Several men, too, had the experience, although no one mentioned whether they screamed or stayed stoically silent.

The rangers wanted to know the same things homicide detectives did in other cases brought to us: Were they dealing with one perpetrator or multiple ones? How were they going to locate him (or them)? And what the heck was going on?

The last part of that was easy. John Douglas was up to date on scatophilia and gave them a full explanation of the disorder. As to the number of perpetrators, we concluded after a cross-table talk, odds heavily favored a single source. The geographic spread was relatively tight, given how far apart outhouses were in those settings, and if feces excites you, it probably doesn't matter much whether it is male or female generated. We also offered some advice on how they might trap such an individual, and that worked so well that they caught both perpetrators. Yes, *both*! In retrospect, we should have realized that a latrine-rich environment is to scatophiliacs as a beehive is to bears—irresistible.

A happy outcome, in short, but also a reminder that the commonplaces of our job at the BSU stretched to the far ends of human aberration.

Another case seemed to go almost beyond the possible. I was minding my own business at the BSU when John Douglas sent a visiting police officer down to tell me about a case he and his partner were working.

"Fire away," I told the guy, having no idea what weirdness lay ahead.

The case began innocently enough. A state policeman down in Georgia notices a car sitting beside the road with the engine running and a taillight out, so he stops to write up one of those citations that will disappear after the guy can certify the light has been fixed. Routine stuff, in short, except the driver immediately begins to act strangely: furtive eye movements, all the little tells that something isn't quite right.

Finally, things get so quirky that the trooper pulls his gun and says, "All right, let me look in your trunk." And with that, the driver takes off running, but not very fast or very far before the trooper catches up with him and leads him back to the trunk, which this time the guy has no choice but to open . . . to reveal a bunch of dead animals and a collection of suggestive women's clothing.

Among the dead animals is a chicken wearing a dress and pearls. Also, a dead buck still warm to the touch and dripping semen that eventually is matched to the driver. And there's also a video, which the visiting policeman was kind enough to bring along with him to Quantico.

Turns out, this upstanding citizen and father of three was deeply into having sex with a variety of animals, but he had a special thing for chickens, as the video recorded and the trooper and local police soon learned. The filming was done with a stationary dashboard camera, and the seduction (if that's the right word) all takes place in the front seat.

"Hey, darling," he says in one segment, "you look nice tonight," and on and on. The chicken, of course, can reply only "Baaak, baaak, baaak" to these endearments, but she's wearing the same dress and pearls found in the car trunk, and that apparently is enough for this particular Don Juan. Before long, intercourse begins, and however much that might satisfy the man, it definitely kills the chicken, but the video doesn't stop there. There's also footage of him having intercourse with lambs, pigs, and other decomposing farm animals—no longer, I should add, confined to the front seat. The chickens, though, are the only ones he dresses beforehand.

The policeman allowed me to keep the video overnight, so at

the end of the day I gathered the entire BSU in the conference room and said, "I want to show you this video. I have my thoughts, but I want your opinion," and let it roll. Even the guys were grossed out.

Afterward, contrary to official FBI rules and codes of conduct, I brought out a jeroboam of very nice wine a cousin had sent me, and we all raised a glass—or more likely a chipped mug—to the total weirdness in our world, but more than a little uneasily for me and maybe for almost everyone else in the room, given what we had just witnessed.

I never bothered to find out if this sort of bestiality was a crime in Georgia at the time, but did I really want to live in a professional world where something like that would even come up for consideration? More and more, I found myself answering, "No." True, I had been privileged to gain a PhD-level education in the reality that human beings are capable of almost anything, but in my line of work that was not necessarily a good thing.

17.

... AND NORMAL IS HELL

AS HARD AS THE WORK WAS AND as emotionally and psychologically taxing as it could be, most of my colleagues stayed with the BSU until retirement age, which in the FBI is fifty with twenty years of service or a maximum of age fifty-seven. For much of my time there, I thought I might do the same. It was an elite posting, no question about that. But as my fifth year wore on, I began thinking that I had always loved new challenges and was ready to reenter the FBI "mainstream": investigations, operations, and leadership. That's only part of the reason I moved on, though. The other part, harder but necessary to acknowledge, is that I was starting to focus much too much on the dark side of life.

I loved walking and jogging through the woods on the Quantico campus, but it got so that every time I saw a plastic bag flickering in the breeze or glinting alongside the footpath, I couldn't stop wondering if it contained a body part—a head, fingers, some inner organ. I'd seen too many of them just like that: detached, severed, cut out, then bagged and tossed away as casually as you might chuck your McDonald's cups and containers.

At home, too, I was having trouble. America is a gun culture by and large, but the people I focused on mostly favored knives, perhaps because knives are quieter, or prolong the torture, or can be dual-purpose, for killing and sectioning afterward, or just because they are often at hand in a house break-in or a fit of domestic rage. ("Weapons of opportunity," we call them.) I had recently worked a number of homicide cases where the victims had been killed at home by their own kitchen knives, and I started thinking if a killer was able to gain entry to my house, I at least wanted him to have to use his own knife to do me in.

To that end, I took every knife in our kitchen and hid them—where else?—in the basement dryer. No one would think of looking for them there, not even Dale . . . as I discovered when I found him scrambling through the kitchen drawers, trying to find a single flat blade to make a peanut butter and jelly sandwich.

On the subject of common household dangers, about halfway through my time with BSU, we were asked to do a link analysis on a somewhat bizarre burst of murders committed with or involving steam irons. In one case, the offender had bashed a woman in her own kitchen with her ironing board, then crushed her skull with her iron and left what were obviously iron burn marks on her body. In case two, an intruder had strangled two family members with their iron cord and left the iron and cord hanging around one of the victim's necks like a noose. In case three, the victims had been shot to death and covered with iron burn marks all over their bodies. The medical examiner couldn't determine whether the burns preceded or followed the deaths, but we all hoped for the latter.

Amazingly, all these murders had been committed within a single week, but they were geographically so separate and each had enough distinctive elements that we concluded this was almost certainly the work of multiple perpetrators. Still, the cases stuck with me, not in the best way.

I suppose if I had been completely round the bend by the time my tenure at BSU was drawing to an end, I would have hidden Dale's and my steam iron away, too, or more likely driven up I-95 to the Occoquan Reservoir and tossed it in there, since that's where I believe all steam irons belong—at the bottom of large bodies of water and completely irretrievable. (My mother's compulsion for ironing did not transfer to me: I consider dry cleaning one of the seven wonders of the modern world.) I didn't do that, but that's a low bar for measuring a healthy psyche.

IT WASN'T ONLY AT QUANTICO and on the home front where things were getting more than a little edgy. I'm all for situational awareness, especially for women. Whether it's day or night, a city you're visiting or a town where you have lived in all your life, if you want to go for a walk or take a jog, don't wear a headset, and make sure you have all your senses on the alert—in front of and behind you, but on the periphery as well. If you hear something behind you, turn around and check it out. You're not being rude; you're being wise. If you don't sense danger, go about your business. If you do, and the danger seems real and present, this is no time to be passive.

The same goes for dating apps. Meet your date in a public venue, protect your flanks, keep your antennae up and active, and leave yourself a clear path out if things turn bad. I've seen too many times, in my professional capacity, what can happen when a "good vibe" about someone's character is fatally wrong.

There is, however, a thin line between being situationally aware and situationally over-aware, and as my time with the BSU drew to a close, I was clearly losing the capacity to distinguish one from the other.

This took place in Los Angeles, during my last year with the BSU. There had been a multiday conference of some kind, thick with FBI agents I had known for a decade or more, mostly all of them men, as was the case with the Bureau back then. Afterward, we would find the hotel bar and have a drink to wind down. Then, while some of the guys settled into second and third adult beverages, I would excuse myself and head for my room . . . except, it dawned on me, I wasn't heading *exactly* to my room anymore. Instead, I would take the elevator to a floor or two above my room, have a good look up and down the hallway, then rush to the stairs and walk back down to my floor and from there to my room, keeping an eye on both ends of the hallway and on all the room doors in between.

If you're James Bond, operational, overseas, and on Dr. No's hit list, evasive procedures like that might be justified. But that wasn't me. That I was doing it at all gave me the cold shakes; that this was becoming a pattern of behavior kept leading me to a word I could no longer silence: "paranoia."

And then there were the photographs. The dead can't talk to you, but photographs of their brutal murder sites or mortal remains often can. One time, when Dale was away on extended Bureau business, I brought home a bunch of 8 x 10 sadistically graphic crime scene photographs—all in living color—of a case I was working on and taped them to the dining room walls, much as I'd do in my office. I hoped they would begin telling me their secrets during the two weeks I was living alone. When Dale returned, he noted that normal people did not wallpaper their dining rooms with human carnage. Maybe I needed to back away. I took his point.

DALE TOOK MY POINT, TOO, when I cited examples of how he was beginning to normalize the abnormal—his Stockholm syndrome moments, for example, with Salvatore "Sammy the Bull" Gravano.

Gravano had a résumé as long as your arm, all in the wrong direction. Born in 1945, he got his start with the Colombo crime family in New York and later with the Brooklyn wing of the Gambino family, where he played a key role, along with John Gotti and others, in the 1985 murder of Gambino boss of bosses Paul Cas-tellano. But that was only the icing on the cake. Along the way, Sammy the Bull took part in another eighteen murders—at least, that's the number he eventually confessed to.

By 1991, Gravano was an underboss for Gotti, working his way nicely up into the executive mob ranks. That's when federal pros-ecutors who had been dogging Gotti for years invited Sammy to listen to a wiretap segment in which Gotti not only badmouths his supposedly much-loved underboss but also implicates them both in more than one murder. And that's when the Bull sticks a finger to the wind, votes for his future instead of his past, and decides to turn state's evidence and testify for the prosecution against Gotti in what would become one of the most closely watched mob tri-als in modern history. All of which raised the problem of how to keep Sammy the Bull Gravano alive until and hopefully through his testimony.

The U.S. Marshals Service oversees the widely known witness protection program, which helps those who endanger themselves by testifying to establish anonymous new lives, but for super-risks like Sammy, the FBI provides protection up to and through court appearances. I can't tell you the where of any of this—suffice it to say, the locations provide considerable extra security—but I can tell you that in this case the FBI provided not only a secure spot but round-the-clock, outside-the-door, and inside-the-room hand-holding by multiple special agents, one of whom was my hus-band, detailed in this case (as were the others) from the Bureau's elite Hostage Rescue Team.

I admit to having had more than a little professional curi-osity about Dale's new assignment. As I mentioned, serial killers tend to create all sorts of excuse mechanisms to shield themselves from their actual behavior and its consequences, but while Gra-vano had murdered or helped murder more people than many of

BSU's prize subjects, he was a comparatively uncomplicated man. There was no sexual component to his murders; he wasn't playing some kind of sick control game. To him, these were people who by their actions or lack of action had drawn a target on their backs and, frankly, deserved to be hit and at some level probably even expected it. Business is business.

For his part, Dale was not a happy camper when the assignment came down.

"I'm going to hate this duty," he told me. "This guy's despicable."

Maybe, in the hope that Sammy was an early-to-bed kind of guy, Dale volunteered for the in-the-room late shift. But, like Dale, the Bull turned out to be a night owl and a movie fan, and it wasn't long before the two of them were watching films into the wee hours of the morning.

I could tell the balance was shifting between the two of them by the casual comments Dale made on the rare evenings he was back home with me. Things like "You ought to hear Sammy when he calls his family. The things he says—he's actually a really good father." And "You know what? We like the same movies!" The clincher came when Gravano had finished testifying and Dale's six weeks of babysitting finally came to an end: "I think I'm actually going to miss the guy."

"Oh, stop it," I said. "This guy's been involved in more murders than Jack the Ripper!"

That at least put an end to any outward signs of overidentification with Sammy the Bull, but fast-forward to a couple months later when Dale and I are at home, trying to figure out what movie to play for our evening entertainment.

"Let's watch such-and-such," I say to him.

"No," he says, "we already saw that."

"I did not see that."

"Yes you did."

And then it dawns on me: "That was you and Sammy, Dale. That was not me."

"Oh, you're right," he says, but that was not the end of it. On at least three more occasions he did the same thing until I began to wonder if every time Dale looked at his wife, he was seeing a notorious mob hit man instead. That's an exaggeration, of course, but this was yet another way in which the strangeness of the world Dale and I occupied kept bleeding into our lives.

I WASN'T EXACTLY INNOCENT MYSELF when it came to overidentifying with less-than-optimal human beings. Informants on the whole are not model citizens. They tend to have shaky lifestyles and are frequently in the company of shady characters, which is why they have access to people you want to get information about. That's part of the deal, but maybe the best informant I ever had was a complete sociopath. He wasn't a professional hit man. He didn't have sex with cadavers. He did, however, lie from the moment he got up in the morning until the moment he went to bed, and probably in his dreams. Still, he had what was for me a redeeming sense of humor. More important, for all his lies, his information was frequently golden, and for that I spent more time with him than with any of my other sources, I laughed harder at his jokes than they fully deserved, and I never once suggested that if he buffed up the good parts of his personality and toned down the sociopathic ones, he might not have to make ends meet by slipping nuggets of information to someone like me at the risk of getting his knees broken, or worse. You make pacts with the devil, in short, but you always have to remind yourself that the devil is not the baseline of human behavior.

Sammy the Bull Gravano, I should add, got a sweetheart deal from the Feds for ratting on John Gotti, but he wasn't through with crime. In 2002 he was sentenced in New York to twenty years in prison for his part in a drug ring but was let out in 2017 for good behavior and went on to launch his own YouTube channel. Last I looked, this ruthless mob murderer had 460,000 subscribers and had logged nearly 70 million views. Talk about normalizing the abnormal.

I understand why such websites and related TV fare are so popular. They're a window into extremes of human behavior, and extremes are always fascinating, whether it's extremes of athletic endeavor, extremes of natural beauty, or extremes of human horror and suffering. Throw in supersized murders, and the subject matter is simultaneously compelling and repulsive. A girlfriend of mine loves serial-killer–related shows. She's constantly recommending one or another to me and baffled by my resistance.

"Oh my God, it's so riveting," she tells me. "If I get too scared, I just pull a blanket over my head."

But in a way that's the point. She *can* pull a blanket over her head, just like the people who follow Sammy the Bull's website can hit the mute button if they don't want to hear about how some father of three was sent to swim with the fishes in the East River because he ran afoul of a bad-tempered mob boss, just like the people who slow down to a crawl at highway wrecks will crane their necks to look for evidence of human mayhem but are rarely tempted to stop on the shoulder and help pull the dead and nearly dead out of all that convoluted metal.

Things that repulse and compel in almost equal measure will always have an appeal so long as they remain in essence one-dimensional—so long as they are seen through a car window or on a computer screen or between fingers that cover the eyes. These things had stopped being one-dimensional to me long before I pulled the plug on my BSU career.

When I turned on a favorite TV show like *Law & Order* and saw a battered and bruised body lying on a coroner's examining table, my nose filled with the smell of formaldehyde or whatever it is they use in morgues to wipe examining tables down once the examination is over. My imagination went flying to similar bodies—real ones, not actors' artfully made-up torsos—at real crime scenes where real people suffered real and excruciating pain. I had no windows left to see things through, no psychological blanket I could throw over my head. At least for me, "riveting" no longer applied—or maybe it just over-applied. Six of one, half a dozen of the other.

Add that scene to the stories I told earlier and my concern that I was going to find body parts on my runs through the lovely Quantico woods and those knives I stored in the dryer and how I had started taking the elevator to one story *above* my hotel room before walking back down the stairs to my own floor, just in case who knows what, and maybe now you will have a better sense of why I was ready to give it all up and begin a new and different adventure. I was like an emergency room doctor who had no capacity to treat the broken and maybe dying bodies that flooded his cubicles. All I could do was ask why, why, why?

18.
LOW CRIMES IN HIGH PLACES

WE INHABITED A DARK WORLD at the Behavioral Science Unit, literally and metaphorically. We worked underground in artificial light, breathing air pumped two floors down to us, unraveling crimes that beggared the imagination and regularly kept me awake at night, even before I started filling the dryer with kitchen knives.

My next posting, in San Diego, was almost the exact opposite. Beautiful California sun streamed in my office window most days. There was a hint of ocean in the air, a festive, touristy feel to the streets, and anything-goes Tijuana was just over the border. That part of the new job appealed greatly to me. After five years in the BSU, I needed sunshine in my life, literally and figuratively. I also wanted to enhance my leadership skills, and in the FBI in those days there were precious few opportunities to do that as a woman and even fewer models to look up to and learn from, especially in the operational side of the Bureau. I wasn't going to be the boss in San Diego, but as a supervisor, I would at least have an upward rung on the career ladder.

Yet, as nice a place as it was, and remains, San Diego was not my first choice. Most of my expertise by then was in violent crime, so I put in for a number of positions that would have had me heading up a squad that investigated murders, serial rapes, violent bank robberies, and the like, including a position that I really wanted in

Dallas because I had never gotten over my early teenage fascination with the Texas Rangers and also because, let's face it, Texas has
never been short on violent crimes.

Naturally, I assumed the powers that be back at headquarters
in downtown DC would see the logic in all this as well. Something
along the lines of *Let's see. We've spent five-plus years turning Jana
into a maven of mayhem. How can we put this to best use now?*

Headquarters, however, didn't reason exactly that way, as I
learned one gray, underground afternoon at Quantico when Burdie
(short for Burdena) Pasenelli, the Bureau's personnel boss, called
me and said, "Congratulations, Jana, you're going to San Diego!"

"San Diego?" I remembered seeing the posting. "That's a
white-collar squad. I've never worked white-collar."

"Well, are you an accountant?"

"Nowhere close," although the FBI did employ a ton of
accountants.

"Maybe you once worked in a bank?" Burdie asked hopefully.

"I once ran down a bank robber barefoot in Tampa," I told her.

"Ah," Burdie said, delighted. "That explains it!"

With a job like Burdie's in a bureaucracy as massive as the
FBI, a sense of humor is a vital survival skill. Besides, I knew San
Diego from growing up in Long Beach, an hour up the road (or
three, depending on traffic). Better still, I would be able to check in
on my mother with some regularity. She was now in her eighties,
all alone in Upland, California, since my dad had died. Best of all,
Dale was sure to be transferred with me: the Bureau was very good
about doing that with dual-agent couples. Apart from our own
domestic happiness, this would give him a break from the meat
grinder of Washington politics, which had been set on hamburger
mode ever since Ruby Ridge.

That didn't quite work out the way we expected, either. We
had no trouble selling our house in Virginia. Washington-area real

estate was going gangbusters in the mid-1990s, and we quickly found a nice rental to get us started in San Diego, but by then Dale wasn't part of the moving package—at least not yet.

Dale was on tap to be commander of the SWAT team in San Diego, a natural outgrowth of his work with the Hostage Rescue Team, but the FBI refused to transfer him until he had appeared before the Senate committee looking into Ruby Ridge, and that wasn't expected to happen for another four months or so.

"That's what planes are for," I told the Bureau personnel people. "You can fly him back east when it's time to prepare and deliver his testimony."

"Oh, no," I was told. "We have to be prudent with the taxpayers' money. We'll put him up in a room at the Quantico campus until he's through testifying. But don't worry: The room will be free of charge!"

The "free" part sounded less generous when Dale called to report on his new living conditions.

"The room has been condemned," he told me.

"Condemned?"

"Literally. I can see the pipes."

"Well, just shut off the light."

"There is no light!"

Moral: Beware of having the federal government, or the Federal Bureau of Investigation, for your landlord. All is not gold that glitters.

Second moral: Sometimes it's better just to let old memories alone.

MAYBE IT WAS COMING BACK to Southern California, where I had launched myself into law enforcement. Maybe it was a recessive gene that craved a little street action after all that time in my underground bunker in Quantico, or simply the fact that I was no longer that eager-beaver quick-draw policewoman begging for a taste of the action, or just sheer curiosity. But when one of my old policing buddies asked me, a week after I got to San Diego, if I wanted to ride along on a Friday night patrol in Escondido, I said sure, signed all the necessary paperwork, and climbed in the shotgun seat—without, I should add, asking the Bureau, probably because I didn't want to hear that answer.

In any event, I marveled at all the new, computerized gizmos in the car, and we had a lot of catch-up chitchat to fill the time of what was essentially a pretty boring night of policing. Then, at about 1:30 in the morning, near the end of the shift, a call came in that shots were being fired in a nearby neighborhood, and off we sped just in time to see a guy silhouetted by the moonlight as he raced across the local rooftops, followed as we soon saw by two other guys climbing up after him and firing as they went.

The most dangerous situation anyone can encounter in policing or in war is being in the middle of gunfire, with no idea of what's going on, and that was exactly us. Who's bad? Who's good? We had no idea as we crawled toward the action. Then my partner identified himself, and the guy who was being chased breathed a huge sigh of relief from the roof and called down that he was a fugitive from justice and would gladly surrender to us. Meanwhile, the two guys chasing him owned up that they were bounty hunters . . . and clearly disappointed with our intervention, which had ruined their night and cost them however many thousands of dollars in reward that had been offered for bringing this felon back, dead or alive.

As we were filling out the paperwork afterward, I kept envisioning a headline reading "FBI Supervisor Killed by Bounty Hunter" and just how that would play back at headquarters. As it was, I had to endure getting briefly chewed out by the Escondido police chief. Ride-alongs aren't supposed to be armed, but

FBI agents are supposed to always carry their weapons. It was, I explained to him, a dilemma wholly of my own making.

As for my day job—the one the FBI expected me to devote full attention to—instead of being surrounded on all four walls by photographs of corpses, I suddenly found myself in charge of an FIF (financial institution fraud) squad that was huge: nineteen agents in all, twice the normal squad load, and all of them accountants. All male, too, except for one lone female . . . or two, now that I was on board.

"Financial institution fraud" sounds like a purview limited to banks, savings and loans, and the like, but the larger ambit of the white-collar-crime squad includes public corruption as a whole. Not to sound overly cynical, but wherever you have a public, you're going to have public corruption. So I got together with two of the agents who had already shown themselves to be top talents and told them to find some public corruption for us to investigate right here in good old San Diego.

"How?" they asked.

"Why don't you start with the daily newspaper. Give the *San Diego Union-Tribune* a good read every day, and not just the sports section and the opinion page. You guys are accountants. You've been trained to smell something fishy in long columns of numbers. See if you smell anything fishy in long columns of print."

So they set up an operation that they code-named QUARTER-PAST (the roots of which I never understood) and started poring over the newspaper and asking questions around town, and before long an informant voluntarily called one of the agents, John Gillies, and said that the deepest well of public corruption in San Diego could be found in the one place you might be least inclined to look for it: the local courts. The informant didn't have proof to offer up, but he had the names of judges we should focus on, particularly their dockets and the lawyers who appeared before them, and their particular cases and outcomes.

Focusing on these leads was so promising that John redoubled his efforts to coax the informant into identifying himself and finally succeeded: Our informant was unwilling to meet in person with any old agent. He wanted to talk with the head of the squad, so out I went to La Jolla, met with the informant several times, and took a ton of notes, and that was the beginning of a two-year stretch that involved six of my agents full-time as well as six prosecutors ponied up by the U.S. attorney's office—a rare commitment of resources for such an investigation—a grand jury inquiry, and a long list of indictments against local Superior Court judges G. Dennis Adams and James Malkus and one prominent attorney, Patrick Frega, who was accused of liberally sprinkling bribes among the judges in return for favorable outcomes in their courtrooms. (A third judge, Michael Greer, saw the writing on the wall and turned witness for the prosecution before the indictments were handed down.)

A scandal, in short, but far from embarrassing the local legal establishment, our diligence and success seemed to have convinced many of its most prominent members that the FBI and U.S. attorney's office had gone way overboard and ought to just shut up and preferably get the hell out of town.

The investigators had stumbled upon "horribly indiscreet behavior" and assumed it was a crime, one well-connected lawyer told a reporter for the *Los Angeles Times*. Other lawyers claimed that the investigation took too long, went way too far into the weeds, and—tellingly—was conducted by a bunch of outsiders who didn't understand how the bench and bar had always intermingled in a highly friendly fashion in San Diego. Robert Walsh, the special agent in charge of San Diego's FBI office, had arrived only in 1994. Assistant special agent in charge Grant Ashley showed up in the fall of 1995, just about the same time FIF squad chief Jana Monroe (not mentioned in the *LA Times* article) transferred from ghoul duty in Quantico, Virginia. What's more, all three judges, including Greer, had already been pulled from their benches by state oversight agencies by the time the indictments came down. Enough is enough already!

As if to underscore just how chummy the bench and bar were in San Diego, surveillance captured our own U.S. attorney paying a home visit to one of the judges in question well after normal office hours. That was enough for me to insist to the special agent in charge that our U.S. attorney recuse himself from the case going forward and turn this over to his number two.

Despite all this supposed mitigation, we at the FBI continued to labor under the assumption that low crimes in high places are as deserving of attention as high crimes in low places, so we prepped for trial, knowing full well that this was going to be a hard case to present to a jury. Frega wasn't handing out bundles of money to the judges. He was rewarding them and/or their family members with automobiles, car repairs, money orders, an apartment, health club memberships, even a queen-sized bed. To make our case, we had to show a clear cause-and-effect relationship between these benefits and decisions handed down by the various judges in favor of Frega's clients—far from an easy thing to do. I spent days serving as a mock jury, shooting down any approach that wasn't going to pass muster with the lowest common denominator of those likely to serve.

Whether or not that made a difference, I have no idea, but the defense gave it their all. Malkus took the stand to profess complete ignorance of Frega's various expenditures on behalf of himself and his family. Adams, through counsel, contended that while he had indeed accepted Frega's many payments and benefits, he did so without corrupt intent. Frega's lawyers, as expected, characterized those payments and benefits as gifts, not bribes—acts of friendship and generosity. And in the end the jury was utterly unconvinced.

All three were found guilty of violating conspiracy charges under the RICO anti-racketeering act, which—surprise!—applies equally to mob bosses and judges and lawyers. Frega was convicted of an additional thirteen counts of mail fraud, Malkus of six of the same, and Adams of five. Add in an additional conviction for Frega of committing a "substantive RICO offense" and cap the whole thing off with a United States court of appeals decision affirming the entire package, and it was a slam-bang win for justice.

My only complaint was with the sentencing: Frega and Adams drew forty-one months' imprisonment; Malkus got off lighter with thirty-three months. We had solidly shown that Frega doled out and the judges accepted more than $100,000 in bribes. Indications suggested a much higher figure, but we wanted to keep our presentation to the jury tight and solid. Where I come from, that's real money, and in the venues I had previously worked in, crooks were not given extra-credit points for being supposed pillars of the community.

When those sentences were handed down, I immediately thought of all the people doing hard time in serious prisons for being stupid enough or strung out enough or otherwise desperate enough to rob at gunpoint a convenience store where a good haul might be a hundred bucks and any till excess over, say, $600 gets dropped in a safe.

Yes, the gun is intimidating. Yes, the clerk was probably scared stiff. The dopes who do these things deserve to see the inside of a cell. But white-collar fraud isn't a victimless crime. Look at the string of suicides that Bernie Madoff's high-finance crimes spawned—the lost jobs, the depression that followed. However the money gets stolen—at the point of a gun or by cooking the books—there are ramifications and repercussions that the law is too ready to ignore when the crook works in a paneled corner office and belongs to all the right clubs. And I would argue that was especially the case in our San Diego fraud investigation.

Not to over-preach, but I strongly believe in ethics. Those to whom law enforcement and justice have been entrusted—police officers, FBI agents, district attorneys, especially judges—are obligated to comport themselves unwaveringly with integrity and honesty and to consistently abide by this moral compass. When they don't, they deserve no better treatment than a guy who tries to knock over a 7-Eleven.

They don't deserve a better jail cell, either—which is another way of saying don't get me started on Martha Stewart and the two years (of a two-year, five-month sentence for insider trading) she spent on "supervised release" at her Bedford, New York, mansion, with forty-eight hours a week away from home allowed for business-related purposes. Department of *Injustice*, anyone?

ODDLY, THOUGH, JUSTICE DOES GET done more often than not, and often with the help of the perpetrators themselves. San Diego offered up a good example of that as well while I was still there.

This case began far away in South Africa with a split-up between two men who had been in business together. One of the businessmen relocated to San Diego. The other stayed behind, convinced that his former partner had grabbed most of the money the two had accumulated and run with it to the United States.

Whatever the merits of his accusation, threats from afar were producing no results other than frustration and anger that eventually boiled over sufficiently for the South African stay-behind to hire an Italian hit man, with instructions to travel to San Diego, locate his tormentor's office (in a handsome old Spanish-style building, as things turned out), and put an end to things. The hit man had no trouble locating his target, conveniently sitting at his desk with a clear line of fire right through the front window.

But all Italian hit men are not created equal, and this one failed to notice before he emptied his .22-caliber pistol that the window he was about to fire through was made of double-pane glass. The bullets had no trouble penetrating the window, but the glass had no trouble deflecting the rounds, either, and once inside the office, they flew every which way but true and left the target undoubtedly stunned but completely unharmed.

For the hit man, though, the bollix was just beginning. A bystander saw the assailant race for his getaway rental car, noted the license plate number, and passed it on to police, and the Los Angeles police found the car just as its driver was meeting with his South African employer, who had flown to the West Coast to make sure the job was done before he paid the tab—a two-for-one arrest that saved taxpayers lots of money and the LAPD a lot of extra effort. Shortly afterward, a South African–born informant Dale had used in the past called him to say that he had done business with both men and knew there was serious bad blood between them, which pretty much tied the package up with a bow and just goes to show that Italian hit men and the people who hire them are thankfully not always the sharpest tools in the shed.

ONE MORE TALE FROM SAN Diego because it illustrates something I feel deeply about: fire discipline. SWAT teams and a financial institute fraud unit would appear to live on different planets: White-collar crooks resist arrest with lawyers, not guns. But when my guys requested SWAT help because the man they were about to arrest had pulled a gun in a previous situation and would likely be armed this time around, I immediately said yes, and I'm eternally grateful I did so. (I was also, I'm sure, recalling the SWAT team that I had been refused when I went out to arrest James Huntze in Tampa a decade and a half earlier—the time I nearly got a hole blown in my head.)

The target was living in a low-rise apartment complex, and the SWAT team was not able to clear the unit next door: The landlord wouldn't let them in, and the woman living there never responded—maybe because she wasn't there, but that was chance our team couldn't take. So, after identifying themselves and forcing the door, the two lead SWAT guys worked with extra care to clear the rooms until they came to the final refuge, a back bedroom, and sure enough, when they threw that door open, the guy popped up from the far side of the bed with his pistol held in both hands, saw our two guys armed and in body armor, calculated the odds, and dropped back down again.

All in all, our guys told me later, this might have happened in no more than a few seconds, but now they knew the guy was in fact armed and had a record of previous gun use in similar situations, and that was, by the books, all they needed to tear that bed apart with gunfire. Instead, one of them quietly worked his way around the bed, saw the guy quivering behind it, and basically jumped on him, breaking his arm and bringing the incident to a peaceful conclusion (if you ignored the perpetrator's whining about his arm).

I was, of course, thrilled with the outcome and proud of the two guys for having the courage to hold their fire, but I soon started to hear rumbles that they were taking a lot of crap from their colleagues for putting themselves at risk when they had every right to just blow the perpetrator away. Now the guy was sure to sue the FBI over his arm, and God alone knows where it will all end.

Sure enough, it wasn't long before the two guys showed up in my office, second-guessing themselves.

"Maybe we should have just shot him and got it over with," they told me, heads hanging down.

"Absolutely not," I replied. "The guy might be the world's biggest a-hole, but you don't take a life when you don't need to."

To underscore the point, I went to the special agent in charge in San Diego and told him these two needed to be recognized and acknowledged for their fire discipline.

"Fire discipline?" he said. "I've never heard of anyone being recognized for fire discipline."

"Well, you have now," I told him.

So I wrote up the commendation, and once it had passed muster with headquarters (because of the cash reward involved), I had the assistant SWAT team leader—not Dale, who was out of the office then—make the presentation at a little ceremony, and the guys walked away each richer by $500 and a gold star in their records for intentionally and bravely placing themselves in danger so that the life of an alleged crook might be spared.

Sometimes in law enforcement less is more.

19.
HELP IS ON THE WAY

BY NOW, IT SHOULD BE obvious that mine has not been a life easy on the psyche. I have been forced to look closely at things people should not have to see, to contemplate acts that one might hope we humans could never commit on our fellow humankind, to sift through the debris of too many hearts of darkness.

I'll never forget my first clear look at how the human body falls apart. I was still the new kid at the Chino Police Department when we were called to respond to a violent automobile collision. Everybody in one of the cars—a family, I was told—had been killed. In fact, as I neared the car it seemed clear that no one could have possibly survived the impact. The car was severely compacted. And then I realized that what I had been staring at on the pavement was the remains of a human brain.

With that, I hurried off to the side of the highway and vomited. Partially, of course, it was the sheer shock of what I had just realized, but the brain matter also brought home to me the awful finality of what had happened here. I had no idea what had caused the accident. Driver inattention? A mechanical failure? Someone asleep at the wheel, or drunk, or high on drugs? For all I knew, the real cause of this tragedy was another twenty miles up the road, perhaps even unaware that his or her swerve had caused someone else to swerve, etc., etc.

What I did know for certain was that no family gets in a car expecting never again to get out of it alive, and now this family was dead. And as I thought about that, I also couldn't stop thinking about the uncles and aunts and grandparents and friends and other loved ones who were going to be affected by this—the whole ripple effect of this terrible event spreading out across a neighborhood, schools, maybe a church, across a state, a country, maybe even in a diminishing way across borders and even continents.

I felt much the same way, including the nausea urge, when I saw the bloated and distorted Rogers family females being pulled out of Tampa Bay, and when I watched those 737s plowing into the World Trade Center towers and read about the shootings at Sandy Hook Elementary School in Connecticut and on so many other similar occasions in these carnage-filled times we live in. I have no children of my own, and I wasn't at Sandy Hook and wouldn't have wanted that case in any event. But I remembered from my own childhood how excited I was to attend kindergarten, to be with other kids my age, to have all those activities to look forward to every day, and I could easily imagine all those mothers and dads sending their little ones off to school with hugs and kisses, sure that they would see them again before the afternoon was over—not knowing their little loved ones in a quiet New England town would have had a greater chance of survival if they had been deployed to Afghanistan that morning.

The point I'm trying to make—the one that kept being reinforced with me time and again by the violence I witnessed—is twofold. First, the victims of violence are not just data points in some national tally of crime. Those data points are flesh and blood; they're men, women, and children. They had lives that were violently extinguished, and they cry out for our attention. Second, the first responders who deal with so many of these gory events— cops, SWAT teams, firefighters, EMTs, and the like—are not just data points, either. They're flesh-and-blood humans, too. They feel up close and personal the horror that most of us only feel second-hand, watching the after-footage on our TV or computer screens. And like any human being, they have to process those moments and rearrange their lives around them so they can go on.*

LEAVING THE BEHAVIORAL SCIENCE UNIT and starting up the executive leadership track at the Bureau didn't exempt me from the American carnage—if anything, it gave me a closer view of even more heinous acts—but doing so did give me a more holistic point of view. One example might suffice here.

April 20, 1999, marks one of the darker and more ominous moments in American history. After a year of detailed planning, Columbine High School seniors Eric Harris and Dylan Klebold chose that day to murder in cold blood one of their teachers and twelve of their fellow students and wounded with gunshots another twenty-one people before taking their own lives in the school cafeteria.

Two powerful bombs, also placed in the cafeteria, had failed to detonate, as had bombs meant to weaponize both shooters' cars in the school parking lot. Had any of those homemade explosives succeeded, the toll would have been in the hundreds. Indeed, topping the death toll at the Oklahoma City bombing almost four years to the day earlier had been one of Harris and Klebold's motivations. Instead of reading about history, they wanted to make it,

---

* Typing those words just now reminded me of Anders Behring Breivik, the Norwegian mass murderer who spent years consciously, in his words, "dehumanizing" himself before shooting and killing sixty-nine people, mostly teens, on an island summer camp. Describing one victim at his April 2014 trial, Breivik told the court, "When I make a follow-up shot, his cranium bursts and there are brains flowing out. I remember that very well." Breivik's voice at that moment was every bit as emotionless as Ed Kemper's voice at his terrifying worst. Dehumanizing is the last thing we want in first responders. Rather, we need to fully recognize and honor their *humanity*.

and in a sense they did. The Columbine shootings were the first of what has become an epidemic of similar events at high schools all across the country. (Recall, too, that the Oklahoma City bombing was in retaliation for the perceived heavy-handedness of the FBI and other federal agencies at Waco and Ruby Ridge. Both of those events have careened through American history ever since.)

The sheriff's office of Jefferson County, Colorado, just to the west of Denver, had primary jurisdiction over the shooting and took a lot of flak in the aftermath for what many considered a slow response.* But five different agencies in all were involved, including our FBI SWAT team, which was the first unit to actually enter the school building. And for those team members, the shootings were as personal as such moments can be.

One of them had a son and another a daughter who were students at Columbine. As they entered the school, they were looking to see if their kids were there and still alive. One of them, in fact, had been injured—not by a gunshot, thank God, but in the stampede to get out of the building. The sharp edge of a table had ripped a hole in his leg, and he had bled profusely enough to make everyone around him assume he had been shot.

I learned of this a few days later, the result of another bump up the Bureau career ladder. After nearly four years in San Diego heading up the FIF squad, I had been named assistant special agent in charge of the Denver Office, one stop short of the coveted special agent in charge (SAC) slot and about as high as a female dared to aim in those days if she didn't want to risk a mountain of frustration and disappointment.

---

* The far more recent deadly school shooting at Uvalde, Texas, appears to have been tragically magnified by a similar slow response. How Uvalde School District Police could have been so clueless twenty-three years after Columbine and the active shooter safety resources made available by the FBI to all law enforcement is, as of this writing, a mystery.

For the moment, though, I had actually gotten there. The new SAC, soon to be my boss, had not yet arrived, which put me in the driver's seat, and it was immediately obvious to me that the traditional FBI solution for events as unsettling as the Columbine shootings—*Go have a beer and get over it!*—wasn't working. Those SWAT team members didn't find their children cut to ribbons, but they had seen something that wasn't yet almost commonplace in America—school kids lying shot up, wounded, and dead in their classrooms, cafeterias, libraries, and hallways—and that wasn't sitting easy with them . . . not easy at all.

After a couple days of this, I met with the SWAT commander in my office, expecting that I would have a hard sell.

"Whether you and your guys are cognizant of this or not," I began, "you've been through something extremely traumatic. You were looking at dead teenagers. Some of you were terrified of seeing your own children among them. So I'm going to retain an outsider, a counselor, a psychologist. I'm going to strongly encourage every one of you to go talk to him or her."

True to my expectations, the SWAT commander replied point-blank, "They don't need this or want to do this." His jaw was set; his face, stern. *What next?* he was probably thinking. *Group therapy? Kumbaya sessions? Tea and scones in the canteen room?*

"Well," I told him, "I think you're from a different generation, because I've seen the looks on their faces, and those looks tell me a lot of them are having a very hard time getting over this." And it turned out almost every single one of those SWAT team members except the commander took advantage of the arrangement, and some of them continued with the counseling sessions for several months.

This wasn't the first time counseling had been advised and provided for FBI personnel following such a traumatic event, but I can say for certain that this was not a common practice. In fact, it was shunned—by, among others, my own husband.

Dale was then SWAT commander in the San Diego office, set to follow me to the Denver office in a few months. When I told him by phone that night about what I had set up for my SWAT team members, his response pretty much echoed what my own commander had said: "You did what?"

"Yes, absolutely. They're going to counseling."

"I don't think they need that," he replied.

"Well," I said, "I do."

And I could use it, too, every time a new Columbine or Parkland or Sandy Hook or Uvalde or too many other school shootings go down.

20.
THE TEXAS SEVEN

LIKE OTHER SPECIALIZED INTELLECTS, CRIMINAL minds are often ingenious when it comes to malfeasance but incapable of coping with—or sometimes even imagining—a world outside of murder, theft, and mayhem. Take the Texas Seven. (Henny Youngman would make that: Take the Texas Seven, *please!*)

Between the seven of them, Joseph Christopher Garcia, Randy Ethan Halprin, Larry James Harper, Patrick Henry Murphy Jr., Donald Keith Newbury, George Angel Rivas Jr., and Michael Anthony Rodriguez had been convicted of a breathtaking array of crimes: murder, sexual assault, aggravated child abuse (including breaking the arms and legs and fracturing the skull of a sixteen-month-old), robbery and aggravated robbery, and hiring the hit man who murdered his wife.

As of December 13, 2000, when the seven escaped from the John B. Connally Unit, a maximum-security prison in South Texas, Rivas was serving eighteen consecutive fifteen-years-to-life sentences; Rodriguez was in for ninety-nine years to life, and Newbury for ninety-nine years only. Three of the others were serving fifty-year sentences. Halprin, the youngest at age twenty-three, had pulled thirty years for grievously injuring that child.

These were, in short, men with little to lose, and their escape from the prison was in many ways a work of genius. First, the seven methodically subdued four correctional officers and nine maintenance supervisors, mostly by calling them over one at a time on some pretext or another, then whapping them over the head until they were unconscious, tying and gagging the inert bodies, and storing them in a utility closet.

Next, three of the seven set off for the back gate of the prison, wearing the clothing of their civilian victims and posing as workmen sent to install video cameras. Instead, they used that ruse to raid a guard tower and stole all the weapons they could find. Meanwhile, the other four made a series of distracting calls to prison guards, pretending they were the officers trussed up in the closet, then stole a prison pickup truck, loaded up the others at the back gate, and off they all went. Thus, the Texas Seven were born.

Outside the prison walls, the seven quickly exchanged the truck for a car Rodriguez's father had left for them in a Walmart parking lot and lit off for bright lights and big cities. In Pearland, part of Greater Houston, they robbed a Radio Shack to secure some walking-around money. On the day before Christmas, now in Irving in Greater Dallas–Fort Worth, they walked en masse (think of the Seven Samurai) into a sporting goods store, bound and gagged the staff, and were helping themselves to forty-plus guns, heaps of ammo, and $70,000 in cash when an off-duty employee standing outside the store became suspicious and called the local police. Officer Aubrey Wright Hawkins, who responded, never had a chance. He was shot eleven times and, for good measure, run over as the seven were escaping. Aubrey was twenty-nine years old, married, the father of one. Suddenly the Texas Seven had a $100,000 reward on their heads, a figure that would climb to half a million dollars.

So far, so good, one might say, at least from an escaped convict's point of view, but there were holes in the thinking of these criminal masterminds that would eventually come back to bite them. For starters, they never split up. There is strength in numbers, to be sure, but an all-points bulletin that advises *Be on the lookout for seven men, heavily armed . . .* is likely to stick in the mind more than an APB that says be on the lookout for one man.

Also, among the seven, none seems to have had any experience in or around hair salons. All dark-haired, the seven decided to disguise themselves as blondes. Instead—as so often happens with home dye jobs—their dark hair turned a striking orange.

Still, the land west and north of Dallas–Fort Worth is wide-open country, easy even for seven orange-haired escaped convicts to lose themselves in, and it wasn't until *America's Most Wanted* aired a January 20, 2001, segment on the Texas Seven that a possible sighting was made, in Woodland Park, Colorado. That's when I came into the story, and when events tragic at their heart grew plain whacko in practice.

I was still assistant special agent in charge of the Denver office in January 2001, but the special agent in charge was frequently gone, leaving me running the show, which is why one of our best agents, Greg Groves, called me at one in the morning on January 21 to report that we had a solid lead on the whereabouts of the Texas Seven.

"How sure are you on a scale of one to ten, with ten being the most sure?" I asked, as I frequently did in these circumstances.

"Nine point nine," Greg answered.

"That's good enough for me," I said.

Chain of command still began with the absent Denver SAC, but when I couldn't make contact with him, I called Greg back with the only viable plan of action open to me.

"I'm assuming command and deploying SWAT," I told him. "Where are we going?"

"The Coachlight Motel and RV Park in Woodland Park, Colorado," Greg told me. "A bunch of guys in a RV there fit the description. They've been posing as evangelists or something, blasting Christian music out of a boom box."

Uh, oh, I thought, for two reasons, neither having to do with religion. First, it was two degrees outside, and the road to Woodland Park was sure to be slippery with snow and ice, as indeed it was. What should have been a ninety-minute drive took closer to two and a half hours. Second, our public information officer was on vacation, and I anticipated this situation would draw a lot of media attention.

The slight upside to all this was that Dale was already at the RV park with the FBI SWAT team out of Denver. Maybe we could wrap this up in a hurry and take off later that day for a planned visit to see friends in California.

Lots of law enforcement agencies had gathered in Woodland Park by the time I arrived just around daybreak—sheriffs' offices, local police contingents, even a small SWAT team from Teller County—but we had brought the real firepower, so I set up a command post in the RV park's tiny office and did a quick briefing there to get everyone on the same page. And then our SWAT team, including Dale, did a knock-and-announce on the RV door, and a shot rang out from inside.

And it was at that very moment that my phone rang. On the other end of the line was the deputy director of the FBI, Tom Pickard.

"What the hell is going on?" he said. "You haven't called this in."

"I'm sorry," I told him. "Shot fired. Gotta go."

With that, I hung up and got on the radio.

"Anyone down?" I asked.

"No," came the answer. "Do we have approval for entry?"

"Yes, go ahead," I said.

And just then the phone rang again, and this time Tom Pickard was really angry.

"Please," I told him, "we don't have a media person here to do this, and I just can't brief you right now."

"Do—not—hang—up," he replied, through obviously clenched teeth.

So I handed the phone to the still-wet-behind-the-ears agent sitting beside me and said, "Here, you talk to the deputy director of the FBI!" (a move I might have learned, now that I think of it, from none other than Demi Moore). That taken care of, sort of, I got back to my job, which was trying to keep as many people alive as possible.

By then the SWAT team had stormed the RV. One of the fugitives was dead by his own hand—that was the shot that had been fired—and it wasn't long before our small army of law enforcers spotted four of the other escapees trying to sneak out of the RV park in a Jeep Cherokee and arrested them when they stopped for gas.

The Texas Seven were now down to the Texas Two, so it seemed reason enough to send the SWAT team back to Denver. The potential shootout at the RV park hadn't happened. Dale could make our flight to California, and with a little luck I might be able to join him on the plane. How far could two orange-headed fugitives get?

But the chase wasn't over—not by a long shot.

Almost a full day later, and after running down a dozen or more leads, we finally found the remaining Texas Two hiding out at a Holiday Inn in Colorado Springs, but our stealth approach went afoul, and before we could storm the room, they took two motel employees hostage and laid out for my negotiators the conditions of surrender if those hostages were going to have any chance of seeing the sunrise the next morning:

1. They demanded access to a radio station so they could broadcast to the world how awful prison conditions were in Texas.

2. They both wanted a hamburger and French fries, which drove home for me just how horrible conditions must be in the Lone Star state prison system. As I told our chief negotiator, Dwayne Fuselier, I would have at least asked for a great bottle of red wine, knowing that I was never, ever, ever going to be released from prison again once this was over—even rarely released from solitary confinement where the meal and beverage choices are severely limited.

But a deal's a deal, so we got them the best burgers and fries we could find within reason. We also found the least-listened-to radio show at the worst possible hour for broadcasting, and at 1:00 a.m. the next morning the Texas Two described the horrors of their incarceration to an audience that the show's host generously estimated at "about six people." I was not among those six, I should add, much as I wanted to listen. For law enforcement in situations such as this, phones never stop chiming, reports have to be filed, and spectator status is almost unheard-of, something the media rarely seems to understand. For the Texas Seven, though, the 1:00 a.m. little noted cri de coeur was the end of it, and basically of them. In addition to the one gang member who had taken his own life at the trailer park, four have since been electrocuted and two, as of this writing, remain on death row.

There is, however, a final chapter to this tale.

At this point, it was about two in the morning, and I had been up for a little over seventy-two hours—which I do not recommend under any conditions but especially not if your backup public information officer, Jane Quimby in this case, has been besieged by interview requests and is leaning on you to agree to at least a few of them. Apparently, the Texas Seven takedown was very quickly blossoming into a leading national news story.

"No, no, no," I kept telling Jane. "I'm too tired, I haven't had a shower in days, and this is generally not my best look."

"Please, please, please," she kept saying in return. "This is a great moment for the Bureau. Let's celebrate it."

Finally, we compromised. I would do one interview, but it would be big-time: one of the national morning shows, although I can no longer remember which one. In fact, I was going to lead the show, at 7:00 a.m. Eastern Standard Time, which translated to 5:00 a.m. Mountain Standard Time where I was, which meant I had to race to the studio in Denver with the window down in two-degree weather so I wouldn't fall asleep at the wheel. And thus, less than five hours after the final Texas Two had been arrested, I found myself alone in a room with my hat hair, rumpled clothes, and probably half a frost burn on my face, waiting for the host's introduction to end and her first question to pop into my earpiece, and you'll probably never guess what it was.

"Why did they dye their hair orange?"

Honestly. Prison officers had practically had their skulls bashed in during this escape. Customers and clerks had been terrorized at two stores back in Texas. An officer had been killed in one of the robberies. Dozens of law enforcement officials had risked their own lives to finally bring this arrest about. And the burning question in America's mind was: Why did these guys dye their hair orange? Whatever producer was whispering in the host's earpiece must have had a similar feeling, because she quickly moved on to question two: "And where did the Texas Seven break out of?"

Uh, Texas? Okay, admittedly I was utterly exhausted.

I was still exhausted four hours later when I boarded a flight to California to join Dale and our friends for the tail end of what was to have been our festive mini-vacation, and I had no hope of catching up even two hours of my lost sleep in the air because, at least back then, I was an alert/vigilant flier, always ready to help the pilot with any air bumps, takeoffs, landings, etc. Also, as a LEO, as law enforcement officers are sometimes known, I was obliged to identify myself to the crew and, since the FBI did have jurisdiction in the air, stay on the alert just in case. For that reason I always insisted on an aisle seat so I wouldn't have to scramble over fellow passengers if push came to shove somewhere in flight.

This time was somewhat different, though. I happily settled into a window seat, admired the view of the tarmac for maybe a New York minute, then fell deeply and immediately asleep. When I awoke, everyone had deplaned and the flight attendants were hovering over me, trying to decide what to do.

"Oh my God," one of them finally said. "We thought maybe you'd had a seizure!"

"No seizure," I assured them, "but it's been an interesting few days."

The next year would be more interesting still, in far worse ways.

21.
9/11

EVEN BY THE STANDARDS OF an FBI life, 9/11 was insane.

I had been in Miami for the several weeks before, heading up an internal investigation into a messy shooting. This was another checklist item on the FBI career ladder. As an ASAC, I was required to serve as inspector in charge of at least three field investigations at offices other than my own before I could be eligible to serve as special agent in charge.

We finished our work that weekend, but there still were reports to write, so I called headquarters for guidance and was told either I could stay in Florida and finish the work without the distractions of the Denver office or I could head home and steal time from the office as best I could. For me, that was a no-brainer. I was longing for a night in my own bed and to be with Dale.

I flew into Denver on Monday, September 10, 2001, left word that I would be out of the office the next few days, working at home, and slept soundly (for me) that night. On the morning of the eleventh, I woke up, made a cup of coffee, cleared work space on the kitchen table for preparing the report, and turned on the TV to catch up on the news just in time to see a replay of American Airlines Flight 11 crashing into floors ninety-three to ninety-nine of the World Trade Center's North Tower. The whirlwind had begun.

Dale had worked an all-nighter doing surveillance. We had barely talked at all before he tumbled into bed and fell deeply asleep. That was only a few hours earlier. I hated to wake him, but how could I not?

"Get up!" I said, shaking him hard. "Get up! We're under attack!"

"*What?*"

But we were, and the whole nation was watching it in real time.

I found it nearly impossible to leave the TV that morning—I felt I would be disrespecting the Americans who were dying wholesale in New York and, soon afterward, at the Pentagon and in Pennsylvania if I turned away from the horror—but I had no choice. The special agent in charge of the Denver office was once again gone, in New York City this time, again on Bureau business and unable to return until commercial flights were resumed. That put me in charge, and I obviously couldn't do this remotely. But it might have been the longest drive to the office I've ever taken, not in hours but in the emotional toll of it all.

I'm not a crier, except if it involves animals. (I've never entirely recovered from my grandparents taking me to see *Old Yeller* when I was way too young to handle it.) But I cried the entire thirty-five minutes or so it took to get to the office, hard enough that I probably should have pulled over, but by now I was stoked as much with adrenaline as with grief, and my mind, maybe inevitably, kept going to darker and darker places.

We were just getting the first glimpses of who was behind this, but it wasn't hard to project the ideology that underlay the attack. If the Pentagon had been hit, then surely the White House would have been targeted, along with the Capitol and the Supreme Court—the three seats of our democracy. If New York, probably all of Los Angeles, too: The spoils of capitalism were on rich display in both places. And if LA, why not Vegas? What better symbol of Western decadence?

I had yet to visit Israel, but a number of my law enforcement colleagues had gone over there to study how the Israelis were dealing with terrorism—the frequent attacks, blowing up a shopping mall, shooting up a restaurant, the constant vigilance. *That's going to be our new normal,* I kept thinking. Law enforcement life as we had known it was over.

Within hours of arriving at the office, we had our emergency command post fully operational and, along with every other field office, were chasing leads in all imaginable directions. Simultaneously, we were having to adjust our mindsets to possibilities we couldn't previously grasp: that people would turn the stuff of our daily life—commercial airplanes—into weapons of near mass destruction, that religious beliefs could be twisted to such evil ends.

The soon-to-be-famous FBI Phoenix memorandum, written by my fellow agent Ken Williams, had presciently questioned why all these Middle Eastern flight students were learning to fly planes but didn't seem much interested in how to land one. In hindsight, the answer to that was obvious, but prior to 9/11 we lacked the ability to even imagine what it might be. Now it was hard to stop imagining what else that might portend. I can't tell you how many hours I slept over the next seventy-two hours, but they were few and uneasy, and all on my office couch, wearing the same clothes hour after hour, day after day.

Finally, on day four, I thought: *This is the wrong example to set.* As long as I refused to go home and get some much-needed rest, no one else in the emergency command post would do so, either. So, with an encouraging flourish, I waved goodbye, drove home, and that's where I learned that (a) all nineteen hijackers had been in Las Vegas at the same time, (b) the Las Vegas Division was short on experienced personnel to take over what was sure to be a focal center of the 9/11 investigation, and (c) I was being sent to Las Vegas to run the newest, most major case in the history of the Las Vegas office. So much for that good night's sleep.

By the time I arrived, the small Vegas office was being augmented with twenty-two additional agents out of Los Angeles, and every one of them was needed. The immediate perpetrators of the crime were all dead, but their trail was still hot and littered with leads. Mohamed Atta and the others had made little effort to hide their identities or cover their tracks. That was part of the in-your-face side of 9/11, just as the date 911 itself was: Emergency! Emergency!

I set up a major-case board—basically a wall-size chalkboard—and I and Brent Braun, who had come on as a supervisor out of LA, began assigning leads, and leads that grew from those leads, and so on it seemed sometimes ad infinitum.

Within days, almost nonstop, we were rounding up "people of interest": associates of the perpetrators, casual acquaintances, anyone known to have once brushed shoulders with them. Famously secretive Vegas hotels threw open their guest registers for us—and their hotel room doors. We were working faster than search warrants could be issued, but we did our damnedest to keep up with them as best we could, and under the circumstances everyone was cutting us at least a little slack.

Numbers mattered. Our goal was to interview enough secondary players to begin forming a thorough backstory to the attacks. But reliability was key as well, and we had no sure way to sift our interviewees' facts from their fiction. Polygraphs aren't admissible as evidence in any event, but they can at least help you figure out the broad brushstrokes of events. However, polygraphs work only with subjects who have a conscience and exhibit some kind of emotional response when they lie or get nervous about events in which they have been involved. Far from being ashamed or conscience stricken, many of those we were interviewing, especially those closest to the hijackers, were proud of their associations; they wore them as a badge of honor. Even outright lies to our questions were unlikely to register.

The same applied to non-verbal communication. Normally, the eyes give away a treasure trove of information in interviews: Blinks, flinches, averted eyes—they're all an ongoing road map to truth, evasion, and emotional state. But we were dealing often with people who have been culturally trained not to look you in the eye during a conversation. Barring extralegal means—and we weren't going there—we had almost no way to exploit the potentially valuable sources we had gathered up.

Twice a day initially, there were also two-hour phone calls that linked Las Vegas with other offices following similar leads, and linked us all with Tom Pickard, back to being deputy director after a brief tour as acting director following Louis Freeh's resignation and before Robert S. Mueller's appointment to the post on September 4, 2001. The calls eventually backed down to about an hour per, but this was still unheard-of connectivity for the Bureau.

Meanwhile, I was working on the link analysis that would connect all four of the aerial attacks. Obviously, they were all related, but knowing that and being able to prove it to a Foreign Intelligence Surveillance Act (FISA) court and other vital agencies are two different things, and timing was of the absolute essence.

As opportunity allowed, too, I would check in with Dale. We already knew Denver had several suspected terrorist sleeper cells. Not all the nineteen hijackers had passed through Denver, but most had. Was that a coincidence, or had the sleeper cells become active, or were they about to? Remember, these were days of infinite possibilities. Dale was asked to set up a special surveillance operations group in Denver to keep a eye on the cells and their members around the clock. More important, at his insistence, Dale was given permission to pick his own team members. Historically, surveillance teams in the Bureau were a dumping ground—or, when I first joined the FBI, a place to warehouse women. Dale brought in a first-rate team, many former military like himself; talked his way into multiple vehicles and other resources; and dogged those sleeper cells as they had never been dogged before. In the end, his team was probably the only special operations group in the country allowed to actually make an arrest—a big deal in Bureau culture, as I've stressed before, usually reserved for SWAT teams and case agents. But these were dangerously different times.

For everyone the hours were punishing, to say the least. To break them up, Brent and I and one or two others decided we would eat dinner out and together every night. No Jack in the Box for us. But even then we would talk nonstop about the case. There was literally no escape—in the real world or, almost worse, in my own imagination. The dark place I had gone to right after 9/11 kept getting darker the deeper we burrowed into the case.

The big show was over, I figured: The terrorists were done with airplanes. Now came the long game, the one that would convince Americans that we were no longer safe anywhere within our own borders. I imagined hundreds of suicide bombers scattered throughout the United States but concentrated more in the heartland, not in major population centers where you might most expect them. After all, Timothy McVeigh had shocked America by making his twisted statement in Oklahoma City, not in Chicago or New York, or DC, where the body count might have been even worse.

I didn't have to close my eyes long to imagine a string of suicide bombings and shootings in Iowa strip malls, Arkansas bus stations, an assisted-living center somewhere on the western edge of Missouri, a high school football game in rural Texas where no one in town who wasn't bedridden would dare not be in attendance. Police departments in one-horse towns would be overwhelmed. Communication would be halting at best. People were going to be begging for help, and there wouldn't be nearly enough to go around. None of that happened, thank God, but in the world in which I then lived, we could never assume anything was a one-and-done attack, and of course, in a larger sense, it wasn't. We Americans live with 9/11 still.

BY THEN, TOO, THE USUAL carping and second-guessing had crept back onto center stage. Was the FBI blind to have missed the Phoenix memorandum? (No, as I explained earlier, but nothing previous in American life had given us the imaginative capacity to correctly interpret the information.) Simultaneously, the media and Congress were all over the Bureau and the CIA for not sharing information. *There they go again,* the chorus went, *hoarding information while Osama bin Laden sits chuckling in his cave.* No one seemed to realize that the CIA couldn't share the intelligence it gathered with the FBI without going through an FISA court—no one, in this case, including some of the same members of Congress who had built that wall a quarter century earlier in 1978. And until the morning of September 11, 2001, there was no probable cause for the FISA court to allow such intelligence swapping.

Maybe I was blinded by institutional loyalty or deadened by exhaustion, but I didn't see people in those weeks after 9/11 scrambling to protect their turf or their reputations. I didn't see institutions at war or playing hide-and-seek with vital information. What I saw was different. I saw women and men working eighteen hours a day, day after day, until you had to beg them to take a weekend or even a day off. I saw agents wringing every drop of knowledge they could out of tidbits of information almost microscopically small. I saw a myriad of organizations—from tiny local sheriffs' offices to the giant Bureau—work together for a common cause, on a common mission, in ways I had never witnessed before and would never witness again. I saw pride and patriotism, a country that had been grievously attacked responding as one nation indivisible. And, yes, even amidst the smoldering ruins and horrible loss left behind by 9/11, it was a beautiful sight.

22.
TRAILER TRASH

JULY 4, 2002, HAD ALL the makings of a special day. Eleven months earlier, America had been knocked to the canvas by Osama bin Laden and his minions—down and almost out. Now America was back on its feet and bin Laden was on the run. It would take another nine years to finish that job, but the country had some swagger once again. We were ready to celebrate the nation's birthday without fearing that another attack waited around every corner.

Professionally, too, this was a sweet time. After a short but intense detour to what I had come to think of as "corporate" back at FBI headquarters in DC—more about this later—I had been named special agent in charge of one of the Bureau's prime field offices: Los Angeles. Despite the impressive title, I was only second-in-command. LA, Chicago, and New York each had an extra-level top dog known as the assistant director in charge, or ADIC in FBI terminology. (Pronounced as two words, "a" and "dick." Frustrated agents could grumble quite accurately, "That so-and-so is such A-DIC!")

Fortunately, my ADIC, Ron Iden, was a great guy who would eventually head up worldwide security for Disney. What's more, I had more than enough under my purview to keep me busy and happy: espionage; counterintelligence; counterterrorism; the SWAT team (including Dale) and evidence response team;

the rapid-deployment team, which was helping out as needed in Afghanistan; coordination with my old colleagues at Quantico; and on and on. For a woman who likes a long to-do list, this was near heaven.

Even better, it was glaringly obvious to me that our LA office was severely underutilized. We had so much talent there, so many good agents, so much potential for growth, and I could imagine a clear path forward for me to make that happen: Ron would leave (which he did). I would replace him as ADIC (ironically, given the way it was pronounced). Headquarters would begin cutting us in for our fair share of the Bureau budget, and I would end my law enforcement career near where it had begun. (Little of that actually happened, but, hey, it's nice to dream.)

Finally, there was the personal side of things. My mother was still in Upland and not getting any younger. Now that Dale and I were back in Southern California, I could pamper her in person instead of checking in by phone from distant spots all around the country as I had been doing ever since leaving San Diego. As an early down payment on that vow, Dale and I had planned out a laid-back Independence Day weekend with Mom right at the center. And then, at 11:30 a.m. on July 4 at Los Angeles International Airport, Hesham Mohamed Ali Hadayet pulled out a .45-caliber Glock semiautomatic pistol and opened fire on customers and staff at the El Al ticket counter, and our family moment came to an abrupt end.

Ron Iden, of course, was away and inaccessible—*the A-DIC!* I had to assume command.

IT'S USUALLY (BUT NOT ALWAYS) true that the application of deadly force at the appropriate time produces the best results in highly volatile situations, and that was certainly the case at the El Al ticket counter that morning. Hesham Mohamed Ali Hadayet had shown up not only with his Glock semiautomatic but also with a second 9-millimeter gun in his pocket, along with an extra ammunition clip and a six-inch hunting knife. Before anyone had time to react, he had already shot and killed Victoria Hen, a twenty-five-year-old native Israeli, and forty-six-year-old Yaakov Aminov, a California jeweler who was saying goodbye to a friend headed to Israel. But the killing ended there, far short of where it might have.

As an El Al security guard grabbed Hadayet's arm, Haim Sapir, the airline's head of security, stepped out from behind the counter, shot Hadayet once, then shot him again as he continued to struggle. Sapir himself was shot, not fatally, before Hadayet exhausted his ten-round clip and died shortly thereafter.

Purely from a crime containment point of view, this case was over and done with by the time I arrived on the scene. The dead were dead, the wounded were being treated, the crime scene had been carefully taped and preserved, and the perpetrator would never need to be brought to trial or imprisoned if found guilty, and he would never linger on death row. That was already taken care of. But the circus, trust me, was just beginning.

Almost all law enforcement agencies of any size have mobile command centers. You have to lead from the site, issue orders in real time, meet with the media, and coordinate with other agencies as needed. As a rule, the bigger the law enforcement agency, the bigger and better the mobile command center, and the shootings at LAX, as you might expect, had attracted some of the biggest agencies of them all—federal, state, and local. The LAPD was set up in a beautiful million-dollar bus on-site, along with a bunch of others. The part of the airport parking lot reserved for command centers looked like a kind of crisis-oriented Rodeo Drive.

With one exception: the FBI. We can reasonably claim to be the leading law enforcement agency in the whole world. Our

Los Angeles office was a key part of that, and on July 4, 2002, we rolled into the secure parking lot area in our very own command center—a slightly converted and somewhat aged Winnebago trailer that had been kindly donated to the office.

"Where should I park it?" the driver asked me.

"Out of sight!" was all I could answer, but I was already hearing the theme song from *The Beverly Hillbillies* playing in my ear. Jed Clampett would be pulling his rickety wagon up beside us any minute now, fresh from the Ozarks.

In any event, we didn't get the mobile command center out of sight soon enough because the phone rang before we could escape.

"What in the hell is that?" headquarters wanted to know, having just seen the Winnebago identified on national TV as the FBI's very own.

"It's the command center we have because you won't find us a million dollars to get a decent one," I barked back, deep into bus envy.

"Well, don't let the media inside it."

"Don't worry," I said, "there's no room for them."

Instead, with the great help of the LAX airport police, I set up a media center inside the airport itself and brought in a wonderful public information officer, Voviette Morgan, to get a handle on a story that was spinning out of control in multiple directions and establish a cadence to our media briefings and a logic to who we made available for interviews and when. That first day I worked straight through the night until 7:00 a.m., went home to shower and sleep a few hours, then was back to work through the night the next day, too. Bobbi did the same. Her job was to manage the media. Mine, basically, was to take the heat, and there was understandably plenty of it.

Some media outlets, along with assorted Capitol Hill poohbahs, random talking heads, and op-ed pundits, seemed horrified that there had been armed El Al officials on the other side of the ticket counter even though the official in question had undoubtedly saved a dozen or more lives by acting when and how he did.

Was Haim Sapir a Mossad agent? I was asked, referring to the Israeli equivalent of the CIA. I had no idea, I could honestly answer, but it seemed likely he had been trained by counterterrorism specialists, since he had the good sense and courage to take the fight directly to the perpetrator.

Was this the future of air travel? Garrisoned ticket counters? Armed guards masquerading as check-in specialists? Guns everywhere? I couldn't answer that, either, or say what I really thought: Almost nobody wants that until the moment before his or her life depends on a check-in clerk or a baggage handler or front-of-the-queue greeter who knows his or her way around a weapon that will drop a would-be killer cold in his tracks.

Those kinds of issues would eventually die down. What wouldn't go away was the $64,000 question: Was Hesham Mohammed Ali Hadayet a terrorist and was this a terrorist attack? As the *New York Times* put it in the headline for its front-page story on July 6, two days after the attack: "Officials Puzzled About Motive of Airport Gunman Who Killed 2."

Part of that confusion was the old problem of nuance and exact classification. Hadayet was an Egyptian and a Muslim who appeared to hold anti-Israeli views. One of the former employees of his limousine service told *Times* reporters that Hadayet had informed him that "the Israelis tried to destroy the Egyptian nation and the Egyptian population by sending prostitutes with AIDS to Egypt." Add to that the fact that he had traveled heavily armed to the ticket counter of an Israeli airline and opened fire once he got there, and it would seem likely that he had targeted Jews and was intent on killing them.

But, the *Times* and other news sources reported, Hadayet also appeared to have been personally stressed. His limousine company had suffered in the post-9/11 travel lapse; his marriage had possibly been unraveling under other pressures—his wife and children were back in Egypt when he assaulted the El Al counter—and July 4 was his own birthday, not just America's. Severe depression and birthdays are often not a happy match.

To complicate matters still more, even with the two deaths and suffering he had caused, Hadayet had not been particularly successful by terrorist terms. If anything, it looked like a win for the Israelis. Unsurprisingly, none of the usual terrorism support groups—Al Qaeda, Hamas, etc.—had rushed forward to embrace the Egyptian or claim him as their own.

A crime committed by a morbidly depressed man might be a hate crime, or it could be a hate crime coupled with suicidal impulses or intent, but neither of those conditions necessarily made it an act of terrorism or Hadayet a terrorist, especially in the absence of an acknowledged terrorist sponsor. And here is where criminal, mental health, and geopolitical issues dovetailed with partisan and institutional concerns and made managing the story even more difficult.

As various members of the House Judiciary Committee's Subcommittee on Immigration, Border Security, and Claims pointed out in an October 2002 hearing on Hadayet and his terrorism connections, the Immigration and Naturalization Service (INS) had granted Hadayet political asylum in 1992 even though the Egyptian government contended that he was a member of an Islamic extremist group known as al-Gama'a al-Islamiyya. Nor had the CIA or FBI ever done a criminal background check on this Egyptian, who had entered the United States under a cloud, at least. Did the INS know its rear end from third base? How many more potential Hesham Hadayets had the Bureau and the Agency let slip into the country? And incidentally, why is Congress funding INS, the FBI, and CIA at these budget-busting levels?

Questions like that got to be almost commonplace in the aftermath of the El Al attack, but they were far from easy to answer, frankly, without stumbling over the Bureau and Justice Department's own story line, which was in effect that we didn't know what the heck had happened. While a preliminary report by the FBI had labeled Hadayet a terrorist, the Department of Justice's *FY 2002 Performance and Accountability Report* listed no "terrorist acts committed by foreign nationals against U.S. interests within U.S. borders" and further noted that "the reported numbers were compiled through the expert knowledge of FBI counterterrorism senior management at FBI headquarters." (The 2001 report listed four such attacks, counting each human-bomb plane as a separate terrorist attack—weird accounting, arguably.)

Not until April 2003—nine months after the El Al shootings—did Justice and the FBI officially agree that the July 4, 2002, attack fit the "definition of terrorism," and we could officially refer to it as what it had seemed to be from day one. With that, the case could finally be put to rest, and the LA office could turn to other matters, including admiring its brand-new, million-dollar, deluxe bus command center. Headquarters' embarrassment at seeing our ratty Winnebago roll into the LAX parking lot on national TV was apparently and happily terminal.

23.
CRIME AND PUNISHMENT

EARLIER, I WROTE THAT THE Rogers murders—the Ohio mother and two daughters raped and thrown overboard in Tampa Bay— was the only case in which I got "something close to closure." "Something close" is the key phrase there. If I had wanted full closure, I could have been at the Florida State Prison at Raiford when the Rogerses' murderer, Oba Chandler, was executed for his crimes twenty-one years after committing them.

They don't just sell tickets to executions. You have to be invited, but I could have easily arranged that. I even thought about trying to do so—about being a proxy for the three women who couldn't be there and for the other all-but-certain victims of the monstrous Chandler. In the end, though, I couldn't do it.

Part of it, I think, was fear of reawakening memories that never really go away. You need to see only one hideously bloated corpse pulled out of the water to have that image etched forever in some dark corner of your cerebral cortex. To see three, then to learn they were family and finally how they had been assaulted and brutalized, stays with you as long as you breathe. All you can really do is keep those images and that knowledge as dormant as possible.

Part of my reluctance was also tied to an episode of the original *Law & Order* that I first saw in May 1996, just when the corruption investigation was heating up in San Diego, and have watched more than once since. The episode—"Aftershock," the closer of season six—opens with a man strapped on a gurney, getting fitted with an IV, in what looks to be a small examination room. Only slowly do you realize this is inside a prison and the prelude to an execution.

A prison official asks the man on the gurney what to do with the curtain at the end of room.

"Open it," he says defiantly, and there in the viewing room on the other side of the glass, along with a handful of others, are the major cast members of *Law & Order*—Detectives Lennie Briscoe and Rey Curtis, and Jack McCoy and Claire Kincaid from the district attorney's office, the crew that put this guy away in the first place, now come to Attica Prison to witness what I couldn't do.

"Want to say anything?" the Attica official asks, and again the man spits out his words: "Do it!"

With that, a mixture of chemicals is released, and within what seems no more than twenty seconds the man has flatlined—a remarkably serene death, especially for an execution technique that does not always turn out so well in real life.

Later, back in the city, Rey explains to his fellow squad members that there was nothing to it: "He just twitched. Closed his eyes. Case closed."

Except, of course, it's not.

Rey is soon roughing up a punk thug who has been mouthing off to one of his partners. Jack McCoy, the executive assistant DA, has a stiff drink with lunch, then heads straight to a working-class bar, where he can't seem to stop drinking more and talking about his beat-cop father. I had the beginnings of a hangover just watching him throw 'em down.

Claire, the junior DA, pleads the flu on the way back to the office and takes the day off—except she goes to see her former law professor Mac, who also happens to be her father, instead of going home.

Claire is clearly staggered by what she witnessed and hoping for sympathy, but she doesn't get any. Instead, Mac tells her she went to Attica to show off her sense of moral superiority. That wasn't it, Claire counters; it was conviction, a sense of duty that she had to see this case through to the very end. Still, she adds, "What happened up there this morning is going to stick with me for the rest of my life."

Those words sent a chill through my bones, but it was the closing moment of Lennie Briscoe's long, painful sit-down with his adult daughter that really got to me.

"It's just . . . I see dead people all the time, only they're already dead when I see them. . . . This morning, I watched a guy get killed, and there wasn't anything I was supposed to do about it. I don't know. I guess I'm better when they're already dead."

When I first heard that, I was less than a year removed from an office decorated with images of corpses.

And then there was Ted Bundy's execution on January 24, 1989, at Florida's State Prison in Raiford. I wasn't invited to that one, either, but I was in Tampa at the time and happened to be driving to work as one of the local radio stations was broadcasting live from a pasture across from the prison. Within seconds of Bundy's death, at 7:16 a.m., the hundreds of people who had gathered at the pasture began to cheer and sing and dance as fireworks exploded around them, and they kept cheering until a white hearse had carried Bundy's body away and even afterward. The disconnect between the two—the solemn business of state-sanctioned murder and all this gleeful cheering—got to me in a way I hadn't expected—so strongly, in fact, that I had to pull over to the side of the road and compose myself before driving on.

We humans are capable of wonderful empathy, amazing acts of kindness and charity. At our best, we love our neighbors as ourselves and do unto others as we would have them do unto us. But we humans are also capable individually and collectively of barbarous behavior, and this seemed—in the moment—a prime example of that capacity for barbarity. Instead of uttering a silent prayer for all the women Ted Bundy had murdered in cold blood, I found myself thinking of Roman gladiators battling to the death, cheered on by the bloodlust of some crazed Colosseum crowd.

DON'T MISUNDERSTAND. I GET THE economic argument for not warehousing prisoners who have no hope of ever being outside those four walls again. New York and California spend about $70,000 annually per inmate, regardless of the crime for which they are incarcerated. Add further to that the extra $90,000 spent annually per death row prisoner, and you're into very serious money. Imagine what you could do if those funds were put toward, say, improved public housing, community colleges, women's health, and the like. Serial killers can't keep themselves from the dark side. Since there's no way to let them back into society, why not eliminate them permanently from it? Dead men don't dismember their victims or have sex with their dead bodies and then go looking for more and more and more of them. (Put another way, execution eliminates recidivism.)

I also understand better than most, I assure you, the public safety argument for eliminating the very most dangerous among us from the general population, and doing so permanently. Maximum security is not total security—Ted Bundy escaped more than once—and a Ted Bundy or Ed Kemper who went into prison a serial killer is going to come out of prison, if he gets the chance, and resume serial killing. That's what makes life meaningful for people bent that way, and there's not a prison rehabilitation program in the world that is going to change that. The compulsion to murder is too strong. The thrill is too alluring. The sheer joy of watching their victims suffer is too baked into their very existence.

By the common understanding of psychosis, Bundy, Kemper, Dahmer, and the others would appear to be way over the line—totally certifiable, ready for the nuthouse—but more strictly defined, "psychosis" is a severe mental disorder characterized by thoughts and emotions so impaired that contact is lost with external reality. That's the legal threshold you have to meet for an insanity plea, and far from losing contact with external reality, serial killers are able to commit their crimes serially—i.e., over often extended time—precisely because they are so thoroughly *in contact* with the world around them.

Not to insult people who rob 7-Elevens, but they mostly act spontaneously, often under the influence of drugs or out of the need for them. Frequently, they don't even wear a mask or otherwise disguise themselves. They just pull a gun on the attendant, take whatever is in the till, and try to beat it out the door before the police arrive.

Serial killers are precisely the opposite: They do horrible things, yes, but as a rule they put enormous premeditation into each one and go to great lengths not to get caught after they commit it, and they tend to learn on the job. Like a lot of serial killers, Ted Bundy became more sophisticated as the dead bodies mounted up behind him. Bundy manually strangled his first victim. After that, he used a ligature specially designed for the purpose to strangle the women from behind. In what he called his "predator mode," Bundy not only preselected his victims and often prepared the body disposal site in advance; he also had his flight plan, alibi, and evidence disposal strategy decided upon before he ever approached the target.

Bundy favored full moons because he liked to see his victims die. Afterward, he would bury them at least two feet deep and cover the graves with rocks to keep predators from digging up the remains. If he had severed the head, as he often did, he would often bury that elsewhere or toss it into a body of water along with the victim's clothing and any other identifying items. It wasn't uncommon for him to disperse evidence hundreds of miles from the torso. He also followed press accounts of his murders closely, especially any accounts of evidence, suspects, or leads. Once, he destroyed a box of Polaroid photos of his victims after he had seen his own name possibly connected with the murders.

None of this makes Ted Bundy or any of the other serial killers profiled in these pages almost-Einsteins, but securing victims, choosing sites to commit their murders, disposing of victims in inventive ways to minimize the risk of discovery—these are intellectual as well as physical tasks. They require a logical train of thought. The higher the IQ, the better the chance that you will get to murder again. Ed Kemper, for one, was so good at it that he had to call the police *twice* to convince them to drive a thousand miles in order to haul him in. Ted Bundy's courtroom self-defense was so tightly reasoned that the judge lamented that Bundy hadn't gone to law school instead of murdering dozens of coeds.

The capacity to reason and adapt to circumstances, coupled with a savage and murderous appetite, is all the evidence necessary never to let someone like Bundy or Kemper loose on the world again.

I ALSO FIRMLY BELIEVE THAT the punishment should fit the crime, but to fit the crimes of the kind of people we dealt with at the BSU would require a level of grotesque inhumanity that I hope is beyond our collective capacity. How, for example, do you construct a punishment that would fit the crimes of Charles Ng, who has lingered now for more than two decades on death row at California's San Quentin State Prison?

In February 1999, Ng was convicted on eleven counts of homicide—six men, three women, and two male infants—but that barely begins to tell the story. Ng and Leonard Lake, his partner in the murders, sometimes abducted whole families, killed the men and children in short order, then locked the women in a cinder-block bunker behind Lake's cabin in the foothills of California's Sierra Nevada mountain range, about an hour's drive from Sacramento. Once captured and confined, they submitted the women to endless psychological torture while using them, as Lake put it in a homemade video, as "off-the-shelf sex partner(s). I want to be able to use a woman whenever and however I want, and when I'm tired or bored or not interested, I simply want to put her away, lock her up in a room, get her out of my sight, and out of my life."

Lake says this, by the way, via a home video, while lying at his ease on a recliner in his cabin, in a voice every bit as flat and without affect and creepy as Ed Kemper's or Jeffrey Dahmer's ever was in their recorded interviews. In another of his videos, Lake lays out the ground rules for one of the captive females: "While you're here, we'll keep you busy. You'll wash for us. You'll clean for us, cook for us. You'll fuck for us. That's your choice in a nutshell. It's not much of a choice unless you have a death wish."

But no amount of complying with the house rules and satisfying their masters availed for long. In roughly a year, the two murdered a minimum of eleven people, judging by the forty-five pounds of incinerated and crushed human remains found at a burial site near the bunker and maybe as many as twenty-five more as measured by a cache of identification cards and other items also uncovered at the site and nude photos taped to the walls of the bunker.

This might have gone on for years if Ng's kleptomania— he shoplifted a seventy-five-dollar vise at a San Francisco lumberyard—hadn't tipped police to the pair. But even then Ng escaped while police were collaring Lake and eventually made his way to Canada, where he was arrested after another shoplifting escapade (a can of salmon this time) and shooting a security guard while resisting arrest. The arrest, though, was only a blip in what by now seems an almost endless saga. It took six years just to get Ng extradited back to the States so he could stand trial—his lawyers fought extradition on the grounds that Canada has no death penalty for most crimes—and another seven years to bring him to trial in California and find him guilty of his crimes. Twenty-three years later, as I write this, he still lingers on death row.

To go back to my earlier question: How do you even begin to match crime and punishment in a case like this? No punishment can fit crimes of such massive cruelty and committed in such abundance without civilization going over to the dark side. Leonard Lake, actually, might offer an answer.

After Ng's lumberyard shoplifting, Lake was arrested and booked on an illegal-weapons charge. That was small potatoes—an unregistered gun was found in the trunk of his car—but Lake had no trouble foreseeing the larger dangers waiting just ahead. Not only were his various IDs phony; they all came from people who had been reporting missing, some for months. Police were sure to investigate his cabin, and he knew what they would find.

At the station house, he asked for a pen and sheet of paper. Police left him alone in an interrogation room so he could write his letter, and while there Lake fished out a cyanide capsule he'd sewn into his clothing for just such an occasion, swallowed it, and died four days later.

Maybe all the Ngs and Lakes and Kempers and Bundys and Dahmers to come should be offered a similar opportunity. Not at booking—that's a confused and emotional time—but after the jury has come in with its verdict, after they've had to witness the stark reality of what they have done, after they now know what lies ahead. Give them five minutes alone in a room, with a sheet of paper and a pen, and a small bowl containing one cyanide capsule, or whatever might be even faster and surer. And let them go through at least some hint of the psychological torture they put their victims through: choosing between life in a prison cell that decidedly does not cost $100,000-plus a year to maintain and service or an end to it all. I feel certain Aileen Wuornos would have no problem with that decision. She would swallow the capsule, glad to be rid of the killing and the pain. But she, of course, was a woman.

All this is my way of saying that while I have always been an advocate for capital punishment, I increasingly find myself in the throes of indecision. It's no longer black-and-white to me, no longer certain to me that capital punishment as we currently practice it fits the capital crimes the punishment is meant to rectify. That's a seat of judgment we mortals might not want to occupy.

24.
PHISHING TRIP

AS YOU HAVE PROBABLY SURMISED by now, an upwardly mobile
FBI career path in my day was full of twists and turns, cross-
country moves, and sudden assignments that could involve months
of hotel living far from home. (When people asked me where I
lived, I was often tempted to answer, "No fixed address.") The big
ambition on the operational side of the Bureau was to become an
SAC, or special agent in charge, at one of the field offices, but the
time frame for getting there was tight, given the mandatory retirement age of fifty-seven and all the hoops you were expected to
jump through before you could be considered for an SAC slot. In
fact, the only way you could really qualify for consideration was to
do two or three jobs at the same time.

My time as assistant special agent in charge (ASAC) at the
Denver office was typical. After multiple weeks in Miami super-
vising an inspection into a shooting incident, I returned to Denver
just before 9/11 struck and was immediately detailed to Las Vegas
only days after the attack to head up an investigation of all the
suspects who had lived there prior to the hijackings and terrible
deaths. When that duty wound down, I assumed I would resume
my post as ASAC in Denver. Instead, I was sent to Washington to
help with the investigation into the 9/11 attack on the Pentagon—
code-named PENTBOMB—but before I could even report for

that, I was yanked away again, to rescue the Bureau's huge computer upgrade program that had been code-named PROJECT TRILOGY. (Within the FBI, the program was widely known as PROJECT TRAGEDY and might also have been called PROJECT TAKE THE MONEY AND RUN, since a lack of oversight and general mismanagement had produced cost overruns in the many millions of dollars.)

If the PROJECT TRILOGY posting had required actual computer knowledge, I would have been completely at sea. Moreover, if we had looked inside the Bureau for help just a few years earlier, my job might have been handed to Robert Philip Hanssen, the infamous Soviet mole who was widely considered the FBI's go-to computer guy until it became apparent he was using the Bureau's ambient tech ignorance to rob the place blind. But the job had already been contracted out to external vendors, and my job was to manage them, stop the bleeding, and ensure that whatever system they came up with would be user-friendly enough for an agent workforce that still circled desktops and keyboards cautiously, as if afraid they might rear up and bite them. We didn't need to reinvent the wheel, but we desperately needed to get all four tires back on the rims and fully inflated.

To that end, I put together an in-house team of computer experts—twelve agents, all male since that was still mostly the state of computer education/experience then—and together we did a mess of field interviews with the people in the trenches who would actually be using and depending on whatever systems we came up with. Collectively, I think we can claim that we had successfully nudged the FBI ever so reluctantly at least into the opening years of the new century. Director Robert Mueller must have felt the same way because my next posting was to the Los Angeles office as special agent in charge: the SAC slot I had been shooting for, and practically in my hometown after all that roaming around.

The Monroes—Dale and Jana—with FBI Director Bob Mueller, who had just asked me to head up the Bureau's new Cyber Division.

But as the old saying holds: No good deed goes unpunished— or at least that's what I first thought when Mueller subsequently offered me what should have been my dream FBI job of all time.

I DON'T KNOW WHERE I picked up this statistic, but I love it: Eighty-five percent of women will not take a job unless they can meet eighty-five percent of the requirements in the job description, whereas eighty-five of percent men *will* take the job if they meet only twenty-five percent of the job requirements.

Is it social conditioning spread out over generations that accounts for the stark difference? Are men just inherently more confident or more willing to fake it or less concerned about failing? I have no idea, but I intuitively believe those numbers to be on the mark, and I proved as much (to myself, at least) when Bob Mueller, then the new director of the FBI, interviewed me to head up the soon-to-be-established Cyber Division of the Bureau.

Being a division assistant director in the FBI is a big deal for anyone, and it was especially so in those days for a woman. For an operational division like Cyber—Crime and Counterintelligence are the other two—a female AD was unheard-of. That didn't scare me. Nor was I particularly intimidated by the reality that cyber-security itself was suddenly at the center of the storm in a post-9/11 world. The higher the stakes, the more reason to take on the job and pursue excellence.

In short, I didn't lack confidence in my ability to be a leader, and I took the fact that I was now being interviewed for such a key position as the institutional and personal compliment it was meant to be. If the director then and there had asked me to take charge of the Bureau's entire violent-crime arena, I would have said, *Count me in. I'm your person and I can start this afternoon.* Same thing if he had asked me to head up forensic interviewing. I knew how to do it. *Put me in, Coach!*

But the PROJECT TRILOGY posting that first brought me to Mueller's attention was about defining capacities. What did the agents/users need? And how were we going to supply that in the most efficient, cost-effective way? "Director of cybersecurity" sounded as though it might require some actual knowledge of the systems themselves, and in that regard I was still very old-school FBI. In fact, for the entire half hour or so that Bob Mueller talked with me about this new position, two thoughts kept nibbling at the back of my conscience: *Is "cyber" spelled with a c or an s? And what the hell is "phishing"?*

As I mentioned earlier, the FBI under Louie Freeh was famously computer averse. In preparing for this book, I came across a note I had written to the FBI's career board regarding an in-house applicant's qualifications for a new position. "I apologize for this being handwritten," I explained at the end. "However, some of us have not been furnished with computers yet." This was in 1994. Apple was just about to introduce the Power Macintosh. Within two years, email would overtake U.S. Postal Service mail in total volume. We were the nation's frontline collector and disseminator of crime-related information, and in comparison to the private sector we were living in caves, chiseling facts and figures on stone tablets and keeping a wary eye out for saber-tooth tigers prowling by the entrance. By 2002, when this interview with Bob Mueller took place, I could log on, send emails, and do basic online research, but did the FBI really want someone who was tempted to laugh whenever she heard the word "gigabyte" running that particular show? I thought not, and I felt confident I had made that clear to the director.

"There are people far more qualified than me in this building," I told him. "Thank you for the opportunity to interview, and good luck in your search!" But the search, it turned out, was already over. The next day my flight from Washington back to Los Angeles had just landed when Bob Mueller's executive assistant, Wanda Siford, called.

"The director would like to speak with you," she said cheerfully.

I thought immediately of calls from your doctor's office after some potentially ominous test: If the nurse delivers the news, it's generally good—"You've passed with flying colors!" If she says, "The doctor would like to speak with you," it's likely not what you want to hear. This was one of those latter calls: "Congratulations," the director told me. "You are the new assistant director of our Cyber Division!"

I'M AN OPERATIONAL PERSON. GIVE me a dozen defined missions to accomplish in a day, and I'll prioritize them, start at the top, and not stop working until number twelve is over and done with. My first stop after I retired from the FBI in 2006 was with KPMG, the global business services giant. The compensation was bountiful after my quarter century on the government payroll. The office was beautiful. Everyone could not have been nicer, but . . .

In one sense I had everything to do and everything I might ask for to do my job with: I was hired to create and sell a suite of security services—including forensic investigations—to firms large and small around the nation and the world. I could travel where needed in pursuit of clients. When I was back at corporate in LA, the boss and I would occasionally linger over dinner late into the evening, at some fancy restaurant, discussing strategy, next moves, all that.

In another sense, though, I had absolutely nothing to do. There were no fifty action items waiting for me every morning. I wasn't solving problems. I was trying to create a business sector for KPMG, so I might have problems to solve sometime in the future, but I was directionless and absolutely miserable. Sixteen months into the job, I tendered my resignation and felt a huge burden lift off my back. Setting up the FBI's Cyber Division was exactly the opposite experience. I was overwhelmed with action items and happy as a lark. Also exhausted as could be.

Setting up a division is programs. It's a budget for OMB (the Office of Management and Budget). It's finding off-campus space—in this case, an anonymous office building in the DC suburbs where our new cyber army would work while my management team and I set up shop at FBI headquarters on Pennsylvania Avenue. It's also hiring personnel, and in large numbers. Remember, this was right after 9/11, when photos of Mohamed Atta and the others had to be FedExed between FBI offices because even faxing was too high-tech for us. Going forward, we wanted to assure we had a cybersecurity presence and up-to-date capacity in all fifty-six field offices, and we had few human resources to draw on from inside the Bureau.

Fortunately, techies by then were just starting to pour out of our colleges and universities, but hiring outside the Bureau created its own set of problems. Within the Bureau, we were still wrapping our mind around cybersecurity as a whole. How did we know if we were even asking the right questions of all these bright young people who were overwhelming our personnel staff with applications and queries? How did we ensure that people we had little experience with would not be security risks themselves within our off-campus cybersecurity nerve center? How did we fit them in with the FBI's existing culture, which was anti-techie sometimes to an extreme? And how did we make the knowledge that was second nature to them accessible to those still struggling to catch up? Me, for example.

These experts in their late twenties and early thirties whom we were bringing on board understood all about phishing schemes. They were comfortable prowling the dark web. Bots, Trojan horses, and P2P networks were old hat to them. But they had a really hard time speaking comprehensible English to me. "My job is doing translation," I told them, "but you could make this a lot easier for me."

Finally, I realized that many of them were far more comfortable returning to their desks at our remote location and emailing answers to whatever questions I had posed rather than answering aloud sitting across from me. So I compromised. "You cannot go back to your own cubbyhole," I said. "That would take too long and follow-up would be difficult. But you can go to another room not far from my office [in the headquarters building] and email me an answer from there."

That actually worked in many cases. I could study the answer after I received it, call them back in, and ask the specifics I needed to know for my purposes: *What does this mean? Define that? How is that relevant? What are our current real-time capabilities? What* is our long-term strategy for these capabilities and how do we implement/operationalize them? And am I actually going to tell a senator this? Will he care? How will he care? Why? Often the answers were super long, so then I would move into phase two of blending their culture with ours: *Here's how an executive summary works.*

Phase three of culture blending was FBI-wide but a particular problem for us, given our much younger and more diverse workforce than the Bureau as a whole: bridging the gender gap. We were hiring based on brains, experience, and the potential to grow on the job. Gender had nothing to do with our decision-making, which set us sharply apart from the "beer, guts, and glory" mythos that had built up around the FBI and still spilled over into many parts of the organization, including the executive ranks I had just joined.

I and Cassi Chandler, who headed up Congressional Public Affairs, were the only two female agents at FBI headquarters in the Senior Executive Service (SES) at that time. A third woman who eventually joined us from the National Security Administration once complained to Cassi and me that nobody was paying attention to her at the meetings she attended.

"It's always been done like that," Cassi told her. "You just have to be heard."

"But nobody invites me to join in," this woman went on.

"I've never been invited into anything here," I said, "and I've been around eighteen years!" (See my earlier comment about bringing your own folding chair to the table if no one offers you a seat.)

That's an old story for women in the workplace, but there was neither time nor space to dwell on it for long. If meetings were gold, my two years as head of the Cyber Division would have put me right up there on the wealth charts with Elon Musk and Jeff Bezos.

There were the daily meetings with my deputies; more briefings with Director Mueller for his every-other-day White House meetings with the CIA's George Tenet, President George W. Bush, and a select few others; and what seemed like almost constant interfacing with all the relevant players as the Department of Homeland Security was being set up. Cybersecurity was a big part of all that. So were the inevitable turf wars. *What belongs to this new DHS? What to the CIA, the U.S. Secret Service, NSA, FBI?* You don't want to get caught in that crossfire, but I was on a daily basis.

Cybersecurity also was often a key player in whether the new FISA courts would allow electronic surveillance of American citizens. The government can't just wiretap phones, because, hey, you never know what you'll find. You need reasonable cause, and pursuing the roots of the 9/11 attack sometimes stretched "reasonable" to the breaking point.

Simultaneously, I was doing a crash course on navigating the always complicated political landscape "inside the Beltway" and especially on Capitol Hill. If you wanted to get anything done at the highest levels, you had to go through all-powerful chiefs of staff, without whose approval you were never likely to reach the principal player he or she was protecting. Okay, that's political reality. But who was this person in the shadows? What were this person's leanings, his or her soft points? Sometimes I felt like I was back in the BSU, probing mysterious people for points of entry.

There was always pressure from above as well. I have great respect for Director Mueller, but he was not an easy person to work for. The Marine in him never receded entirely, nor did the urgency. When I got called into his office on the seventh floor, I could be pretty sure that his first question was going to be some variant on *Has there been something going on in the last ten minutes that I don't know about?* I had the overwhelming sense that I was supposed to know everything, in real time.

• • •

THE HARDEST PART OF THE job, though, was one that took little actual time as measured by a clock but enormous numbers of hours preparing for and worrying about: testifying before the relevant congressional committees. Congress has oversight, and senators and representatives have the right to know what the FBI is up to and why they should approve budget outlays for the Bureau. That's especially true for an expensive start-up like the Cyber Division. Someone needed to justify the division on Capitol Hill and argue for its mission, if necessary, and that someone was me: the first assistant director of the FBI Cyber Division, a pioneer in a field that was definitely our future.

Sure, I was still learning about cybersecurity when I first testified before the all-powerful Senate Commerce Committee, but I figured that might work to my advantage. Most of the committee members had only the dimmest idea of what a phishing scam was; some probably still couldn't log on to their own computers without summoning a twenty-something aide to help. And more than one, I'm willing to bet, might have actually spelled "cybersecurity" with an initial *s* if you put them to the test. Hey, we'd all be learning together!

I was also going to be heavily "back-benched," as the expression goes. While I would be testifying by myself, my chief of staff would be by my side, and key staff members who actually knew this subject matter cold would be sitting in the row behind me, ready to confer on any arcane points that might arise as the hearing proceeded.

True, I still recalled as if it were yesterday the four-hour drubbing Dale and his colleagues endured when the Hostage Rescue Team members from Ruby Ridge were summoned before the Senate Judiciary Committee, and Arlen Specter, Fred Thompson, Larry Craig, and others barely gave any of them—Dale in particular—a spare minute to respond to a torrent of allegations. That was awful, but this was different—way different, in fact.

Ruby Ridge was a fraught moment in modern American history. Lives had been lost on both sides of the standoff. Feelings were still running high three years later when the Senate Judiciary Committee summoned the HRT. You've got to expect some fireworks in a situation like that. I wasn't going before the Commerce Committee to get anyone angry or to help them settle grudges and score political points. I was going before the committee to bring the members up to speed on a dangerous crime trend that was sweeping across not just America but the world.

On the one hand, traditional criminal activity such as fraud, identity and credit card theft, trade secret and intellectual property violations, extortion, and child pornography was increasingly migrating to the internet and spreading like wildfire once it did. On the other hand, the internet and World Wide Web were enabling whole new classes of crimes and criminals: everything from cyberterrorism to terrorist cyber threats, trolling by foreign intelligence operatives, illegal intrusions into American and international computer networks, and the theft of highly sensitive data. The growth in all these crimes was almost exponential. By the time I appeared before the committee, our new Internet Fraud Complaint Center was logging 9,000 complaints a month, over 100,000 annually.

That was the bad news I had to deliver. The good news was that the FBI was finally catching up with cybercrime. In addition to our new cybersecurity units, we were expanding our international investigative capacity, joining with the United States Customs Service to co-lead a new National Intellectual Property Rights Coordination Center, partnering with the private sector across a wide range of efforts to merge its expertise in these matters with our investigative umbrella, and lots more.

In short, I had a happy, proactive story to tell lawmakers about a problem that touched almost all facets of American life. What could go wrong? This would be democracy in action!

ALLOW ME TO SET THE scene: Senator John McCain has invited me to testify about cybersecurity and our new stand-up division before the body I earlier mentioned, the Senate Commerce Committee. I take my job seriously, I believe the subject is of serious importance, and I respect John McCain. And thus I have prepared my testimony with great care, with one eye to informing America's lawmakers on a subject that poses significant risks at a global scale and with another eye to alerting the American public generally that "phishing" is not an outdoor sport for people who can't spell while also assuring all present that the FBI is on top of cybersecurity issues as it has never been before.

The doors close. A hush settles over the room. I thank committee members for inviting me and launch into my presentation, and . . . no one in front of me, so far as I can tell, pays the least bit of attention to what I have to say. Senators are getting up and walking out, or their aides are whispering in their ears, and they're whispering in their aides' ears, or maybe checking last night's baseball scores on their cell phones if they know how to work them, or who in the heck knows what. But one thing seems certain: I am testifying into an absolute void.

"Should I continue?" I ask after a while.

"Oh, of course," comes the response. "We can hear you. We're listening."

No you're not, I'm thinking. *Your body language says you are not.* My eyeballs say the same thing. I've had far more civil and engaged exchanges in interview rooms with subjects who saved body parts of the people they murdered. But in the FBI you have to be very cautious about what you say or don't say in a public forum like this, and so I say none of that. Instead, I bury my nose in my prepared remarks and read on for fifteen or twenty minutes until my mic suddenly goes dead and my chief of staff taps me on the shoulder and kindly whispers in my ear, "That means you're dismissed"—or basically phished right out of the pond.

Democracy in action, indeed.

ON A MORE POSITIVE FRONT, during my tenure as head of cybersecurity I was able to do a great favor for the Rolling Stones, Ray Charles, Cyndi Lauper, Jon Bon Jovi, Boy George, Aretha Franklin, the Sex Pistols, and thousands of others—though I never received a direct word of thanks from any of them.

It all began innocently enough when the Recording Industry Association of America (RIAA) came to me with a problem. Digital technology had been a godsend to the music industry— CDs were far cheaper to produce and ship than vinyl LPs, and they were flying off the shelves—but digital technology also made copying a lot easier and playbacks almost untraceable, and that was costing a lot of recording artists serious money in missed royalties and a lot of recording companies huge losses in missed sales. What to do?

To me, the answer seemed obvious. This was another instance where technology had outflanked existing statutes, so we created a new anti-piracy violation, and I had the Bureau wordsmiths come up with a warning that most readers have probably seen a thousand times without ever entirely reading:

The unauthorized reproduction or distribution of this copyrighted work is illegal. Criminal copyright infringement, including infringement without monetary gain, is investigated by the FBI and is punishable by up to 5 years in federal prison and a fine of $250,000.

And for those forty words, the RIAA sent me my very own mounted platinum record "in appreciation and acknowledgement of [my] significant contribution to the creation" of the FBI anti-piracy seal and warning. Can a spot in Cleveland's Rock & Roll Hall of Fame be far behind?

My very own platinum record! Not for singing, alas, but for shepherding through the FBI bureaucracy the anti-piracy seal and warning label that has saved real recording stars untold billions of dollars.

25.
FORK IN THE ROAD

AS 2006 BEGAN, I WAS SITTING PRETTY at the FBI. The Cyber Division was up and running, and I had gone back to the field—not to Los Angeles, where I still would have been number two to an ADIC, but to another sweet posting where I was running the whole show: special agent in charge of the Phoenix office, hip-deep in combating terrorism and, increasingly, cyber-terrorism, which put my recent grounding in cybersecurity to vital use but also challenged me almost daily with the sort of management issues that kept my desk calendar full and honed what I think (or at least hope) is my natural instinct for finding common ground between often warring factions.

The Phoenix office's purview encompasses twenty-two separate Native American reservations and has federal law enforcement authority over every one of them.* But a whole host of other federal agencies—the Bureau of Indian Affairs; the Alcohol,

---

* The U.S. Constitution recognizes Indian tribes as distinct governments, and they have, with a few exceptions, the same powers as federal and state governments to regulate their internal affairs. There are nearly six hundred federally recognized American Indian tribes in the United States, and the FBI has federal law enforcement responsibility on nearly two hundred Indian reservations. This federal jurisdiction is shared concurrently with the Bureau of Indian Affairs' Office of Justice Services. As a general rule, state laws do not apply to Indigenous Americans living in Indian country. Instead, tribal and federal laws apply.

Tobacco and Firearms people; the Department of the Interior and the Department of Education; the Centers for Disease Control; and others—have an interest in and responsibility for various parts of reservation life and often guard their interests and prerogatives jealously. Hell hath no fury like a federal agency scorned. Part of my job was to make sure things never got to that point and that we were all singing from the same hymnal so that we weren't separately pursuing identical goals.

Reservations also have their own law enforcement agencies and tribal police, who quite reasonably feel that, as those closest to reservation life and residents, they are better able to deal with local crime than any outside authorities. (The cable TV series *Longmire* got this just right.) I agreed, but justice ultimately had to prevail, and more than once that meant stepping on toes and unleashing centuries of pain and resentment.

Overhanging all this were the same conditions of reservation life that I had encountered at my first FBI posting in Albuquerque two decades earlier: poverty, cultural resentment, dismal economic prospects, domestic abuse, incest, and other crimes so often tied to alcohol abuse. It seems nutty to write it, but I was on the whole happy with all this. I had accumulated over my FBI career a set of skills that I felt were being put to good use and could do real good. And the calendar was decidedly on my side.

I HAD TURNED FIFTY-ONE JUST about the time I arrived in Phoenix; in six years, I would hit fifty-seven—mandatory retirement age for everyone at the Bureau except directors—and could head into the sunset with a government pension that, if not lavish, would still help keep the wolf from the door. But I wasn't all that comfortable with the prospect—or with certain other elements of my current circumstances.

For starters, I never quite understood the mandatory age-fifty-seven-and-out-the-door policy. If the Bureau were still all about busting down doors and nabbing Al Capone, sure, youth mattered, but that was an ever-diminishing part of the Bureau I lived and worked in, and the FBI was saying goodbye too early to way too much accumulated experience and expertise—a reality that the cable news channels and Fox have happily seized upon. Much of the most insightful commentary I hear on news shows these days comes from men and women who had achieved high positions in the Bureau for the best of reasons: They were smart as whips and dedicated patriots.

I'm also achievement oriented, and I was beginning to feel that I had done all there was for me to do within the FBI. At least in my own mind and I hope in the perception of my colleagues, I had met and come out on top of every challenge thrown my way, from those early struggles with the Bureau's sometimes caveman culture to my later posts in the Senior Executive Service. Like other female agents I served with, I had helped move the bar for women generally in the Bureau. We all—and maybe me in particular—went to sometimes ridiculous extremes to prove that a woman's place in the FBI was in the field, at the heart of the action, not just behind a desk, typing up and filing away the results. I wouldn't say the playing field is level yet, but the once vast distance between male and female roles in the FBI and law enforcement generally has clearly narrowed, as has the once vast distance between the opportunities for white agents and officers and those available to other races and ethnicities.

If I am to be completely honest here, I also had to acknowledge to myself that I was never going to become the first female director, no matter my experience and qualifications. As I said, I'm achievement oriented, and as I climbed the ranks, it was only natural that I would allow myself to imagine, however briefly, scaling that summit. But the simple fact is that every FBI director since J. Edgar Hoover has boasted a law degree and often prosecutorial experience, while only one—Louie Freeh—has ever worked the streets as a special agent. I had honed my credentials the wrong way to get to the top of that mountain.

Practical considerations were at play as well. A lot of Americans think of the FBI as one huge building on Pennsylvania Avenue in DC, halfway between the Capitol and the White House, but the Bureau sprawls all over the country and Bureau careers sprawl with it. In my then quarter century with the FBI, I had already been assigned to nine offices: Albuquerque, Tampa, Quantico, San Diego, Denver, Los Angeles, two stints back in DC, and now Phoenix, plus extensive travel for inspections, assignments, meetings, assorted crises, and more. Like a lot of military families at this point in their service, Dale and I were ready to have someplace to really call home. And for both personal and professional reasons, I didn't want to wait too long to make a move.

Age discrimination exists in the workplace for all of us who are getting on in years, but every metric shows that it lands more heavily on women than men. If I stayed at the FBI until mandatory retirement of fifty-seven, I would be leaning heavily toward sixty—not exactly a prime age as far as executive recruitment services are concerned. If I left now, I would be just over age fifty, with a lot still to bring to the table.

And then opportunity knocked on the door, with a compensation jump that made it almost impossible to say no. My time with KPMG was brief and bumpy, in some ways even ill-considered, but it paved my way out of the FBI—on the last day of February 2006, to be exact—and has led to a very rewarding career since.

• • •

TWO OTHER FACTORS, HARDER TO write about, also sent me packing. From day one with the Bureau, I bled FBI Blue (or, as it's known inside the Bureau, "Hoover Blue"). I might have chafed over small insults—my high heels, those old female body armor vests that failed to protect anything much below our breasts—but when it came to big, Bureau-wide policies, I saluted and charged off into battle whenever summoned. Post-9/11, though, the FBI took a turn that I found increasingly hard to support.

America is a multicultural society—a nation of immigrants, the fabled "melting pot" of other nations and their peoples. I get that, and I love that about my country. I also know that in the aftermath of the September 11, 2001, attacks on the World Trade Center, the Pentagon, and wherever the fourth plane was ulti-mately headed, American mosques were vandalized and Muslim Americans taunted and attacked. Nor were they always given the full protection of the law due them. During those hectic, terrifying days in Las Vegas just after the attack, the nation was effectively at war. We had no idea if another onslaught was coming and, if so, from where. Legal niceties were sometimes skirted in the search for answers.

On paper, the FBI's decision to team with the Council on American-Islamic Relations (CAIR) seemed like a good way to undo some of this damage and sensitize the Bureau to the nuances of a culture that has an increasingly large American presence. CAIR would annually arrange for imams in the vicinity of our major offices to meet with agents at a local mosque; a healthy back-and-forth would follow; and both sides would leave a little wiser.

Except there was no back-and-forth. I went through two of these sessions—one in Los Angeles the other in Phoenix—and all we got from the imams was an endless litany of dos and mostly don'ts. An investigation has led you to the house of a Muslim fam-ily, and there's only a woman present? Forget it: You cannot go in.

Same thing with subpoenas. You cannot—repeat: *cannot*—serve a subpoena to an Islamic woman; she's not allowed to look at such things. You must wait for the man of the household to be present. As for pursuing a suspect into a mosque itself, *NO*. A mosque is holy ground.

Again, I understand the desire to preserve one's culture and the need for law enforcement to respect those cultures. If I had occasion to visit a Japanese American home in my role as a special agent, I tried to remember to take my shoes off at the door. I had no trouble pulling a scarf over my hair if an investigation led me to a Muslim man I knew would be uncomfortable otherwise. If I had ever had occasion to arrest an Amish perpetrator—as unlikely as that seems—I would have tried to dress in as plain a way as my wardrobe would allow. But these imams were telling us not only that we had to respect their culture but that we could not do our jobs in the most efficient way—which is almost always the safest way, too—if doing so interfered with Islamic mores and religious law.

That irked me, and I wasn't alone. By the time I got to Phoenix as special agent in charge, the agents there had also been through the CAIR ringer once and were openly grumbling about the prospect of being harangued again. A quandary? Yes, but enter Captain Problem Solver!

"Instead of going through the same process," I told the local CAIR representative, "why don't we reciprocate this time, and your community can learn about how our law enforcement community works and the rules and customs we live under? That way, we'll both get to know each other better."

What I had in mind was a mini-version of the fabulous new FBI Citizens Academies then being established in Phoenix and elsewhere to provide community leaders with a holistic understanding of what the Bureau does and detailed information on how we do it. Unlike the FBI academies, which offer three-hour classes held weekly for up to eight weeks, this would be a one-day event, just like the imam-led seminars. I promised we would do our very best to open our doors to the Muslim American community and help them see the world through our eyes.

The CAIR representative promised to get back to me in a timely fashion, and for a fleeting day or two I harbored hope that I might have actually gotten through to him. But what got back to me first was Director Mueller's office.

"I hear you're being resistant," a familiar voice (*not* the director's) said.

"No," I explained, "I'm offering up an alternative. The agents are dejected at the thought of going through the mosque seminar again."

"Going to the mosque is our practice. You have to do this."

"No," I said. "I am respectfully declining to do this."

Years earlier I had told myself that if I ever reached a point where I would not jump on board with anything any FBI director really wanted to do, I would ride off into the sunset. A week later, out of the blue, KPMG made me that offer I couldn't refuse, not having any idea how primed I was to accept it.

THE FINAL FACTOR THAT UNDERPINNED my decision to leave was in a way even more compelling: I was tired—tired of rushing everywhere, tired of packing and unpacking, tired of both Dale and me being in constant tension mode and wholly worn down by a schedule controlled less by Dale's and my own wants and needs than by the sum total of madness afoot in the world at any given moment.

Over the years during casual business conversations, I had asked more seasoned agents, or those already retired from the Bureau, how I would know when it was time to retire. Amazingly, the response was almost always the same, even from agents who had never met each other.

"Oh, you'll know!" they told me. "The situations that used to excite and motivate you will become a chore and an intrusion on what you'd rather be doing."

That's the moment I had reached, and it's how I knew it was time to bid farewell and begin the next chapter. The only problem was that there was no further guidance on what to do next.

26.
NEVER ENOUGH TIME

I WOULDN'T TRADE MY QUARTER century with the FBI for any-thing. I certainly didn't get rich in the monetary sense, but when it comes to stories and experiences, I'm a billionaire. The years before the Behavioral Science Unit, when I was learning law enforcement at the street level and trying to figure out how a woman could pos-sibly fit into and help change the fossilized male culture of the FBI; the years after my time with the unit, when I dealt with the emo-tional trauma of the shootings at Columbine High, the horror of 9/11, and other events etched on my memory more from the per-spective of a senior executive than an agent on the scene; and the years in between, the ones I spent wandering among the hearts of horrible darkness that are all too common in America today—it's all been one heck of a ride. But every life has costs—the things not done, the paths not taken, events that shape you in ways you might not have foreseen—and mine had been no exception.

As you might have already guessed, it seemed almost impos-sible for Dale and me to make long-range plans. Not that we didn't try. We would sketch out vacations here and there. We would even buy tickets and book hotels. Sometimes we almost got to where we thought we were going. But Dale and I were both at the mercy of unpredictable events and sometimes highly volatile people and circumstances.

There was, for example, the time Dale and I set foot on Ellis Island. Notice, I wrote "set foot," not "visited." This was supposed to be day one of a long weekend in and around New York City in the beautiful spring of 1992. First we would see the Statue of Liberty and the new National Museum of Immigration. Then it was off to Broadway shows, museums, people-gazing in Central Park, lazy dinners, and plush hotel bedding and linens—the whole Big Apple extravaganza. Except, as so often was the case, none of it happened.

We had literally just stepped off the ferry onto Ellis Island when Dale's pager went off. Within a few seconds he was making a little turn-around sign with his finger, so we stepped back onto the ferry and returned to the New Jersey side where we had left our car, and I drove Dale to Newark International Airport and kissed him goodbye. He was flying to Phoenix. I would be heading back down I-95, back to our home in Virginia, where I would try to cancel as many reservations as I could while also preparing to eat the cost of those I couldn't wiggle out of.

A month earlier, Danny Ray Horning, who was serving four life terms for bank robbery, kidnapping, and aggravated assault, had escaped from the state prison at Florence, Arizona, about an hour southeast of Phoenix. Ever since, he had been leading local police and park rangers on a merry chase in and around Grand Canyon National Park. Then, on June 25, he took a Flagstaff, Arizona, couple hostage, forced them to drive him—in their truck—to Grand Canyon Village, where the three spent the night in one of the Village lodges. The next night, rangers spotted the truck and gave chase until Horning started firing through the back window of the cab at them. The next night they found the couple handcuffed in their truck, along with a cassette Horning had left behind, demanding $1 million and the release of his brother, who was serving a twenty-nine-year sentence for sexual misconduct involving a minor, who happened to be his own son.

All that was enough for the FBI's Hostage Rescue Team, including Dale, to once again be called in on the chase, and not only was our mini-vacation over, but I wouldn't see my husband again for almost another three weeks. But more galling by far was that as the chase went on, Danny Ray Horning was becoming something of a national cult hero.

Park rangers, who presumably knew the territories better than the backs of their hands, couldn't corral the guy. The HRT members, once they arrived, couldn't keep up with Horning, either, and these were guys paid to be in top physical condition, at the prime of their lives. Sure, the guy had terrorized the Flagstaff couple, but he had left a note along with the cassette, apologizing for stealing their truck. Sure, he had later abducted and terrorized a couple of British women who had traveled across the sea to visit the Grand Canyon. And, yeah, he was also wanted for questioning in a 1990 California case in which a robbery victim had been dismembered.

Forget all that, though. To read some news dispatches, the guy was Rambo incarnate. Like Rambo, he had learned survival skills in the military. Like Rambo, he backtracked in circles and figure eights to frustrate bloodhounds and their handlers. Since my husband was one of those pursuing Horning, I couldn't help but note that Rambo (aka Sylvester Stallone) had also been ultra–heavily armed and had killed what seemed like dozens of people during that two-hour movie.

Most galling of all, Horning was clearly enjoying himself. He was on the news every night, he was having a great time, and really he had nothing to lose. If he was caught again, he was just going to go back to serving out his life sentences. For the time being, he had the public's attention and could pose as some kind of rogue philosopher-king. Early on in the chase, he described himself in one of his left-behind messages as a "good guy, with a heart that does bad things," if I remember correctly. After he was finally run to ground by the HRT and caught—following yet another car chase punctuated by his gunfire—Horning told reporters, "I would have liked to have prolonged it."

Charming to the end, in short. If Horning had known he had ruined yet another of Dale's and my carefully plotted vacations, he probably would have apologized for that, too, and maybe even sent flowers. And, by the way, we've never been back to Ellis Island since.

THE VAST MAJORITY OF FBI special agents have never discharged a weapon outside of a firing range or for recreational reasons. Agents are far more likely to be paper pushers than gunslingers. Even Dale, who was frequently in dangerous situations and could probably shoot the head off a dandelion at four hundred yards, never once fired his weapon in a hostage situation.

But all FBI agents are nonetheless required to constantly carry or be in close access to their guns 24/7, and doing that is a constant reminder that other people have weapons and might just be inclined to aim them in your direction. The closest I ever came to being shot was that time in Tampa, early in my career, that I described earlier—when a bullet fired through a door actually split the hair on my head—but another incident, this one in DC, was in some ways more haunting.

Back in 1994, shortly after Director Louie Freeh assumed his position, he set about downsizing FBI headquarters operations, including the headquarters division at Quantico where I was working. Headquarters agents who were eligible to retire were given added incentive to do so. Others were encouraged to get closer to the crime we dealt with every day by relocating to the various field offices around the country.

I had been assured that I was soon headed into the senior executive service, which would mean eventually moving into the headquarters building in downtown DC that Director Freeh was trying to thin out, but in the meantime I said to myself, *Hey, for a change of pace, why don't I help the director's numbers along by temporarily going back into the field.* Before long I was assigned to the Washington Field Office, and soon after that, I suffered the rude awakening of having to force myself out of bed at 3:30 in the morning so a squad of us could meet at 5:00 a.m. and head into DC for a dawn arrest.

Mustering up for that is when I realized what a dinosaur of a "street agent" I had become. Everyone else on the arrest team had already transitioned from clunky revolvers to sleek new pistols— everyone except Jana, that is. Out at the BSU we were practically last in line for this significant upgrade, and the sidearm I was toting on this mission was my trusty old Model 66 Smith & Wesson revolver, which was to my colleagues' sidearms roughly what a Dodge Grand Caravan family wagon is to, oh, a Lamborghini.

Now, if we had been doing this dawn arrest in Georgetown or Cleveland Park or any of the other elegant neighborhoods of Northwest DC, odds are my gun fashion faux pas would never have drawn attention or the arrest itself a crowd at such an early hour. But this was in the rough streets of Southeast DC, where people can sense law enforcement arriving from blocks away and where the kids are quick to gather to witness a little excitement and are alarmingly knowledgeable when it comes to weaponry, especially the ginormous revolver being carried by the blond woman special agent assigned to stand on the stoop outside the building in question while other agents made the takedown inside.

"Oh, look," I remember one kid saying, "she's got a wheel gun, not no pistol"—i.e., a gun with a rotating chamber, not a magazine.

"I've never seen anything that old," another kid added (referring, I hope, to my Smith & Wesson, not me). And keep in mind, these were real kids—not more than ten years old, by the looks of them.

"Hey, lady, what's that thing fire? Oranges?"

And it was just about at that very moment when a guy comes around the corner, spots me, and pulls a gun (one of those slick "pistols") on me just as I'm pulling my "wheel" gun on him. And there we are, staring at each other with an audience of kids whipsawing their heads back and forth between the two of us.

I was a blond white woman standing at the doorway of a building in a predominantly Black part of town, so he couldn't have had much doubt about who I was in a macro sense and what I was doing there, but what else was going on in his mind, I can't even guess.

For myself, we were trained in the FBI not to think about "killing the enemy" but rather "eliminating a threat." The distinction is subtle but important. Not every enemy is a threat. And, for that matter, not all threats are created equal. There is no doubt that I felt threatened by this man's pistol—and no question, either, that he felt threatened by my wheel gun—but was the threat an artificial one created by the fact that we had surprised each other and drawn and leveled our weapons simultaneously? The fact was, he looked as confused as I felt.

How long did this standoff last? Maybe fifteen seconds, maybe thirty. I have no idea. Long enough for him to lower his weapon and walk quickly down the street and out of my life. And long enough for me to decide that I would rather die than take an innocent person's life and lower my weapon as well. But was I scared? Of course I was, and that kind of experience doesn't disappear with the next cup of coffee, any more than getting shot through the hair does. Those experiences become part of the fabric of your life.

THEN THERE'S THE MATTER OF families. The FBI—at least, the FBI I knew—was hard on them. J. Edgar Hoover ran the Bureau with an iron hand and shaped its culture in ways that far outlived his long tenure as director—forty-eight years, to be exact, and the reason Congress placed a ten-year term limit on any new director. Hoover was also a lifelong bachelor who had no apparent interest in children and made no accommodations within the Bureau for childbirth and certainly not for childcare. Switchboard operators, secretaries, file clerks, and other female employees who went through childbirth could use their two weeks of vacation time to adjust to motherhood; then it was back to the grind. Hoover had been gone for almost thirteen years when I joined up, and women were slowly beginning to infiltrate the ranks of agents, but the same rules still applied.

That was one reason Dale and I never had children. There seemed to be a big sign hanging at the end of every hallway that read: "Don't even think about it!" The other, bigger reason was that we could never see a clear path to raising kids.

Doing that job the right way is time intensive, and when you are working a major case, as I often seemed to be doing, or responding to some sudden new outbreak of hostilities—Danny Ray Horning, say—you have to be ready to leave on a moment's notice, put in long hours, and hole up far away for weeks and sometimes months at a time. More than once—during the Branch Davidian standoff in Waco, for example—both of us were on extended duty almost 24/7 at the same time, albeit fifteen hundred miles apart.

Who's going to look after the kids in a situation like that? The nanny? The au pair? Not on the FBI pay scale unless you have wealthy parents, which wasn't us, or a lot of side hustles, which were not allowed. That pretty much leaves the dog, but who's going to take care of the dog that's taking care of the kids?

Then there were the accumulated pressures and liabilities of our work. Again, one example to stand for many.

Earlier, I detailed Dale's involvement in the events at the 1992 Ruby Ridge standoff that resulted in the death of Vicki Weaver. I also described the relentless browbeating Dale took from Pennsylvania senator Arlen Specter and other lawmakers at a 1995 hearing on the siege and shootings. But that was far from the end of the matter. Lon Horiuchi, who fired the fatal shot at Ruby Ridge and was eventually acquitted on manslaughter charges in the case, had his life repeatedly threatened in the immediate years that followed. The Oklahoma City bomber Timothy McVeigh regularly handed out cards at gun shows listing Horiuchi's home address and expressing the hope that someone in the "Patriot movement" might assassinate him. Dale didn't come in for that level of threat, but to varying degrees he has been trolled by Randy Weaver sympathizers and Ruby Ridge never-forgetters ever since, especially after he retired from the FBI and began seeking employment in the private sector.

In 2013, for example, Dale was hired by Troy Industries as a contract instructor for its asymmetric training group. (Troy then was manufacturing a popular standard-capacity magazine for AR-15 assault rifles.) The matchup made perfect sense: Dale had spent a professional lifetime doing just this kind of work. Dale's hiring, however, did not go unnoticed. Within hours of the news going public, it seemed, a website calling itself GunsSaveLife. com began posting a series of vitriolic responses that reduced Ruby Ridge to a black-and-white tale in which only the Hostage Rescue Team members had been armed and Randy Weaver and Kevin Harris were emissaries from the Peaceable Kingdom. As one poster put it:

Remember Ruby Ridge?
FBI snipers Lon Horiuchi and Dale Monroe tried to kill these men. Judge, jury and executioner.

And Horiuchi just "accidentally" murdered Vicky [sic] Weaver.

And Dale Monroe said he was ready to take that same shot but Horiuchi fired first. What a couple of shining examples of courage and bravery, right? Shooting down a woman armed with nothing but an infant in her arms.*

Steve Troy, the company namesake and owner, initially did the right thing in response, defending Dale in an August 22, 2013, Facebook post and bringing reason to the discussion:

We are saddened by the events at Ruby Ridge and recognize the significance of the tragedy. If you've never worn a uniform, you might not understand why Monroe was in the situation he was in, but if you have worn a uniform, you know how it is to follow orders in a fluid situation.

But in practical terms, there's no reasoning with these people. Two weeks later, a commentator on the website The-OutdoorsTrader.com called Dale a "jackbooted thug . . . [who] if he were a mere civilian like the rest of us would still be in prison for murder." And there's no statute of limitations, either. Six years later, as recently as 2019, a Reddit contributor and former Troy Industries customer added to the discussion: "Troy is still a pass for me. Hiring the [Ruby Ridge] guy wasn't the only retarded thing they did."

By then, Dale hadn't worked for Troy for six years, as the company explained in an early 2016 Facebook post:

---

* As noted earlier, there is absolutely no evidence backing up that last assertion. In my opinion, it was introduced into the record by Weaver's defense attorney, Gerry Spence, solely to muddy the waters.

In August of 2013 Dale Monroe was retained by the Director of the Training Division as a training consultant to TROY Asymmetric. Dale Monroe has not been affiliated with any division of TROY, in any capacity since August 2013. He was never an employee and he never worked a day representing TROY to our client companies.

If we had started a family at the normal time for such things, our children would likely have been in their teen years when all this was breaking. My sense is that it's hard enough to raise kids right without the added pressure of anonymous online ignoramuses coming after the family's dad.

See what I mean? The more you dig, hoping to find normality in a life like ours, the deeper the hole. Instead, we ended up with cats—mostly self-sufficient and easy for friends to look in on occasionally. But 9/11 stretched even our feline family, not to mention ourselves, almost to the breaking point.

I WROTE EARLIER ABOUT THE feverish, nightmare-driven pace of my time in Las Vegas, just after the attacks. In memory it feels like months. In fact, my tour there lasted only sixteen days: not because the job was done—how could a job like that ever be done?—but because in my line of work, in those days, crisis fed into crisis, one need into another, and there was always something pending just around the corner that could blow up all to hell if we weren't on top of every last detail, every imaginable possibility, no matter the dark places it led us.

The day I was pulled off the Vegas job, I was told to return to Denver and given all of twelve hours to pack before I flew to DC and reported to work on PENTBOMB, the not-too-secret code name for the Pentagon attack. When I got to my hotel that night, I flopped into bed still wearing the business suit I had flown in and fell asleep without brushing my teeth, which for me, an obsessive tooth brusher, is the absolute apex of exhaustion. And when I woke up in the morning . . . I was no longer on PENTBOMB! Instead, Director Mueller had drafted me to rescue PROJECT TRILOGY. I wouldn't see Denver—Dale's and my home!—again for the next four months, and then only for twenty-four hours before I was detailed to Salt Lake City as one of four on-scene FBI commanders for the 2002 Olympic Winter Games.

That's something else about this life I've led. I love the Olympics. Winter or summer, bobsledding or pole-vaulting, figure skating or floor exercises, track or pool—it doesn't matter to me. I like to watch women and men at the very peak of their athletic ability trying to be the very best in the world. It thrills me. But like other major events—think Super Bowls, presidential inaugurations, etc.—the Olympics are a massive crime scene waiting to happen, involving huge numbers of law enforcement personnel and massive protection strategies. If anything, the 2002 Winter Games were all that on steroids. America was only six months removed from 9/11 and at war with multiple enemies willing and quite possibly able to wreak havoc on our nation yet again. The slalom skiing might have been pure magic, the speed skating breathtaking. But if I were Al Qaeda and wanted to further destabilize America in front of the whole world, I couldn't think of a better place to do it.

I never could have been a world-champion athlete, but I am definitely a world-class owner of responsibility and accountability, and I spent those two weeks in Utah mostly glued to monitors that were concentrated far less on the events than on the dark shadows from which attackers might emerge.

The recent history of Olympic Games in America was also not comforting, including the fact that the perpetrator of the last attack on the games was still at large.

I was on the other side of the country, newly installed as

supervisor in the San Diego FBI office, when the bomb exploded in Atlanta's Centennial Olympic Park on Saturday, July 27, at 1:20 a.m. eastern standard time, near the start of the 1996 Summer Games, killing two (one of a heart attack), injuring another 111, and terrorizing the entire city. But I had a family stake in all that. Dale was part of a special Hostage Rescue Team put together for the Atlanta Games and might well have been in the park at that moment if the explosion had not taken place so late at night. (Many more also would have been killed or injured if the attack had come earlier.) As it was, he and the rest of the team had already scrambled and were on foot in Centennial Park before I even got word of the attack.

It wasn't long, also, before my former colleagues at the BSU and I were conference calling about Richard Jewell, the security guard who at first had been hailed as a hero for discovering the bomb and helping to partially evacuate the park before the explosion and now was under heavy suspicion of being the actual bomber himself. Did what we knew about Jewell in those early days after the bombing fit with that of a would-be mass murderer? Was he a bomber who had had second thoughts? Or was he trying to be villain and hero at the same time—creating both crisis and rescue?

The top of the FBI food chain, beginning with Louie Freeh, seemed to have decided that Jewell fit the profile of a "lone bomber" and wanted to create a ruse to pull him in for questioning—something about a training film for bomb detection. Enough of all this suspicion, meanwhile, leaked to the media that for almost three months Richard Jewell's life was basically holy hell, and for no good reason. The real Centennial Olympic Park bomber, Eric Rudolph, was a domestic terrorist who, in his own words, wanted to "confound, anger and embarrass the Washington government in the eyes of the world for its abominable sanctioning of abortion on demand."

Rudolph would go on to bomb three other venues—abortion clinics in an Atlanta suburb and Birmingham, Alabama, and an Atlanta lesbian bar—and spend five years on the FBI's Ten Most Wanted Fugitives list before being arrested in 2003 while pawing through a dumpster for food in Murphy, North Carolina, and the Monroe family would be involved in that as well. Not only was Dale present in Atlanta at the Centennial Olympic Park bombing; he and the San Diego SWAT team he commanded were the lead team pursuing Randolph seven years later when he went dumpster diving in Murphy and was easily collared by an alert rookie local officer.

OUR WORLD, IN SHORT, AND welcome to it. But as I wrote earlier, I wouldn't trade it for any other life—not in a million years. Nor would I trade the people I knew at the FBI—friends, colleagues, bosses, even some bona fide pains in the neck—for any other human assemblage I can possibly imagine.

There was a special quality to the Bureau I knew and worked in, and I think it's best captured in the character of the director under whose tenure I worked the longest, Louis Freeh. Louie was anything but glitzy, but he was always genuine and he had rock-hard values he wouldn't stray from, no matter how much pressure was brought to bear. Bill Clinton, for example, hired Louie early in his first term, then spent much of the rest of his presidency regretting the decision. Louie knew who he was, and he was true to his word. He also knew that his job and the job of the Bureau he led was law enforcement and that prosecutorial decisions were the province of the Department of Justice, not the FBI, a line never to be crossed—something one of his successors, James B. Comey, never quite got down.

Maybe most important to the Bureau as a whole, Louie invoked a bright line for all of us, from rookie agents to the senior executive service, to follow. From the outside, some parts of that bright line might look petty or like throwbacks to the iron-fisted leadership of J. Edgar Hoover. Agents were to use their government cars for business and for nothing else. Agents were not to drink on the job unless it was undercover work, and they should drink only in moderation in their off-hours because a DUI charge or worse would embarrass the Bureau, and embarrassing the Bureau weakened it in the eyes of the American people it was charged to protect from crime.

Whatever their private opinions about politics and politicians, agents were also to remain apolitical in any and all public ways: no bumper stickers, no yard signs, no preaching politics on the job. The only agent I can recall from my time at the FBI who openly thumbed his nose at that was one of the greatest calamities the Bureau ever suffered: Robert Philip Hanssen, the longtime Soviet mole, who plastered the family van with pro-life stickers and lectured secretaries on sexual abstinence until marriage while selling some of the Bureau's darkest secrets to the enemy. (I know about Hanssen only secondhand, I should add. The Russian section, where he worked, was a world apart.)

I thought of all this when I heard that the Los Angeles office of the FBI, where I once served as special agent in charge, had called off plans to host a summer 2022 fundraising event for a Democratic candidate for state office. Sisterhood probably played a role in that: both the ADIC and the candidate are females, and I'm all for women supporting each other. But any such gathering would almost certainly have violated the Hatch Act, which prohibits federal employees from engaging in blatant political activity while on the job. Far more to the point, it would have grossly violated the principle of political neutrality. Like the U.S. Supreme Court, the FBI has to stand apart from politics, because doing otherwise will delegitimatize it.

Just how different this world was and is from the larger out-side world quickly became apparent when I left the Bureau for the private sector. I was in my first month at KPMG when one of my colleagues told me how great a proposed new initiative was going to be for the company, then completely contradicted himself a few hours later when our "big boss" panned the initiative over dinner.

"Absolutely," my colleague chimed in. "A terrible idea. I couldn't agree more."

The next day I asked him what that was all about. "You were so enthusiastic about it," I told him. "Then you completely threw it under the bus."

"It's simple," he replied. "I need this job. I'm not going to fall on my sword over something like this."

Ethically, it was like I had landed on the moon.

I saw some of the same in my next private-sector position as security director for Southern California Edison. We had a bona fide crisis while I was there, a horrible event. On December 16, 2011, an employee went rogue at one of our office buildings in Irwindale, California, and shot and killed two of his coworkers and wounded two others. Part of my job was to untangle what had actually happened so we could protect our people against similar events in the future, but time and again what I was told in one-on-one interviews with employees close to the incident and/or shooter was contradicted by what the same people had written in their interoffice emails. (Another all-points bulletin: Job-place emails are *not* private.) What was true? What was a lie? Whose word to trust or dismiss? It was a horrible mess to untangle.

I'm happy to say the ethical climate was far healthier—as was the canteen food—in my most recent role, where I was vice presi-dent in charge of security services. (A sample morning's lineup of worries: entire facility closed by a server failure, arranging for an employee to be medevaced from Europe back to the States, and an extortion threat against one of our senior executives—and this was all on a *Sunday*, before I'd even had my coffee. The private sector was not dull!) But even there I had to accommodate myself to a workforce sometimes built more around individual advancement than the common good.

Don't misunderstand: I am aware that people have to look out for their own interests. I realize that private-sector capitalism inevitably has elements of a survive-or-die mentality, that sometimes to make a living good people end up in enterprises that don't always reflect their own beliefs or interests. (That last point was brought home to me recently when someone called to measure my interest in becoming director of security for PLBY Group, Inc., the successor to Hugh Hefner's old Playboy empire. "It's not what it used to be," I was assured. "No Hefner anymore, no Playboy Bunnies. They're going more after the transgender audience and marijuana-based wellness.")

But as much as I understand all that, I can't help but miss a world where you knew that everyone above and below you had your back; where people did what they said they would do; where there was no reward for showboating and none for shirking duty, either; where valuing your life over theirs seemed the norm, not the exception. My husband says his Marine Corps service and experience was much the same, so it could be a rewarding common baseline for those of us who have a calling to serve others.

Yes, there was never enough time in that world—I hope I've successfully shown that by now—but I've never known anything better than that kind of trust and camaraderie. We were a band of sisters and brothers, and there's never enough of that.

EPILOGUE

MY JOURNEY IS FAR FROM over. The people and events I have described in these pages are part of the embroidery in an ever-forming tapestry that both defines and drives me. Like all of us, I'm the sum total of my experiences, shaped by the past—the good, the bad, and the ugly, to return to my childhood fascination with Clint Eastwood—and hopeful of a future that will allow me still more chances for personal growth and service to others.

Not long ago, a girlfriend who happens to be a psychologist pointed out to me that there seemed to be an incongruence between the artwork that overflows in Dale's and my home and the life we have both led to this point. Professionally, Dale and I have been knee-deep in some of the darker moments and personalities in modern American history. Personally, we had made the decision early on not to have children; yet, as my girlfriend pointed out, our walls were hung with art that I often describe as coming from the Norman Rockwell school of American illustration and painting: animals, kids, innocence, family scenes, simpler times, a world different from the one we live in. A world that no longer exists, if it ever did.

"What's with that?" my friend asked.

What's with it, I guess, is that more and more I have found myself living with one foot in the kind of mid-twentieth-century America that Norman Rockwell captured so nostalgically in his many covers for the *Saturday Evening Post* and elsewhere, and with the other foot in a world in which we are no longer surprised when a police officer is killed in the performance of his duties or a gunman sprays July 4th celebrants, dancers in a gay disco, attendees at a music festival, shoppers at a Walmart, fellow worshippers in a prayer circle, or a schoolroom full of fourth graders.

That artificial world of paintings, illustrations, and prints covering Dale's and my walls was my stress release back when acts of darkness were all around me, and they remain so today—a refuge from the daily drumbeat of bad news with which media outlets bombard us, the everlasting antidote to those grisly, gory crime scene photos that once covered my office walls.

Much the same, I think, applies to my love of Sue Grafton's "Alphabet Series" detective novels: *A Is for Alibi, B Is for Burglar, C Is for Corpse,* all the way down to the one she died before she could write: *Z Is for Zero.* My law enforcement friends used to give me all sorts of grief when they found me with my nose buried in the latest adventures of sleuth Kinsey Millhone.

"Those books are so formulaic," they'd say. "She's just regurgitating Ross Macdonald and Mickey Spillane. All that wisecracking from a zillion years ago. Why don't you bury your nose in something worthwhile—something with some believable blood and guts?"

True, there is nothing intellectually profound or revelatory in the Millhone adventures. They are what they are. But I adore seeing the world through the trusty first-person eyes of Private Investigator Millhone, and I've seen, smelled, and worked with blood and guts enough to last several lifetimes. (However, I'll never turn down watching a suspenseful, well-done, murder mystery.)

I told Sue Grafton as much when I finally got to meet her at a book-signing event at Vroman's, a wonderful mom-and-pop bookstore in Pasadena, California, not far from Sue's home in Santa

Barbara. I explained that I had first found her books when I was with the Behavioral Science Unit. "You brought so much enjoyment to me when I was trying to get out of that ugly world. I loved coming into your world."

A long line was waiting behind me with books for Sue to sign—it wasn't the time nor place for a deep discussion—but she gave me a hug and said, "Where have you been all my life?"

LET ME END ON A happier note:

There's an upside to all this exposure to weirdness, to psychopaths, murderers, and rapists too numerous to even begin to remember them all—to these hearts of darkness that were my world for a limited but deeply immersive time. Because I saw so clearly and in such detail the evil of the few, I learned to recognize the goodness of the many.

Being inundated by evil motivated me to read the Bible, to get baptized, to seek out accounts of men and women with convictions so strong, they were willing to die to defend them—people who put their lives on the line to help others, to save total strangers from peril. I sought out the antithesis of the evil that had begun to consume my thoughts and found it all around me, just waiting for me to fully open my eyes and see it. I'm certainly not a Pollyanna, nor would I want to be, but I find it both encouraging and inspiring to be convinced that, on balance, the good among us far outweighs the evil. Unlike Marlow, the narrator in Joseph Conrad's famous novella *Heart of Darkness*, I immersed myself for a time in some of the worst and most troubling the human species has to offer and came out a better, more complete person. For that, I am deeply grateful.

I also emerged from my voyage through good and evil with five personal survival skills that continue to sustain me and that I hope have been woven through this book.

1. Resilience. Be prepared to reinvent yourself over and over again, to successfully change with the ever-changing life landscape.

2. Integrity. Make it your foundation, your moral compass.

3. Perseverance. When the going gets rough, keep going.

4. Flexibility. Without compromising integrity, recognize that there is more than one way to do or look at things.

5. Adaptability. If you don't like change, you really won't like being irrelevant. Adaptability is resilience in action.

Bottom line: Whatever happens, never stop growing. Recognize that negative experiences are indiscriminate and unavoidable and that even the worst can truly be gifts in disguise, agents of self-discovery and life-enhancing change. Evil walks among us. It happens to us all, to a greater or lesser degree. What we do with evil when we encounter it is the pivotal moment.

ACKNOWLEDGMENTS

Shortly after I retired from the FBI, acquaintances began encouraging me to write a book about my three decades in law enforcement. I resisted at first, in part because those were intense years and I wasn't ready to revisit them and in part because I knew most of my police brethren had their own exciting, funny, and often tragic stories to tell. What was unique about my career? Plenty, my dear friend and FBI colleague Joe Navarro finally convinced me: "Hey, bud [our nickname for each other], you *need* to tell this story, and people *need* to read it."

Joe's continual encouragement and support was the catalyst that got me started, and Joe's literary agent (and now mine) Steve Ross has been my invaluable guiding light ever since this book was first conceived.

Having an idea to write a book is one thing; telling the story from beginning to end and shepherding it through publication is another. For that, I could not have asked for a better editor than Chelsea Cutchens. Chelsea saw the potential in my proposal, and she and her excellent team at Abrams have been partners in the creative process every step of the way.

Warranting special thanks is Howard Means, an exceptional writer, who exhibited compassionate tenacity while helping me organize my thoughts into a coherent narrative.

I also want to acknowledge and thank former FBI Director Louie Freeh, the epitome of honesty and integrity, for his passionate and unparalleled leadership of the FBI during much of the time I was an agent.

Likewise, I want to thank John Douglas for taking a chance on me and hiring me in the Behavioral Science Unit at a time when women were not sought after or included in the elite world of hunting violent killers.

In my post-FBI corporate career journey, I have also been inspired by the many women I have met through Women in Leadership and Diversity, Equity, and Inclusion organizations. The longing, the energy, and the enthusiasm of these diverse and accomplished women and their passionate determination to make a positive difference in the world leave me awestruck. Maybe this story of my somewhat unorthodox career will motivate them to move out of their comfort zone and experience the many opportunities life has to offer.

I would be remiss if I didn't thank my friend Dawn Haghighi, who relentlessly encouraged me to keep writing but also tirelessly reminded me to salt these vignettes with "educational moments" for readers not familiar with law-enforcement culture.

Last, but most especially, I thank my husband, Dale, for his love, patience, and support as the writing process consumed much of what had previously been our time together. He reviewed my copy, provided his input and perspective, and always encouraged me.

NOTES

4. Breaking Through

33 *I should add that my class of new agents.* For more on Hogan's Alley, see "Hogan's Alley Turns 30: The Evolution of the FBI's Mock Training Ground," FBI.gov, May 12, 2017, https://www.fbi.gov/news/stories/hogans-alley-turns-30 and "What We Investigate: Tactical/Hogan's Alley," FBI.gov, n.d., https://www.fbi.gov/services/training-academy/hogans-alley.

9. God Is in the Details

89 *In the very early morning of February 17, 1970.* For a more complete summary of the Jeffrey MacDonald case, see "Jeffrey R. MacDonald," Wikipedia, https://en.wikipedia.org/wiki/Jeffrey_R._MacDonald.

11. *The Silence of the Lambs*

103 "'You know,' Kemper said to us." Robert K. Ressler tells this story differently in his book *Whoever Fights Monsters*. In Ressler's account, he and Edmund Kemper are alone in a room when a similar scene takes place. I learned about this encounter from John Douglas and use his account here.

110 *Only two things struck me as particularly off-key about the*

film. Kathleen Murphy, "Communion," Film Comment, January/February 1991.

13. For Better or For Worse

124 *"Forty-five or fifty minutes after selecting our position."* "September 14, 1995: Ruby Ridge Investigation Day 5," C-SPAN, https://www.c-span.org/video/?67153-1/ruby -ridge-investigation-day-5.

14. Hearts of Darkness

142 *"As a young boy, and I mean as a boy of twelve or thirteen."* "Ted Bundy Last Interview," YouTube, https://www.youtube .com/watch?v=sCUQLPOjvxs.

144 *"For much of my upbringing, my mother was sick and angry."* "Edmund Kemper Interview in 1984," YouTube, https://www .youtube.com/watch?v=I8x5PeZZFNs.

145 *"In ninth-grade biology class, we had the usual dissection of fetal pigs."* "Jeffrey Dahmer Interview, Extended Footage," interview with Stone Phillips, February 1994, YouTube, https:/ /www.youtube.com/watch?v=ErB0R4wlB64.

150 *How much of that is accounted for by serial killers.* "Edmund Kemper Interview in 1984," YouTube, https://www.youtube .com/watch?v=I8x5PeZZFNs.

151 *A number of studies built on the profiling.* Abbie Jean Marono, Sasha Reid, Enzo Yaksic, and David Adam Keatley, "A Behaviour Sequence Analysis of Serial Killers' Lives: From Childhood Abuse to Methods of Murder," *Psychiatry, Psychology, and Law* 27, no. 2 (February 6, 2020): 126–37, https:/ /doi.org/10.1080/13218719.2019.1695517.

153 *As state's evidence, I offer you John List.* For a more detailed account of the List murders and of his years in hiding, see "John List (Murderer), Wikipedia, https://en.wikipedia.org

/wiki/John_List_(murderer) and Clifford D. May, "Prosaic Life of Suspect in '71 New Jersey Murders," *New York Times*, June 9, 1989, https://www.nytimes.com/1989/06/09 /nyregion/prosaic-life-of-suspect-in-71-new-jersey-murders .html.

16. When the Abnormal Becomes Normal . . .

173 *"The body of a 57-year-old white man."* Riazul Imami and Miftah Kemal, "Vacuum Cleaner Use in Autoerotic Death," *American Journal of Forensic Medicine and Pathology* 9, no. 3 (September 1988): 246–48.

18. Low Crimes in High Places

193 *Whether or not that made a difference, I have no idea.* U.S. *v. Frega*, Casetext, https://casetext.com/case/united-states-v -frega.

19. Help Is on the Way

201 Footnote. *Typing those words just now.* Victoria Klesty and Walter Gibbs, "Shocking Nation, Norway Killer Describes Island Massacre," Reuters, April 20, 2012, https://www .reuters.com/article/norway-breivik/shocking-nation -norway-killer-describes-island-massacre-idINDEE 83J06S20120420.

22. Trailer Trash

222 *Finally, there was the personal side of things.* In the aftermath of the El Al attack, Hesham Mohamed Hadayet's last name was sometimes spelled "Hedayet," especially in government-related documents. "Hadayet" is by far the more common spelling now.

225 *Those kinds of issues would eventually die down.* Rick Lyman

and Nick Madigan, "Officials Puzzled About Motive of Airport Gunman Who Killed 2," *New York Times,* July 6, 2002, https://www.nytimes.com/2002/07/06/us/officials-puzzled-about-motive-of-airport-gunman-who-killed-2.html.

227 *Questions like that got to be almost commonplace.* "Overview: Mission and Organizational Structure," Justice.gov, https://www.justice.gov/archive/ag/annualreports/ar2002/overview.htm.

23. Crime and Punishment

234 *In February 1999, Ng was convicted on eleven counts of homicide.* "Interviewing Victims: Leonard Lake & Charles Ng Footage—HORRIFYING | #CAUGHTonCAMERA Ep.10," YouTube, https://www.youtube.com/watch?v=IAKhijbFVwY.

234 *Lake says this, by the way, via a home video.* "Interviewing Victims: Leonard Lake & Charles Ng Footage—HORRIFYING | #CAUGHTonCAMERA Ep.10," YouTube, https://www.youtube.com/watch?v=IAKhijbFVwY.

24. Phishing Trip

241 *Within two years, email would overtake.* "Computer History 1996: New Computer Products and Services Introduced in 1996," Computer Hope, updated January 21, 2023, www.computerhope.com/history/1996.htm#computer-products.

26. Never Enough Time

261 *Most galling of all, Horning was clearly enjoying himself.* Dirk Johnson, "Prison Escapee Is Caught After 2-Month Manhunt," *New York Times,* July 6, 1992, https://www.nytimes.com/1992/07/06/us/prison-escapee-is-caught-after-2-month-manhunt.html.

266 *"Remember Ruby Ridge?"* Jboch, "Troy Stands by Their Employee, Lon Horiuchi's Partner at Ruby Ridge! UPDATE #4," GunsSaveLife.com, August 22, 2013, https://www.gunssavelife .com/guess-who-else-troy-has-hired-lon-horiuchis-partner/.

267 *"We are saddened by the events at Ruby Ridge."* Troy Industries, Facebook, August 22, 2013, https://www.facebook. com/TroyIndustriesUSA/posts/we-thank-everyone-for -their-opinions-on-dale-monroe-we-are-still-reviewing -mr-mo/10152162462098986/.

267 *But in practical terms, there's no reasoning.*

(1) *"jackbooted thug."* Roundhouse, "Troy Industries Hired Dale Monroe and Jody Weis WTF," TheOutdoorsTrader .com, September 4, 2013, https://www.theoutdoorstrader.com /threads/troy-industries-hired-dale-monroe-and-jody-weis -wtf.502298/.

(2) *"Troy is still a pass for me."* u/[deleted], Reddit.com, n.d., "Have We Forgiven Troy Industries?," https://www.reddit.com/r /ar15/comments/bknvfd/have_we_forgiven_troy_industries/.

268 *In August of 2013 Dale Monroe was retained.* "Posted 2/9/2016," AR15.com, https://www.ar15.com/forums/industry/Troy -Industries-Statement/397-239784/?page=8&fvx=-1.

INDEX

Page numbers in *italics* reference photographs.

C